Truth Zone:

An Experiential Approach to Organizational Development

By Ward Flynn

SIMON & SCHUSTER CUSTOM PUBLISHING

Printed in the United States of America

10 9 8 7 6 5 4 3 2 1

ISBN 0–536–00753–5
BA 97531

SIMON & SCHUSTER CUSTOM PUBLISHING
160 Gould Street/Needham Heights, MA 02194
Simon & Schuster Education Group

Dedication

To the memory of my mother,
Dorothea, whose love surrounded me with books
and instilled in me a deep appreciation of ideas.
To my father, Howard, the smartest man I have ever known;
and John, my brother—the consultant's consultant.

Acknowledgements

This project would not have been possible without my partners in the Venture Centre: Bill Baker, Gail Hoag, and Glenn Head. *I am grateful for inspiration, support, and the opportunity to learn from these people; not all of whom are fans. I have learned something from each one:* Terry Ihlenfeld, Carl Symons, Peggy Baker, Marian Head, Bob Sherman, Norman Halemano Ing, Jim Dutton, Gregory Hoag, Lois Hart, Susan Adams, Jayne Hill, Michael Chapman, Scott Simpson, Ray Jones, Jacqueline Frischknecht, Sparrow Hawk, Mike Scozzari, Steve Snyder, Ralph LaPerch, Larry Tew, Lamar Graves, Nick Topka, Steve McAlilley, Alec Hemer, Robert B. Roberts, Steve O'Hara, Richard Price, Lloyd Chesney, Jim Fonseca, John Warfield, Pauline Thornton, Arnold Blades, Doug & Carolyn Clark, David Neenan, Marc Woods, John Sanders, Eric Hemer, Frank Clement, Jon & Laurie Weiss, Richard Meyers, Louise Petregnani, John Steiner, Ethel Skinner, Albert Krassner, Linda Rhinehart, Tom & Jill Hall, Phil & Bunny Goldberg, Kaye Barrett, John Reed, Burt Simon, Pat Engstrom, Tim Burke, Scott Simpson, Pete Catches, David Hooper, Peggy Fox-MacKay, Brian Van Duzee, John Gander, Dave Richards, Bruce Wares, Larry Carlisle, Fred Welch, Brian James, Sharon Heinlen, Ann Stone, Marti Belknap, Stacy Thrash, Chuck Milligan, Glenn Copelli, The "no name" team at El Paso, Roger Shuttleworth, Mike Carlisle, Juan Rodriguez, Scott Gates, Grace Kerns, Jennifer Ande, Jack Schultz, the late Richard O'Brien, and the gang at Walnut Cafe for providing me a conference room away from the office.

I wish to honor the people I love who have held me in their hearts: Basil & Charlotte Braveheart, Edina Preucel, Bob Helm, Leonora Smith, Kent McBride, Carol Ann (Wilson) Fullmer, Steve Gerrior, Diana Whitney, Ted Webb, Marie Kane, Michael Gerrior, Dana Wilcox, Dave & Beth Cronin, Ben Walton, Tom & Gail Beavert, David Braveheart, Heather Hemer, Gale Arnold, Phil Webb, Robert Mitre, Gail Horton, Philip Bray, William Harper, Phyllis Kirk, and of course Shaman.

Contributors

Jill Pickett, Ian Kennedy, Jayne Stock-Hill, Cal Wick, Bill Baker, Gail Hoag, Edina Preucel

Editors

Edina Preucel, with Barbara McNichol, Gale Arnold, Dana Wilcox, Timothea Comstedt

My personal truth:
I am not in a position to moralize or judge others.
While I strive for truth, integrity and trustworthiness,
I am not always honest. I keep secrets.
Above all things, I strive to appreciate my place in the universe.
So far I have learned one thing.
I am not at its center.

Section I
Organizational Change

Section II
Seven Steps To Build The Truthful Organization

Section III
Practical Applications

How To Get The Most From This Book

Sidebar essays are not part of the text, but illustrate key points. Sidebars are by the author, unless otherwise credted.

Text columns may vary in width, but will always be found on the inside of each page. Key points are reproduced in the outside columns as an executive summary. Read these for a quick overview before jumping deeper into the "Truth Zone."

Light italics indicate a quote from other authors. Dark italics without an author's name indicates a "pull quote" from the text of the book.

Leadership Vacuum

Many times, while conducting programs on our challenge course in Estes Park, Colorado, I have seen a vacuum in leadership lead to surprising reactions from the team. Often, a clearly defined team problem is actually being solved by one cominant indivdual who takes the lead. The problem is, we are often in the midstw of learning how to work together without a storng central leader. As a result, the "winds of change" blow in and cause this leader to be blindfolded.

Beyond the laboratory, human systems seem infinitely more complicated. The complexity and lack of predictability of human systems is the kernel of truth behind the myth that it is difficult to initiate change in a system. You will recall, a closer look revealed change was fundamental to all systems — the difficult part was controlling the change. Once initiated, change tends to take on a life or at least a direction of its own. Could this be a reflection of some underlying orderliness coming through?

Lets take another look at the ivy trellice. Rather than looking at the trellice and the ivy as separate things, consider the relationship between the two. It is easy to understand that a trellice was created expressly for the purpose of stabilizing an ivy vine, without the ivy, it has no purpose. But as a structure, it exists completely independently from the ivy. It does not need the ivy.a million years before trellices. But look what happens when they unite. A simple, meaningless accumulation of wood slats becomes a thing of beauty when it is embraced by the ivy.

The relationship is more than just a plant and an artifact, it has a power of its own. Anyone who has ever tried, knows separating the ivy from the trellice, mid-summer is a formidable task. Pruning a branch here or there will have little effect because the plant quickly mobilizes itself to fill in the gap. The plant responds, by changing itself. And yet the result is the maintenance of the relationship. Change for the purpose of preserving the status quo is fundamental to life everywhere, its is often called dynamic equilibrium - balance through change. When living things stop changing, they die. But it is more than change, more than growth. Critical relationships must be maintained, whether it is for structural support, nourishment or

Beyond the laboratory, human systems seem infinitely more complicated. The complexity and lack of predictability of human systems is the kernel of truth behind the myth that it is difficult to initiate change in a system. You will recall, a closer look revealed change was fundamental to all systems — the difficult part was controlling the change. Once initiated, change tends to take on a life or at least a direction of its own. Could this be a reflection of some underlying orderliness coming through?

Lets take another look at the ivy trellice. Rather than looking at the trellice and the ivy as separate things, consider the relationship between the two. It is easy to understand that a trellice was created expressly for the purpose of stabilizing an ivy vine, without the ivy, it has no purpose. But as a structure, it exists completely independently from the ivy. It does not need the ivy.a million years before trellices. But look what happens when they unite. A simple, meaningless accumulation of wood slats becomes a thing of beauty when it is embraced by the ivy.

The relationship is more than just a plant and an artifact, it has a power of its own. Anyone who has ever tried, knows separating the ivy from the trellice, mid-summer is a formidable task. Pruning a branch here or there will have little effect because the plant quickly mobilizes itself to fill in the gap. The plant responds, by changing itself. And yet the result is the maintenance of the relationship. Change for the purpose of preserving the status quo is fundamental to life everywhere, its is often called dynamic equilibrium - balance through change. When living things stop changing, they die. But it is more than change, more than growth. Critical relationships must be maintained, whether it is for structural support, nourishment or other sustaining factors, living systems will undergo extraordinary changes in order to maintain those life-giving relationships. Nothing exists independently. Nothing is completely self-sustaining. So at the core of the natural world are relationships.

He who is firmly seated in authority soon learns to think security, and not progress, the highest lesson of statecraft.
—James Russel Lowell

The complexity and lack of predictability of human systems is the kernel of truth behind the myth that it is difficult to initiate change in a system.

Preface to Revised Edition

Based upon responses to the first edition, it may be valuable to define the word truth in the context of this book. Over the past several years, it has been fascinating to observe the response of people to this little word. Some people are strongly attracted, others sneer and recoil like vampires in the light.

As a unifying principle for organization development, truth is much more than simple honesty. The fact is, the vast majority of all transactions are extremely honest. So what is this truth thing? As an avid sailor and whitewater canoeing enthusiast, navigating a true course is vital, and even with a compass, the only way to do that is to have two stationary reference points one ahead, and one behind. An analogous situation exists for organizations. Most have a forward reference point, called a vision, but after years of working with organizations, it is clear that a vision is not enough. The counterpart to the rear reference point is the personal mission of the individuals within the organization. The vision must be compelling enough to exert a real "pull" on every employee toward a shared result. Likewise, the mission of each person must be strong enough to "push" them toward sustainable outstanding achievements. Only when the vision and mission are in place and aligned can an organization be assured of a true course.

In this revised edition, Chapter 11 offers a compendium of sixteen core building blocks and a number of practical tools to build a Truthful Organization. In addition, a series of experiential activities gives the reader ways to develop the building blocks and share the tools in ways that will make them easy to learn and instantly useful.

Ward Flynn
Summer, 1997

The Eleven Big Lies

Which Undermine Quality, Participation, and Teamwork

LIES *Your needs are secondary to those of the organization*	**TRUTHS** *The fulfillment of my needs adds value to the team when my personal mission is aligned with the vision of the organization.*
1. There is no room for your personal life at work; leave it at home.	*1. Loyalty, passion, commitment, and self-management are personal values I learned at home.*
2. Your company protects your safety and maintains a pleasant working environment.	*2. Safety is everyone's business. Only I can make myself happy then I work smarter and more cooperatively.*
3. Conflict in the work place indicates a lack of teamwork and management's loss of control.	*3. I believe conflict is valuable because it is where new ideas come from.*
4. To adapt to the environment in which you work, you must be willing to go along.	*4. When I am made to go along, I feel a loss of commitment and a lack of personal responsibility.*
5. In a competitive environment, there is little or no time for on-the-job learning—you are paid to get it right the first time.	*5. I know learning may be our only competitive edge, and much can be learned from mistakes.*
6. Do your job and stay out of trouble; your company's long-range vision offers security. It will take care of you.	*6. Having security is knowing the value of my contribution and how I share in my company's success.*
7. Your company's big picture is too distracting and should be left to the executives.	*7. I add value to my company in unique ways. It is highly motivational to know how my work impacts co-workers, customers, and the bottom line.*
8. Recruiting motivated star performers builds an unstoppable, high-performing team.	*8. I've noticed that individual "stars" usually lack team skills and lose sight of our common goals while competing with each other.*
9. Rewarding technical excellence and productivity ensures bottom-line results.	*9. Rewarding only technical skills ignores communication, leadership, innovation, teamwork, honesty, and other vital components of our success.*
10. Managers need technical skills equal to or superior to those of their subordinates.	*10. Managers need different skills, including: planning, personal motivation, meeting facilitation, coaching, conflict management, team building, scheduling, and budgeting.*
11. You only improve your skills when you're forced to own your mistakes.	*11. With this approach, blame leads to fear which stifles creativity, innovation, personal responsibility, and participation. I'd rather work where mistakes are opportunities to learn and no one buys into the blame game.*

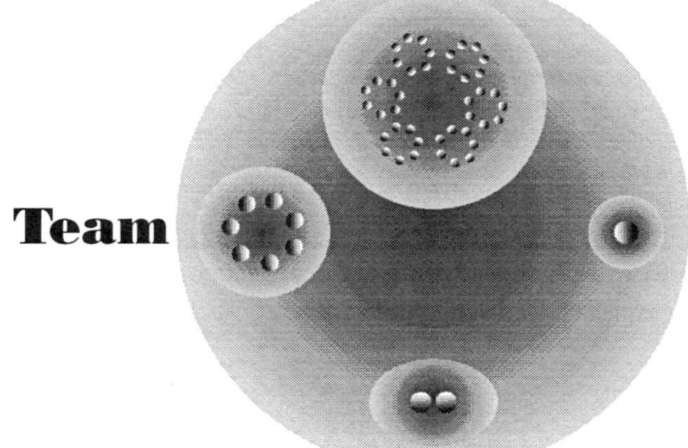

Section One

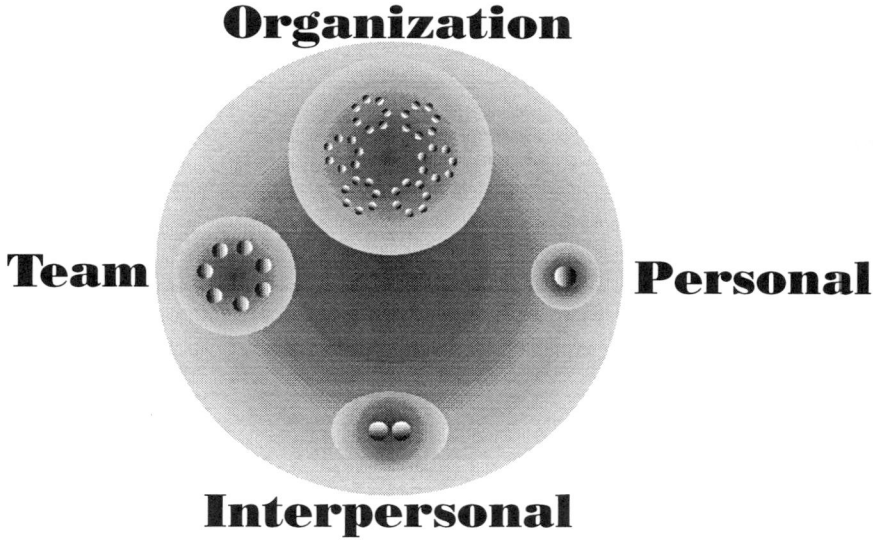

Organizational Change

Organizational Change

Organizational change has been a challenge throughout history. With more and larger organizations of increasing complexity, it has never been more problematical than it is today. Although organizational design and change has been a matter of systematic inquiry only in this century, it has embraced a wide range of disciplines and approaches. Until now, the sum total of that research has led change consultants to the conclusion that change must be initiated, implemented, and managed from the top of the organization.

In the next three chapters, a completely different approach is presented. Individuals who want to create a better working environment for themselves and their co-workers will be given the tools necessary to lead a revolution in their work environment—regardless of whether they are owners, managers, or frontline workers!

Chapter One

1

You Can Make A Difference

You Can Make A Difference

We are in trouble. The new global economy represents a challenge few organizations are prepared to answer. Fewer still are ready to thrive in the new marketplace. The sacred cows have been slaughtered: fair trade, unions, tariffs, lifetime employment, lifelong product cycles, to name but a few. Not since the Industrial Revolution has there been so much confusion, so much chaos, or so much fear.

Many businesses are grasping at straws. The level of experimentation with new methods of management, manufacturing, even finance, is unprecedented. Total Quality Management (TQM), reengineering, reinvention, teams, customer focus, and change management initiatives are but a handful of the programs swallowed by businesses of every size and description. But there is something wrong; few organizations report much success with their ambitious attempts at transformation.

In times of change, people need to pull together. Unfortunately, the way organizations have tried to transform themselves has not engendered support from the rank and file.

We need a revolution! When people do not focus on a common vision and commit to a true course, it is impossible to generate the kind of results businesses seek. If cooperation is lacking in your place of work, in former Chrysler chairman Lee Iacocca's words, it's time to ... "Lead, follow or get out of the way!"

You can make a difference. In fact, you can lead the revolution in your workplace.

If you are tempted to hide behind the words ... "I am only one person," consider this: *The most basic component in any organization is the individual.*

Each of us has a specific zone of influence—each of us in charge of something—some place where we are the master. It might be a specific division, a sewing machine, a back hoe, a shovel, accounts payable, shipping, research and development, or

We need a revolution! When people do not focus on a common vision and commit to a true course, it is impossible to generate the kind of results businesses seek. If cooperation is lacking in your place of work, in former Chrysler chairman Lee Iacocca's words, it's time to ... "Lead, follow or get out of the way!"

maintenance— the opportunity is ripe. Yet how many of us acknowledge our own power and influence?

Too many of us focus on what we lack and wring our hands in disgust. What is worse, we waste time complaining, blaming, and falling victim to the epidemic of cynicism sweeping our organizations. How easily we can sell ourselves short!

Even consultants and business gurus fall into this trap when they rebuke workers for their lack of motivation, saying real change begins at the top. This disempowering bias is as wrong as it is widespread.

I'm plotting revolution against this lie that the majority has a monopoly of the truth. What are these truths that always bring the majority rallying round? Truths so elderly they are practically senile. And when a truth is as old as that, gentlemen, you can hardly tell it from a lie.
—Henrik Ibsen

Change, even from the bottom up, is possible! In reality, the most significant social changes in history were revolutions. And revolutions are, by nature, bottom-up events. For all their reputation for blood, revolutions are not necessarily violent. Nevertheless, revolutions are never easy; change leaders may rightly be called *champions*.

Can organizational change really be analogous to revolution? Yes! And increasingly more business people agree. The trend in recent years is clear: employee-owned businesses, open-book management, self-directed work teams, empowerment, and cooperative relationships between management and unions are just the tip of the iceberg.

Businesses everywhere are part of a large-scale revolution. Today's managers know that timeworn parental management styles of command and control will not work in the 21st century. In the last decade, the old notion that workers need constant, costly supervision has been thoroughly debunked. But how is the workplace transformed into a highly efficient, productive environment peopled by self-directed, motivated workers who really care?

The experience of many companies in the early 1990s proves there is more to transformation than reducing costs and laying off middle managers. The new workplaces must not only stimulate self-management but enhance productivity. A transformed environment delivers creativity, critical thinking, conviction, courage, compassion, service, and a willingness to learn and try new things.

The suggestion that it may be possible to reduce costs, increase productivity, and transform the culture seems too good to be true. In reality, they are a matched set. Downsizing without transformation results in chaos. Transforming the culture without addressing the structure of the organization guarantees turmoil. Companies all over the world have tried to reduce costs and boost productivity without transforming the culture. Perhaps that is why chaos has become a new buzz word in business publishing.

The beauty of transforming the culture is the unexpected dividends which arise from doing so. With blinders off, alternatives to laying off tried-and-true, loyal employees may appear!

The model for this kind of roll-up-the-sleeves, let's-get-the-job-done, how-can-we-work-together organization need not be borrowed from the Japanese. In fact, it as American as apple pie and the Fourth of July.

Organizations are trying to kindle a spark of entrepreneurism in their midst. While the entrepreneurial spirit is historically found only in small businesses, cottage industries, and start-ups, it is not unknown in the annals of corporate America. IBM experimented with this 15 years ago when it shunted some of its brightest people to a Palmetto field in Boca Raton. Their charter: give Apple a run for its money by building a personal computer. And, yes, you can do it your own way; even outsource the operating system to a 20-year-old from Washington state. With the success of the PC and the advent of Bill Gates' Microsoft empire, IBM ultimately decided to pull the plug on its "intrapreneuring" experiment.

Although Big Blue chose not to clone the idea, they proved it is possible to create an entrepreneurial spirit inside one of the largest, most stable, and highly controlled organizations in history!

Kindling the spirit of entrepreneurship in tens or even hundreds of thousands of workers requires a passionate revolution. To bring about a transformation in the values, expectations, attitudes, and skills of workers, nothing less will do. Another top-down improvement program just won't cut it.

Downsizing without transformation results in chaos. Transforming the culture without addressing the problem of the structure of the organization guarantees turmoil.

However well-intentioned, top-down change initiatives may be doomed from the start. The literature is full of disappointing stories describing quality, teambuilding, reengineering, and other initiatives that end up in the weeds. The success or failure of these programs has little to do with management's intentions and everything to do with the motivation of workers. Few people seek change, even when it is for their own good ... most people are wary of the unknown. If change is not off-putting enough by itself, when it is imposed from above, most of us actively resist. The more pressure we feel, the more vigorously we rebel.

Few people seek change, even when it is for their own good ... most people are wary of the unknown. If change is not off-putting enough by itself, when it is imposed from above, most of us actively resist. The more pressure we feel, the more vigorously we rebel.

By contrast, look at the self-generated enthusiasm of entrepreneurs and their teams who regularly overcome the handicaps of small staffs, poor planning, undercapitalization, and lack of experience. In fact, the "handicaps" themselves serve to unleash personal commitment, innovation, courage, and willpower. Sometimes, nothing can hold them back!

And so the search goes on. Leaders seeking just the right strategy or initiative to transform and improve their organizations are tempted to select from a mountain of new management methods and philosophies. But isn't the tail wagging the dog? The problem is not selecting the best improvement program; it's getting buy-in from the team. Most managers have come to believe a mediocre strategy with strong buy-in from the team is better than a smarter strategy with only lacklustre support.

On the other hand, what established company is willing to return to its adolescent entrepreneurial period? Stability is a seductive, if complacent, business partner.

Is it possible to have it both ways? Could workers, burning with entrepreneurial zeal, champion a well-intentioned improvement program in an established organization from the bottom up? Yes! But only after a formidable obstacle is overcome ... a parent-child mindset.

We Have Seen The Enemy ...

Managers and employees historically have a strange relationship. They typically share a singular mind-set which elevates managers above their counterparts, ascribing superior judgment, knowledge, and creativity to managers, and usually simple motives to workers. Managers tend to act like parents; workers like children. Managers enforce the rules, evaluate performance, make judgments about quality, and organize the work effort. Yet no one likes authority! As a result, there is a natural tension between managers and workers.

The problem is not selecting the best improvement program; it's getting buy-in from the team.

When a worker makes a mistake, his or her manager usually responds by exerting more parental control. When a manager is rigid, workers often react with juvenile peevishness or overt resistance. On the other hand, good managers have always known that when workers are treated with respect and viewed as adults, they respond with more mature behavior.

Is it possible to have it both ways? Could workers, burning with entrepreneurial zeal, champion a well-intentioned improvement program in an established organization from the bottom up?

Most of us, however, have difficulty seeing beyond our own experience. The old parent-child dynamic linking manager to employee runs deep. Learned long before people entered the workforce, it represents one of the greatest challenges to organizational change. Because we are locked in a love-hate relationship, those who complain the loudest are often the first to defend the only system they know.

Since the Industrial Revolution, everyone's life has been dominated by parental organizations. These organizations (families, churches, governments, schools, businesses, associations, sport teams, etc.) are so prevalent in our culture that it is all most of us know. While we believe in the dignity of the individual and think of ourselves as self-sufficient adults, the actions of managers and employees support a contrary position. When placed in a position of authority, we tend to treat people like children. It is as if we believe people never really grow up and continue to need guidance, rules, and a carefully monitored system of rewards and punishments.

Sadly, the previous argument is the one dictators and despots use to rationalize their regimes. And after they are deposed, there remain those (and there are multitudes in

Leadership Vacuum

Many times, while conducting programs on our challenge course in Estes Park, Colorado, I have seen a vacuum in leadership lead to surprising reactions from the team. Often, a clearly defined team problem is actually being solved by one dominant individual who takes the lead. The problem is, we are often in the midst of learning how to work together *without* a strong central leader. As a result, the "winds of change" blow in and cause this leader to be blindfolded, silenced, or otherwise incapacitated as a leader. The result is an instant vacuum. But, even with a theme such as "shared leadership" or "team problem solving," only rarely does the team use this opportunity to reorganize and explore alternatives to the single boss model. Instead, someone else grabs the reins of power and picks up where the other boss leaves off. Variations on this activity, including appointing very weak leaders, indicate that most people feel most comfortable when someone else takes command and controls responsibility. Through business simulations such as these, coupled with sufficient time for participants to dialogue about the experience, teams usually come to understand that a strong leader, even a very smart leader, is rarely as effective as a whole team. Once this is understood, teams redefine leadership to focus on communication and coaching as opposed to the old-fashioned, "I'm in command" approach.

Eastern Europe and the former Soviet Union) who are nostalgic for the good old days and pray for a return to *order*.

Insightful, more democratic managers use praise, rewards, and even cash to break this cycle, wanting to inspire workers to participate more fully in the enterprise. While these methods have probably helped, they fall short of the environment Jobs and Wozniac enjoyed when they built the first Apple computer in a garage. Rewards alone do <u>not</u> explain the fever that characterizes the behavior of entrepreneurs. Cash rewards become just a variation on the same old parental models—what managers give they can always take away! The insidious nature of control cannot be overestimated. Even a "good will" attempt to reward workers for greater loyalty or commitment may carry the seeds of the outmoded parent-child relationship!

In Alfie Kohn's book, *Reward as Punishment*, he debunks most of the long-standing myths about monetary and other incentive systems. He points out rewards <u>do</u> work, but we seldom understand how, why, or even what we are rewarding. The result is a series of mixed messages and a confused work force leading to an immobile status quo. Moreover, he proves that behavioral changes lacking corresponding shifts in values and beliefs are usually temporary.

Even leading-edge management schemes have, thus far, failed to close the motivation gap—which brings us to a moment of truth. If the critical missing element is personal motivation, how can a boss, or any external agent, presume to deliver it? You might as well legislate love or enforce happiness. No one can empower, motivate, or fix another person. And since organizations and teams are made up of individuals, how presumptuous to assume any boss, no matter how charismatic, can change a whole organization. Managers who want to make a real impact can begin by reading Peter Block's *Stewardship* where he teaches "revolution to the ruling class."

Even a "good will" attempt to reward workers for greater loyalty or commitment may carry the seeds of the outmoded parent-child relationship!

Genuine change must break through the entrenched, parent-child mind-set. When a change initiative is driven by management, it tends to fortify the notion that managers are in control, thereby preserving the parental model. According to Jeffrey Goldstein, author of *The Unshackled Organization*, real change must be self-generated. He champions the notion that an organization is a system which naturally seeks a state of equilibrium. Therefore, most change initiatives are minor perturbations which are quickly absorbed into the system. Moreover, as they are managed or controlled by management or a facilitator (to keep them from getting out of hand) they rarely pose a threat to the balance. Real change, he advocates, requires an extreme "far from equilibrium" shift.

Top-down change initiatives are usually only temporary fixes, more akin to buying new furniture for a dilapidated house—but nothing really changes.

If a boss cannot make change happen, how can a secretary, mail clerk, or maintenance worker possibly succeed? Clearly a boss is in a better position to "upset the apple cart," but in most cases, the leader we expect to change the system was its author. Besides, the boss has burdensome allegiances to tradition, boards of directors, and other stakeholders who make it difficult to take significant risks. Most bosses are too deeply trapped in their own paradigm to embrace, let alone lead, substantial change. What a boss can do is get out of the way. A boss can help define the problem, then facilitate access to information and resources. He or she hands problems over to the team. Later, the boss can support the process by providing resources, removing obstacles, and offering guidance, encouragement, and coaching.

If the critical missing element is personal motivation, how can a boss, or any external agent, presume to deliver it? You might as well legislate love or enforce happiness.

More often than not, the boss will neither attempt change nor allow others to tackle it. In most cases he or she is the bastion of tradition and the soldier of the status quo. The boss's job is to minimize turbulence and keep the show on the road, motivated by concerns for the bottom line! The question is: if you are not the boss, can you do any better? Can a non-supervisor really make a difference?

Limited authority may look like a liability, but only when you think from the old mindset. In fact, the organization's greatest untapped asset is its people. People like you. When rank and file workers step forward to lead (as opposed to managing or bossing), their peers are more likely to listen. In part, this is because you speak their "language." More importantly, these new leaders do not carry the baggage of the past. The power of peer leadership cannot be overestimated as a motivational aid. When you stand up to be counted, you make a powerful statement to your co-workers.

Lead what, you may ask? Leadership is not a title, but a way of life. Regardless of your zone of influence, your moment of truth arises every day: will you lead or adopt a wait-and-see attitude? Leadership means you know why you are here, you have a personal mission, you accept responsibility for your own happiness and safety, and you realize you may occasionally have to take a stand that puts you in conflict with others. Finally, it means you know the limits of your influence and you set appropriate boundaries that others can see. This is your zone of influence—the area you may choose to transform into a "Truth Zone."

There are others within your zone of influence, such as co-workers, subordinates, even a supervisor, who could benefit from your leadership. The idea of leadership must never be limited to the mere trappings of power: title, parking space, or a corner office.

Leadership

Peer (or situational) leaders lead because of two factors: 1) they are willing, and 2) the team accepts them. Notice that managers and other designated leaders may lack both motivation and acceptance. This is because bosses are seldom taught to lead—they learn from experience to boss and control. As a situational leader, bossing is not your role. In fact, you can lose credibility the moment you start telling, judging, correcting, or acting self-important.

As long as peer leaders can maintain a clear direction and the team's respect, they will be able to *champion* ideas within their own zone of influence. Anyone can have a dramatic influence—with effects reaching far beyond the obvious zone of influence. You and your peers' ability to influence rests on these four points:

What a boss can do is get out of the way.

1. Champions can choose a zone of influence in which they feel comfortable.
2. The credibility they have with their peers guarantees their message will be listened to and heard.
3. Instead of telling others how to act, their own behavior becomes the model others choose to emulate.
4. These champions disquiet an otherwise stable organization, inspiring others to champion change.

Anyone in an organization who seeks transformation can be a *change leader*. When you take a stand, you do it on your terms. It does not mean going into your boss's office and pounding your fist on the desk. You decide how to express yourself. You decide when to speak up, and when not to. You decide how to make your point, how best to be heard. Most change leaders are quiet and unassuming. But even the gentlest stand is visible to others. People will be attracted to your cause. When others join you and all agree to work as equals for a shared vision, the revolution has begun!

Leadership means you know why you are here, you have a personal mission, you accept responsibility for your own happiness and safety, and you realize you may occasionally have to take a stand that puts you in conflict with others. Finally, it means you know the limits of your influence and you set appropriate boundaries that others can see. This is your zone of influence—the area you may choose to transform into a "Truth Zone."

You will have created a pocket of entrepreneurial enthusiasm within the organization. You can craft agreements to guide you and your team in your interactions, assuring open, honest, and direct communication. These pockets of entrepreneurial spirit are Truth Zones because, within these zones, individuals are committed to expressing themselves through their work. Each person has truthfully aligned his or her personal mission with the larger shared vision of the organization. Cooperation is supported with agreements and open, honest communication. People are not afraid to take a stand or venture a risk. People respect each other.

It is possible to create "Truth Zones" within even the most rigid parental organization. For example, Brian, an executive chef in a fine restaurant, was hired and managed by one of the most controlling, tyrannical managers I have ever known. While the manager gave lip service to the notion of employee empowerment, it was going nowhere. When the manager arrived from the corporate office, people were terrified. Watching him walk into the restaurant was a reminder of how people act when royalty enters a room—they seemed to bow. Though two levels removed from the tyrant, Brian took it upon himself to set up a program of empowerment to help his employees participate more fully in the operation of his kitchen. Brian got prep cooks, stewards, and bus staff on the same team in spite of the rigid environment above them. Eventually, the tyrant was removed and, two years later, the restaurant continues to improve on its award-winning track record.

Truth Zones such as the one Brian put in place serve the organization with greater productivity, motivation, and participation. They also serve the workers who enjoy a more supportive natural work environment in which they know their contributions are important.

As these Truth Zones take hold, they tend to multiply. In some organizations, they are supported by upper level managers; in others, they are the product of a single individual working from the bottom up. The result is a patchwork of Truth Zones that link up, exerting an increasingly positive influence on the organization—eventually transforming the organization. Truly revolutionary!

This book does not encourage the overthrow of an organization. There is a big difference between transforming an organization from the bottom up and changing it against its will. It is inappropriate to attempt to move an organization in a direction contrary to its own vision.

Peer (or situational) leaders lead because of two factors: 1) they are willing, and 2) the team accepts them.

Just as individual actions are best propelled by a personal mission, change must always be in the direction of an organization's vision. When both are aligned, individual actions are focused in the direction of the shared vision. If you are unable to align your mission with the company vision, negotiating a change in its vision or altering your personal mission must be considered. If neither is possible, for your own health, peace of mind, and the good of the organization, find a more aligned environment in which to work.

What is the Truthful Organization?

The Truthful Organization is, at its core, a set of tools to help individuals discover their own passion for participation. It is a set of seven action steps that support organizational development initiatives including quality, service, reengineering, customer focus, and others. It is unique in its bottom-up deployment. Any individual, work group, or team at any level of the organization can take the lead, beginning with a pilot program or an organization-wide deployment.

When others join you and all agree to work as equals for a shared vision, the revolution has begun!

As used here, truth does not refer to basic honesty or moral precepts—honesty is a given! While it is easy to cite examples of deceit and larceny, by and large the tens of thousands of interactions occurring on any given day are generally honest. Ultimately, if a team or business chooses to become a Truthful Organization, the level of basic honesty does improve and integrity emerges as a high value among participants. But its primary focus is the alignment of all levels of the organization.

There are four levels of alignment in a Truthful Organization: Personal, Interpersonal, Team, and Organizational.

These pockets of entrepreneurial spirit are Truth Zones because, within these zones, individuals are committed to expressing themselves through their work. Each person has truthfully aligned his or her personal mission with the larger shared vision of the organization. Cooperation is supported with agreements and open, honest communication. People are not afraid to take a stand or venture a risk. People respect each other.

Personal Truth:

In the Truthful Organization, each individual is encouraged to clarify his/her own mission and determine how, and to what degree, participation in the organization supports that personal mission. Likewise, each employee is encouraged to determine how he or she adds unique value. In this way, each person's participation is deliberate, intentional, and therefore, truthful.

There is a direct correlation between a person's understanding of his or her personal mission and the degree of passion brought to the job. When people's jobs contribute to their mission, they bring more of themselves—and their passion—to the workplace.

Interpersonal Truth:

The Truthful Organization establishes criteria and offers tools to improve interpersonal communication. Individuals are given the tools necessary to support situational leadership, collaboration, and the ability to take a stand and resolve conflicts.

Conflicts are less frequent when the quality of relationships is improved up front. Operating agreements permit open, honest, and direct communication, and support a rapid resolution when discord arises.

People in Truthful Organizations are more self-aware. Their relationships are based on the following behavior styles:

Peer - Adult: Non-manipulative, open, honest, and direct in dealing with others.

Boss - Parental: Directive, authoritative, controlling behavior in dealing with others, especially with subordinates.

Subordinate - Child: Subservient, submissive behaviors of those who rely on the authority and direction of others, especially the boss/parent.

Team Truth:

Teams are a part of every organization. How they participate, make decisions, and deal with obstacles are critical to overall team performance. Whether the organization has moved to formal teams, or the team is simply the usual co-workers, specific skills can be applied to enhance team effectiveness. Teams are more than a group. A team can perform at levels greater than the sum total of its members' abilities. The seeming impossibility, where total output exceeds the sum of its parts, is accomplished by creating genuinely interdependent relationships which enhance the performance while focusing on a shared objective.

To achieve real interdependence, team members must move beyond simple cooperation and everyday civility. Real teamwork rests on artful skills of *dialogue, negotiation,* and *contracting* as well as the ability to recognize and resolve conflicts when they arise.

Dialogue is different from discussion. In a discussion, there is a clash of ideas which pits the passion and logic of one argument against another, with the hope that the best one prevails. In dialogue, the passion is not for one's own argument, but for understanding the other person's point of view. In a dialogue, all ideas are given a more equitable hearing. The idea that is adopted will have more to do with its value than the quality of argument.

Negotiation is an important, and often overlooked, tool any individual can use to change things that are not working. Just because something has always been done one way, or because the boss wanted something a certain way does not mean questions cannot be asked. However, the questions should take the form of a negotiation. One might approach the boss with a comment such as, "I am not comfortable with the location of the new watercooler. Would you be willing to hear my reasons and consider some alternative locations?"

Contracting is akin to negotiating, but it is especially important in improving relationships between co-workers, particularly between internal customer-suppliers. All too often, workers (suppliers) assume their job is to do as they are told without asking

It is inappropriate to attempt to move an organization in a direction contrary to its own vision. Just as individual actions are best propelled by a personal mission, change must always be in the direction of an organization's vision. When both are aligned, individual actions are focused in the direction of the shared vision.

While it is easy to cite examples of deceit and larceny, by and large the tens of thousands of interactions occurring on any given day are generally honest.

questions. In reality, employees are far too valuable to leave their brains at the door. Whenever an employee is asked to perform a task, it is important that several key questions be asked to make sure the job will be done to the customer's satisfaction and in such a way that allows the supplier to apply maximum effort to the job. For example, a simple yet critical question in any contract is: "Do you want me to do this job in a specific manner, or may I use my best judgment on how to proceed?" Asking that common sense question up front can save untold trouble down the road—but how often does it get asked?

There is a direct correlation between a person's understanding of his or her personal mission and the degree of passion brought to the job. When people's jobs contribute to their mission, they bring more of themselves—and their passion—to the workplace.

No matter how well team members communicate, negotiate, and contract, occasionally conflicts will occur. Conflicts are natural. But how conflict is dealt with by team members marks the difference between a work group and a team.

Organizational Truth:

Some organizations make it easy for individuals to align their personal goals with the goals of the organization. Others make it difficult by operating without clear values or a long-term vision. Such organizations, even with strong centralized leadership, tend to drift with shifting markets, occupying their workers with short-term projects and crisis management. In such an environment, it is difficult for individuals to know where they stand in relationship to the overall organization; individual and organizational alignment occurs by happenstance, if at all.

The Truthful Organization has a clear vision and operates from a set of well-defined values. Employees are personally motivated to think and act like owners. Organizational assets are invested in an ongoing enrichment of individual employee resources. The Truthful Organization seeks to align individuals within the organization to enhance the overall viability of the enterprise and the experience of the individuals.

The leaders of the Truthful Organization walk their talk. Leaders operate with the same guidelines as all employees. Because there is no need to create artificial incentives, hierarchies, and turf building, sacred cows such as sales contests which institutionalize internal competition are regularly eliminated. In the Truthful Organization, it is enough that the organization itself succeeds. When the organization wins, everyone benefits!

The Level of Quality Cannot Exceed the Level of Truth

Many of us have had to make a decision which pitted one of our values against another. For example, I may have a deeply held value that I should provide for my children's welfare. On the other hand, I may have a value that compels me to report problems in my work. If I have reason to believe that reporting a specific problem will lead to the loss of my job, I face a dilemma. What is truth? To help organizations and individuals grapple with this dilemma, we at the Venture Centre present workshops designed to illustrate the importance of truthful participation and its effect on data collection, quality, and participation.

Any time workers are rewarded for inaccurate or incomplete reporting, or more importantly, have reason to believe they will be disciplined or demeaned for truthful reporting, even the most sophisticated quality measurement system is flawed.

Let us begin by committing ourselves to the truth—to see it like it is, and tell it like it is—to find the truth, to speak the truth, and to live the truth.
—Richard M. Nixon

What is Truth?

Is it my truth? Your truth? Company truth? Situations have a way of undermining people's notion of truth. Some people have not yet discovered that their truth is not necessarily THE truth. Ultimately, each of us must develop, what Steven Covey, author of *Seven Habits of Highly Successful People* and *Principle Centered Leadership,* calls a moral compass to guide us through the complex landscape of business, social, and intimate relationships.

The Entrepreneur's Truth

The lives of contemporary and historical entrepreneurs reveal similar patterns that, when taken as a whole, uncover a handful of recurring themes. Entrepreneuring is the expression of one's self through business. Just as artists use marble, paint, or music,

The Truthful Organization has a clear vision and operates from a set of well-defined values. Employees are personally motivated to think and act like owners. Organizational assets are invested in an ongoing enrichment of individual employee resources. The Truthful Organization seeks to align individuals within the organization to enhance the overall viability of the enterprise and the experience of the individuals.

entrepreneurs use the medium of the marketplace, commerce, and relationships to express themselves. It follows that "to thine own self be true" represents a core axiom of the successful entrepreneur. But how to stay true? How to persevere and not sell out? How to rise above the ridicule, fear, and envy of others? How to rise above one's own pride, greed, and fear?

Again, if we look at the lives of great people—people who, like entrepreneurs, express themselves through their work—we can reap a harvest of powerful concepts, ideas, and guidelines. The **Seven Steps to Championing Truth** that follow encapsulate those recurring themes. They are organized so that others may "true" their own course and enjoy the benefits of aligning their personal truth with the visionary truths of others—the team, the organization, and the larger culture.

These principles can be adopted by people wishing to kindle in themselves a more empowered, more aligned, and more truthful way of living. This is true whether they want to revolutionize their workplaces or just participate more effectively within the organization.

Seven Steps

These seven steps serve not only as guidelines, but as a model for personal and organizational development. They are the application of truth. The first two are *personal.* They deal with inner values, attitudes, and beliefs. The third is *interpersonal*. The fourth and fifth steps are about *team,* integrating the first three in a way that empowers a person to move on to the last two. These last two steps inspire a redefinition of the organization—beyond traditional boundaries. Together, they will lead you on a personal journey of self-discovery, relationship-building, collaboration, and leadership.

Seven Steps to Championing Truth in the Organization

1. **Declare and live out your personal mission.**
The declaration of a personal vision is an expression of a person's commitment. With the knowledge of a co-worker's personal mission in hand, it is possible to craft working relationships that realistically match people's real talents and rouse their passions. In the past, everyone was expected to espouse total commitment to the company and pledge life-long allegiance. That is no longer realistic. Most managers agree that employees with a mission, even ones that will take them out of the organization, are preferable to staff who have no plan, no mission, and no passion.
2. **Accept responsibility for your own safety and happiness.**
Organizations used to want only sheep. Now they need self-motivated, self-aware, and assertive people who have personal values that motivate them to take action—tackling even unpopular causes. Every organization wants people who will stand up to "right a wrong," rather than stand by and watch people hurt themselves or damage the customer or organization.
3. **Acknowledge the value of conflict.**
Conflict is not only a natural part of human behavior but, in groups and organizations, it serves a vital role in stimulating ideas and bringing about change. Employees who understand the difference between conflict and aggression are vital, assuming they have the skills to manage conflict and avoid aggression.
4. **Model truthful behavior by creating "truth zones" within the organization.**
When individual staff members make an effort to improve the quality of the organization around them, genuine bottom-up, buy-in is underway. This effort can

Any time workers are rewarded for inaccurate or incomplete reporting, or more importantly, have reason to believe they will be disciplined or demeaned for truthful reporting, even the most sophisticated quality measurement system is flawed.

Entrepreneuring is the expression of one's self through business. Just as artists use marble, paint, or music, entrepreneurs use the medium of the marketplace, commerce, and relationships to express themselves. It follows that "to thine own self be true" represents a core axiom of the successful entrepreneur.

transform the organization. It may also upset fearful managers who believe change must be controlled from above.

5. **Seek continuous learning for yourself and your organization.**
   An organization committed to learning from its mistakes is an organization made flexible and ready to take on the challenges of a changing marketplace. Unfortunately, an organization cannot learn unless the individual participants are encouraged by an environment in which mistakes are opportunities to learn and learning is valued above getting it right the first time.
6. **Claim a stake in the viability of the organizations of which you are a part.**
   If individual participants do not take a personal stake in the success of the organization, then buy-in will always be limited. A stake is much more than stock options or profit sharing. It is individual "ownership" of every single problem. And it is a proactive search for excellence on the part of staff to improve quality and learn from every mistake.
7. **Champion truthfulness in the organization; be a leader in architecting a truthful environment.**
   The most valuable employees are those committed to the vision that extends over the horizon, beyond today's quotas or tomorrow's goals. When staff members align their personal missions with a compelling, shared vision that transcends growth and profit, then people work with passion and zeal.

Chapter Two

Change Is Easier Said Than Done

Change is Easier Said Than Done

Making personal changes is difficult enough, but leading a revolution in the workplace may seem impossible. Over the last decade, many organizations, perhaps yours, have tried to change, most to no avail. What is it about change that makes it so difficult?

After years of complacency nurtured by a half-century of post-war industrial dominance, American business has found religion. It has happened now because international competition has been giving the U.S. a *devil* of a time. The new religion is *change*—salvation through *improvement* led by the preeminent sect, *Total Quality Management* (TQM). There has never been anything quite like the rush of business to embrace TQM. As evangelist Oral Roberts used to say, "They're coming down all the aisles." As far back as 1993, the Arthur D. Little research organization reported 93 percent of manufacturing and service firms have adopted some form of quality improvement program. Unfortunately it is not working as well in the U.S. as it did in post-war Japan. Even as more and more businesses try to clone the Japanese model, the results are disappointing. Almost two-thirds of 500 executives polled believe their company's quality efforts have failed to generate any significant impact on their competitive position.

A reported 93 percent of manufacturing and service firms have adopted some form of quality improvement program.

TQM is not alone. Teambuilding, leaderless work groups, flatter organizations, reengineering—none have proved to be the elusive panacea management has sought! Why? What's wrong?

Almost two-thirds of 500 executives polled believe their company's quality efforts have failed to generate any significant impact on their competitive position.

The Problem Is In Us

A major problem is businesses' obsession with quick fixes—simple solutions to complex problems. Management desperately seeks a simple formula to yield immediate results. Such a fetish with tens of millions of dollars in consulting fees up for grabs has hatched a remarkable growth industry. Change agents show up at every microphone, on business bookshelves, and in magazines everywhere—all touting their version of change. Each one offers a different recipe but sells the same sweet pudding. These consultant-chefs know management's hunger: reduce overhead, increase productivity, improve quality, gain more loyal customers, keep happy-smiling employees, and earn continuously improving profits. But the hunger will not be satisfied—stockholders, for one, are getting frustrated. No wonder so many companies have given up their subscription to the management scheme-of-the-month club! It's clear that off-the-shelf change initiatives do not work. No recipe is ever completely satisfying. What works in one company usually falls flat in another. The hard lesson to sell is: change is rarely easy, seldom predictable, and never quick.

The Truthful Organization comes at the problem from a completely new angle. Where other change initiatives are implemented from the outside in (driven by external consultants) or top down (driven by upper management), the Truthful Organization gives employees the tools to revolutionize their own workspace from the *bottom up*! This approach overcomes the primary obstacle shared by other change programs—buy-in. When change is initiated by individual workers from the bottom up, passionate participation is assured. What is more, the Truthful Organization can be deployed to enhance TQM, teams, customer focus, reengineering, open-book, and other strategies.

Why Does Change Seem To Be So Difficult?

Beyond businesses' impatience and unrealistic expectations about change initiatives, there is a more fundamental problem. The mechanics of change are poorly understood. Two comfortable old myths illustrate this assessment:

1. Change is difficult to initiate.
2. People fight change.

When change is initiated by individual workers from the bottom up, passionate participation is assured.

Myth #1: Change is difficult to initiate.

Wrong. Physicists assert that change is the only constant. If the basis of everything in the universe is change, how can it be so difficult to bring about change? Change occurs everywhere; no less so in organizations. Over the years, business has coped with innumerable changes; it has often led the way for the rest of society. Consider how information exchange has been facilitated through the introduction of telephones, computers, fax machines, and the Information Highway—innovations introduced by business. The problem is not how to initiate change, but how to manage it. Unfortunately, managing something so mysterious that it is known by myth and superstition represents a leap beyond the capability of most organizations.

The problem is not how to initiate change, but how to manage it. Unfortunately, managing something so mysterious that it is known by myth and superstition represents a leap beyond the capability of most organizations.

Myth #2: People fight change.

Also wrong. People love change. People love anything new. New clothes, cars, colors, foods, vacations. Few things remain popular without changing. Marketing experts know that the three letters N-E-W comprise the most effective packaging alteration to increase sales.

But wait! If people like change, why is the office in an uproar when the manager replaces one water cooler with another? It seems like a paradox but it isn't. Most people like change but nearly everyone dislikes having it imposed upon them. Change on our own terms is OK—more than OK— it is fundamental to life. But when change is imposed

Change On My Terms

As a kid, I remember my old Aunt Alma clucking her tongue at the notion of TV. But every time she came to our house, she would park herself in front of the set, mesmerized by everything from commercials to baseball, her favorite. Eventually, someone gave her a used set which I remember dominating one of her marble-topped Victorian end-tables next to a horse-hair-filled straight-backed chair. She loved it.

Here was a woman who had ridden stagecoaches from Tombstone to Deadwood, seen the introduction of telephones, moving pictures, radio and TV. Who can blame her if she wished to moderate the acceptance of a new technology on her own terms?

by others, people rebel. At the heart of the myth is this truth: when people appear to be fighting change, they are actually fighting the person or system they feel is imposing it upon them. So the office rebellion over the water cooler has more to do with a lifetime of conforming to the influence of institutions, rules, regulations, and company policies than the water cooler incident. It is how staff members demonstrate their frustration with a boss they may be afraid to confront. And, lastly, it is the expression of the powerlessness employees feel, trapped in most organizations.

What is the mechanism that shackles people and groups in such a powerful grip that change seems so unattainable? Let's investigate.

The Architecture of Power and Control

The behavior of individuals, groups, and organizations often seems unalterable. Throughout history, the prevailing wisdom has leaned in the direction of control and the imposition of power by authority figures—generals, priests, parents, and police. In business, the authority has traditionally fallen to owners, supervisors, and union leaders.

While history is replete with a chronology of revolutions, most only changed the color of the authority figure's uniform. The masses have always been at the mercy of unrestricted power imposed from above. Even with the advent of democracies, the state retains the absolute powers of life and death, conscription, and the imposition of taxes. The fact that power in a democracy is subject to certain checks and balances means it is probably meted out more justly. But it does not diminish the fact that the government retains outright authority over its people.

On the widest possible scale, the blueprint for control is duplicated throughout civilization. The life of every living person has been shaped by authoritarian organizations and institutions of every description: families, clubs, religions, schools, hospitals, businesses, and associations. Each has a central governing body (or person) and a charter that frames the boundaries of the organization's authority. Is it any wonder that people are convinced control is central to the well-being of an organization? And when it comes to changing an organization, does it not follow that change, like everything else, must be controlled and managed by a central authority?

In addition to central authority, cultures and organizations are guided by central ideologies. The central ideology of our age is science and technology. Like authority, its influences are everywhere. At the turn of the last century, science found its way into the realm of business management.

Most people like change but nearly everyone dislikes having it imposed upon them. Change on our own terms is OK—more than OK— it is fundamental to life. But when change is imposed by others, people rebel. At the heart of the myth is this truth: when people appear to be fighting change, they are actually fighting the person or system they feel is imposing it upon them.

The Principles of Scientific Management

As a central ideology, science and technology form the very underpinnings of human culture, shaping the ways people think, see, and organize themselves.

Since the Industrial Revolution, science and technology have had an extraordinary influence on how organizations are structured and people work. Science's roots are in reductionism—seeking an understanding of the whole by the study of individual parts. A business example is the widely used organization chart. As charts tend to pigeon-hole workers, technology and the proliferation of machines dehumanize companies where people are treated like objects or machines. How many managers have wished there was a simple on/off switch for the workforce? After all, robots never tire, get sick, or complain.

A mechanistic view of people and a reductionist view of organizations have been around at least since the Industrial Revolution. However, these origins go back to the ancient military science of Alexander the Great, Genghis Khan, and Rome's Caesars. But it was the Industrial Revolution that joined man and machine, science and organization. Eventually, a book entitled a *Scientific Approach to Management* was published in 1911.

It's Not Nice to Fool Mother Nature

Science and a technological approach to harnessing nature has been the preoccupation of the "first world" cultures for the past few hundred years. Yet many thinkers question the wisdom of this "man against nature" approach. As of late, there are more and more examples that cast doubt on the notion that science and technology can fix anything!

Many of the great rivers of America have been subjected to engineering "improvement," but it has become more and more obvious that natural engineering is hard to beat. Apart from flooding on many of these rivers, in Florida, the ambitious plans of the Army Corps of Engineers and the Central and Southern Florida Flood Control District have been called into question. Their grand plan to regulate the great Kissimmee river by straightening it and controlling it with a series of levees and dams has proven more catastrophic—bringing Okeechobee, one of the world's great freshwater lakes, to death's doorstep. This is not about too little technology or too few resources—it is about too much of both. The meandering, marshy old river naturally filtered the run off of millions of acres of nutrient-rich farmlands far more efficiently than any computer-driven water control system. The Army Corps of Engineers is now charged with returning the river to its unimproved state. Unfortunately, there is no guarantee the effort will save the lake.

To his credit, the author, Frederick Taylor, recognized the inherent dignity of workers. He was dedicated to "the development of each man to his state of maximum efficiency, so that he may be able to do, generally speaking, the highest grade of work which his natural abilities fit him." Unfortunately, he also diminished the value of individual contribution to that of the proverbial cog in a wheel with his words, "In the past the man has been first; in the future the system must be first." The system of management Taylor created organized the workplace in a way that afforded management unprecedented leverage to control workers.

Scientific management was accomplished by analyzing each job and reducing the task to its most basic components. His work eventually resulted in stop-watch-driven, time-motion studies which focused entirely on the mechanical aspects of a job—treating each worker as if he or she was merely a machine. Taylor's influence cannot be overestimated. Families, churches, schools, factories, and service organizations follow his approach to this day. However, as successful as industry has been in the last hundred or so years, it may be that success has not been facilitated by a scientific-mechanical view of the workplace. It is even possible that success has occurred in spite of it.

Until his death, Dr. W. Edwards Deming, America's celebrated architect of Japan's extraordinarily successful quality movement, railed against Taylor's "scientific" model.

Deming said organizations must be understood and managed as a whole system. Any attempt to reduce an organization to its component parts, in the way Taylor advocated, leads to what Deming calls *suboptimization*. To illustrate the point, he described a scenario in which one department optimizes itself, but sets in motion a series of events which ultimately results in suboptimization of the whole organization. For example, if production is optimized, purchasing must keep up. If sales, shipping, and service are unable to meet the demands of the new production schedule, the company's overall viability is jeopardized; hence, suboptimization results.

Dr. Deming was also concerned about Taylor's legacy of control. Deming compared Taylor's workplace to a prison where workers could not be trusted and were assumed lazy—each needing to be controlled by manager-guards.

There are times when we must sink to the bottom of our misery to understand truth, just as we must descend to the bottom of a well to see the stars in broad daylight.
—*Václav Havel*

The impact of Taylor's brand of scientific reductionism and the arrogant belief that systems should control people cannot be overemphasized—the influence is everywhere. Nearly all institutions and organizations are, to some degree, organized in accord with Taylor's principles.

A lesser known but equally influential management scientist of the 1920s was sociologist Max Weber. Weber, a German national, was the father of bureaucracy! Although his work was not translated into English until after World War II, his ideas were widely interpreted, disseminated, and adopted in the U.S. by the early 1930s. If bureaucracy is a bad word today, its origin is generally misunderstood. It is often assumed that bureaucracies are an unavoidable, if unsavory, by-product of organizational growth. Not so. The principles of bureaucracy as developed by Weber were *designed* to improve efficiency and make organizations more humane in their dealings with employees and customers.

Bureaucracies use strict organizational boundaries, auditable paper trails, and specific rules and regulations to maintain order, predictability, and uniformity of operation. All these attributes were contrived by Weber to bring about equitable treatment for all employees by management.

One of the key aspects of bureaucratic management is the idea that "nothing is personal." All decisions are made rationally—without bias, prejudice, or emotion—no exceptions!

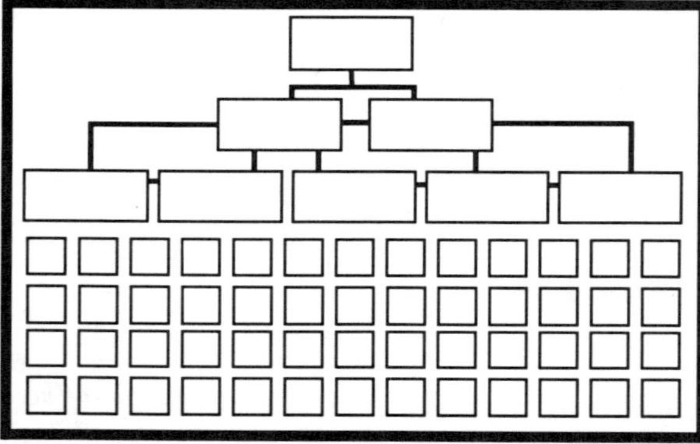

A typical organization chart

An example already cited, and in keeping with the thinking of Taylor and Weber, is the omnipresent organization chart. Companies everywhere use a series of boxes and lines to describe their organization and manage people and resources. The fact that these charts bear little similarity to the relationships between actual people, departments, and processes is beside the point. Ironically, apart from those people who create the charts, everyone else seems to understand the real organization operates parallel to, but rarely within, the chart.

In most companies, there is a conspiracy of silence that allows upper management to draw their boxes and move resources around like so many chess pieces. Meanwhile everyone else knows these actions have little or no real effect. Workers figure out how to get around the "block head" in box three and develop alternate routes to acquire necessary information, guidance, and resources. End-runs like this are an everyday occurrence with middle managers and front line workers in all organizations. Terrence Deal and

William Jenkins, in their book, *Managing the Hidden Organization*, point out that as long as behind-the-scenes, so-called support staff remain hidden, they also remain largely untapped and uninvolved. All too many people waste precious resources maintaining or improving their position on an organization chart which does not serve the customer, does not add value, and may have no real meaning at all.

In the Truthful Organization, there is no hidden organization sapping workers' energies and diverting their focus to office politics. People should not have to waste energy preparing to work. Their careers should not be on the line when they go outside the system to get the job done. But neither should a departure from the system be considered a heroic act. In or out of the structure, an organization must support staff to get the right job done in the best possible way. In most organizations, the people with the know-how to do the job are the ones doing the work, not the people drawing boxes on a chart.

Plato is dear to me, but dearer still is truth.
—Aristotle

In the Truthful Organization, structures are naturally semi-permeable. Boundaries exist, but they are never barriers to change and growth. The organization responds organically, as a whole, by learning, growing, and responding to the vagaries of the marketplace.

It would seem that the organic structure of the Truthful Organization is far removed from the scientifically managed systems espoused by Taylor, Weber, and their followers. But, in reality, no organization was ever scientifically controlled or organized according to an ORG. CHART. Between every box on every chart, behind every memo, manual, and directive, exists the real organization—its people and relationships. And because of the inherently intelligent nature of people, the job gets done—sometimes despite organizationally imposed impediments.

Real organizations are like an ivy plant growing on a trellis. People in the organization represent the ivy while the organization chart represents the trellis. No one overlooks the ivy on a trellis, yet the natural, human aspect of organizations is routinely overlooked during change initiatives. Is it any wonder TQM fails? The way TQM and other change initiatives are generally implemented is analogous to a gardener painting the lattice and expecting the ivy to change its leaves.

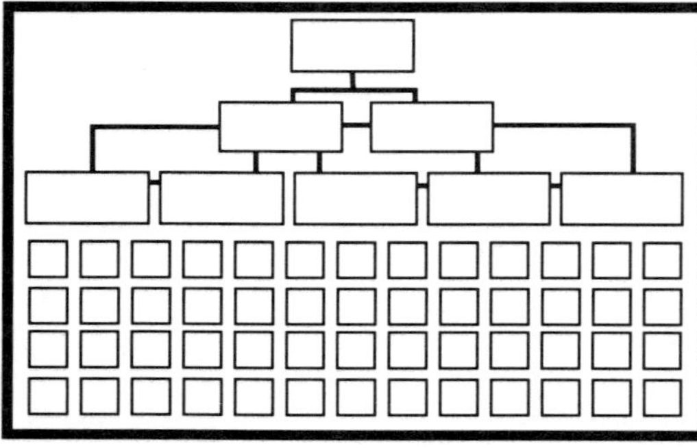
Organization Chart

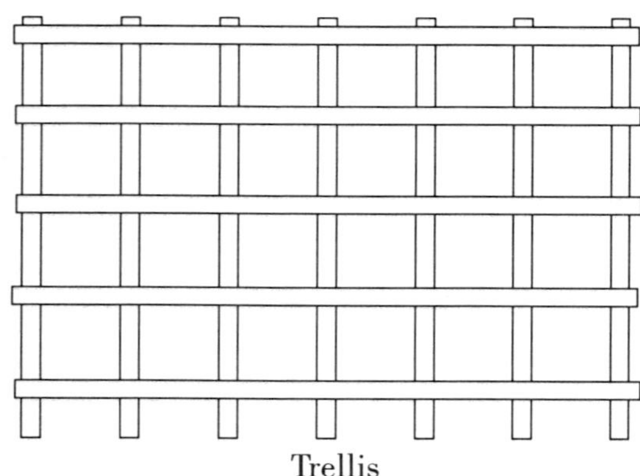
Trellis

Analogies or not, science still holds the hearts and minds of many people. Science and technology deliver the goods. There are planes, phones, faxes, gene splicing, space shuttles, recombinant DNA, and the Internet. The reductionists' understanding of the whole from an analysis of component parts is so deeply ingrained that the possible benefits of a fresh approach is beyond most people's imagination. Interestingly, various scientists are in the same boat. Thinkers in many disciplines are beginning to understand the limitation of reductionism. Some of them are searching for an alternate approach which will incorporate a systemic or wide-angle view.

New Science

New trends in science may offer clues to help understand the mysterious nature of change, and the resistance of organizations and people to fully participate.

Some scientists are abandoning the "divide and conquer" brand of science for a big-picture version. They are seeking insights into what appears to be an inherent order in the universe. One of the most influential exponents of this approach is the physicist, David Bohm, author of *Wholeness and The Implicate Order* and *Thought As a System*. His work integrates thought, communication, and social interaction in ways that have impacted a variety of disciplines: business communication, psychotherapy, and strategic planning, to name but a few.

Any non-reductionist approach represents a drastic departure from the traditional Western approach to knowledge. Science has historically described a chaotic universe that first needs to be understood (through its component parts) and then conquered (with technology) for eventual exploitation (for profit).

If science is flirting with new approaches, organization development specialists are in the midst of a dramatic revolution. Some managers even see workers as intelligent, committed partners instead of unruly children. The ivy and trellis example further illustrates the point. People (even scientists) have sometimes been culturally biased to see the trellis as orderly and the ivy as natural ... and therefore chaotic and insignificant. Yet the ivy exhibits a remarkable level of orderliness and even intelligence. It not only systematically grows by replicating its architecture; it does so in a way that optimizes its own success as an organism. It sends out tendrils that latch on to the trellis, feeling its way as it weaves itself up the trellis—all the while maximizing its exposure to the sun and minimizing its vulnerability to the wind and other elements.

The orderly simplicity of the trellis is in no way diminished. It is now joined with a different kind of orderliness in the form of ivy. Scientists have developed the ability to see the elegance of both systems.

The big question facing these new thinkers is: if there is an architecture or orderliness underlying the apparent chaos of nature, how does it manifest itself? Books on fractal geometry and chaos theory reveal thousands of naturally occurring patterns. A head of broccoli organizes its buds in the same pattern as sunflowers arrange their seeds into blossoms—all according to the same mathematics found in a nautilus shell. The universality of natural architecture is beyond chance—its orderliness is subtle but unavoidable. What is more, natural orderliness is not imposed from the outside; it emerges from within the structures themselves. It is not a technology, but an innate quality of natural systems to organize themselves in an orderly fashion.

Trellis and Ivy

While the idea that systems are self-organizing flies directly in the face of scientific management, what are its implications for managers? Is it possible that social systems are self-organizing as well? Is it possible that "less management" has value beyond the reduction of overhead costs? Is it possible that principles of cooperation, collaboration, and teamwork are naturally occurring? Might they have been at play before teambuilding, leaderless workgroups, and self-management became fashionable?

Some managers even see workers as intelligent, committed partners instead of unruly children.

Self-(Re)organization in Complex Systems

The effects of self-organization are real—they surround all of us. Amazingly, scientists have been discovering self-organizing properties beyond the world of biology. Even non-living chemical systems demonstrate properties of self-organization. Dr. Ilya Prigogene, author of *Exploring Complexity* with Gregoire Nicolis and *Order Out of Chaos,* won the 1977 Nobel prize in chemistry for his work on *dissipative structures*. His ideas shed light on the paradox between mechanical systems which, over time, run out of steam and come to rest, versus evolving biological systems which, over time, become better organized and more complex. His work, and the work of others inspired by his lead, has led to an understanding that self-organization is not limited to living systems. He has even described self-organizing behavior in the molecular motion found in puddles of fluid. The description of his experiments involving catalysts and self-catalyzing processes lead the reader to striking parallels with social and business systems—especially factories.

This personal field incorporates a vast array of individual qualities (confidence, values, intentions, fears, desires, etc.) and projects the individuality of a person beyond the mind and body into the surrounding space.

While Prigogene frequently uses the term self-organization, I believe it is more descriptive to call it *self-(re)organization*. Ultimately, it is one aggregation (no matter how disorganized) reorganizing itself into another usually more orderly system.

This line of thinking may appear to have taken us far afield. It began with the notion that prevailing management theories traditionally presumed workers were essentially automatons, devoid of intelligence. Now we have intelligent ivy vines, sunflowers, and even sea shells! If it is difficult for some people to see intelligence in their fellow human beings, acknowledging it in a head of broccoli may be asking too much. Dr. Margaret Wheatley, author of *Leadership and The New Science,* built a solid bridge between the newest trends in physics and mathematics to contemporary approaches to management and leadership.

Orderliness is a natural phenomenon. Orderliness and naturally organized systems pre-date Frederick Taylor, Max Weber, management science, and even human beings. The notion that nature is chaotic and without structure is a bias that obligates us to maintain the illusion of "control," preventing any natural tendency for self-reorganization to appear.

What does self-reorganization look like in the workplace? In a March 18, 1996, *Fortune* magazine article, two Hewlett-Packard managers, Mei-Lin Cheng and Julie Anderson, received a reengineering assignment. They chose an unorthodox and courageous strategy. They "bought" autonomy from their bosses by promising measurable results in less than nine months. They brought together a team of 35 people and explained a chosen mission. Then they got out of the way—earnestly refusing to tell anyone what do. The specifics of how the team self-reorganized was beyond the scope of the article. What is important is they met their deadline *and* their goal.

Natural orderliness is not imposed from the outside; it emerges from within the structures themselves. It is not a technology, but an innate quality of natural systems to organize themselves in an orderly fashion.

Obstacles to Self-Reorganization

The complexity and lack of predictability of human systems is the kernel of truth behind the myth that it is difficult to initiate change in a system. You will recall, a closer look revealed change was fundamental to all systems; the difficult part was managing the change. Once initiated, change tends to take on a life or at least a direction of its own. Could this be a reflection of some underlying orderliness coming through?

Let's take another look at the ivy trellis. Rather than seeing the trellis and the ivy as separate things, consider the relationship between the two. It is easy to understand that a trellis was created expressly for stabilizing an ivy vine. Without the ivy, it has no purpose. But as a structure, it exists completely independently from the ivy. It does not need the ivy.

Orderliness is a natural phenomenon. Orderliness and naturally organized systems predate Frederick Taylor, Max Weber, management science, and even human beings. The notion that nature is chaotic and without structure is a bias that obligates us to maintain the illusion of "control," preventing any natural tendency for self-reorganization to appear.

What about the ivy? Does it need the trellis? No, the ivy could grow along the ground, up a tree, over rocks, just as it did for a million years before trellises were built. But look what happens when they unite. A simple accumulation of wood slats becomes a thing of beauty when it is embraced by the ivy.

The relationship is more than just a plant and an artifact. It has a power of its own. Anyone who has ever tried separating the ivy from the trellis in midsummer knows it is a formidable task. Pruning a branch here or there will have little effect because the plant quickly mobilizes itself to fill in the gap. The plant responds by changing itself. And yet the result is the maintenance of the relationship. Change for the purpose of preserving the status quo is fundamental to life everywhere. It is often called *dynamic equilibrium*—balance through change. When living things stop changing, they die. But it is more than change, more than growth. Critical relationships must be maintained whether it is for structural support, nourishment, or other sustaining factors, living systems will undergo extraordinary changes to maintain those life-giving relationships. Nothing exists independently. Nothing is completely self-sustaining. Everything is interconnected and interdependent. At the core of the natural world are relationships. The very thing science has sought to nullify in its objective, reductionistic approach may turn out to be vital, not only to organizations but to life itself. Nevertheless, change initiatives of all sorts routinely ignore the importance of relationships and systematically fail to enroll people or foster interdependent relationships!

A team usually generates a field by incorporating to one degree or another the qualities of every individual on the team.

As described earlier, human relationships are extraordinarily complex. People have relationships with other people, animals, objects, ideas, places, art. Now there are statistics which state almost three quarters of the U.S. population believes in angels! Human history is replete with grand achievements, self-sacrifice, and, on the dark side, murder and even war—all in the name of relationships. With people, like all living things complicated or not, *relationships are everything*. The Lakota Sioux have a saying that is at the heart of their entire culture and way of life. *Mitakuye Oyasin* means "all my relations," or "we are all related!"

So what is the glue that binds people so tightly to a host of relationships that the slightest change can feel like an intimate, personal threat? Personal and interpersonal "fields."

Personal and Interpersonal Fields

The "glue" in a relationship is akin to a magnetic field generated by each person. Everyone has a personal field which is an amalgam of values, intentions, desires. It may also include an array of beliefs that define who we are and what we do in the world. Moreover, each person has assumptions about others—their intentions and motives.

This personal field incorporates a vast array of individual qualities (confidence, values, intentions, fears, desires, etc.) and projects the individuality of a person beyond the mind and body into the surrounding space. I cannot explain the physics behind this phenomenon, and I am not suggesting it is necessarily anything more esoteric than what is known as *charisma*. A charismatic person may just be a person with an unusually powerful personal field. On the other hand, most people have had the experience of walking into a room just *after* a heated argument occurred. Something often remains that is tangible enough to be sensed. What is it? Nearly everyone has, with minimal direct contact, sensed something about a person, group, or company that either attracts or repels. Labeling these experiences as intuition, "vibes," or charisma adds little to our understanding. It is my belief that people generate a personal field which broadcasts the sum total of their feelings, values, attitudes, intentions, and desires. While everyone has a personal field, we most often recognize fields when they are strong or powerful such as those of charismatic leaders, politicians, or entertainers. Our personal fields exist regardless of how potent they are, although fields do fluctuate when we experience strong feelings.

Once initiated, change tends to take on a life or at least a direction of its own. Could this be a reflection of some underlying orderliness coming through?

A relationship or interpersonal field is an unspoken set of agreements that make it possible to share the same space while maintaining the integrity of each person's personal field.

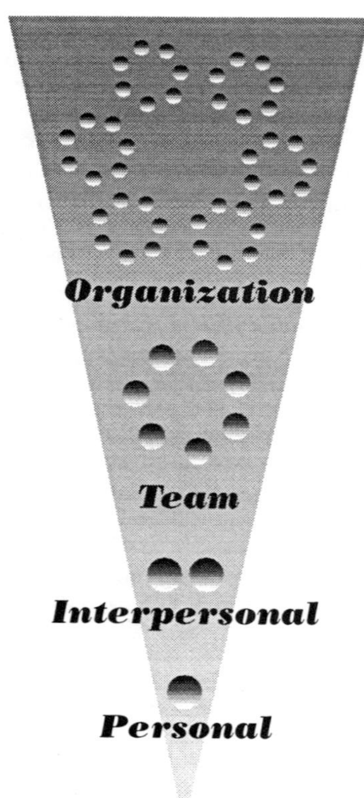

A relationship or interpersonal field is an unspoken set of agreements that make it possible to share the same space while maintaining the integrity of each person's personal field. On one end of a spectrum, the agreements may be comprehensive, intimate, and loving. At the other end is an unspoken agreement to participate in an antagonistic or even hateful relationship. In between are tens of thousands of variations characterized by varying states of acceptance, mild annoyance, or simple indifference.

As long as fields remain intact or change very slowly, they are invisible. However, if something occurs to shift the fields, the agreements and the quality of the fields become apparent. Even if it may be difficult to describe in words, both parties usually *feel* a disturbance in their field.

Team- and Shared Fields

When I enter a room and join a meeting, I immediately come into contact with the personal fields of others in the room—and they with mine. Beyond anyone's awareness, our fields automatically seek a natural state of equilibrium that accomplish two things:

1. There is an attempt to maintain the integrity of each person's personal field.
2. We unconsciously seek points of agreement with the fields of others. We seek to integrate the fields of others to promote enough harmony to permit the fulfillment of our individual intentions.

In addition to personal and interpersonal fields, there are also team-fields composed of three or more people. A team usually generates a field by incorporating to one degree or another the qualities of every individual on the team. Additionally, the team's charter and the context in which team members work can have a profound impact on the quality of the team-field. For example, a work team in a prison will share a different field than a group of entrepreneurs in Silicon Valley.

Organizations typically incorporate multiple team-fields. Thus, a business generates an organizational field which incorporates qualities of all teams. In addition, the organizational field is influenced, to some degree, by the surrounding meta-field in which the business operates. It includes vendors, customers, industry, geo-political, and other influences.

Not everyone's field seeks equilibrium in the same way. Some fields are only in balance when they dominate others. In these cases, our personal fields are challenged to give the other field what it wants, while maintaining its own integrity. These are challenging relationships that can make going to work an ordeal. If only we could just change fields ...

Unfortunately, the power of fields is in their resiliency. The more effort you put into changing another's field, the more enmeshed you are likely to become. It is like Uncle Remus's tar baby.

Remember when Brer Fox decided to teach Brer Rabbit a lesson with a bunch of sticky tar shaped and dressed up to look like a baby? Rabbit comes across this tar baby while Brer Fox watches from a ditch ... "where ... he lay low"... .

Rabbit says "Mornin'" to the tar baby, expecting a polite and cheery response. Brer Rabbit feels snubbed because the tar baby, "He ain't sayin' nothin'." Rabbit sets out to teach the tar baby a lesson in civility. In turn, the tar baby teaches Brer Rabbit a lesson in humility. No matter how much force Rabbit puts behind his change efforts (punches), the tar baby just absorbs the energy and further incorporates Rabbit into his sticky "field" until Brer Rabbit is totally stuck to the tar baby and cannot get free.

Relationships are similar—they are sticky. Every person's field is affected by every other field with which they come in contact. A relationship shifts both participants' fields; a team's field has some components of each individual—yet no individual, regardless of how overbearing one person might be, completely dominates the team-field. Even though some fields are characterized by overpowering behavior (such as abusive relationships), no one can control or predict the behavior of an interpersonal field with accuracy. When it comes to team or shared fields, predicting their future may be no more accurate than long-range weather forecasting. Not only is it impossible for executives or managers, no matter how powerful, to completely dominate a team-field, but they cannot reliably control

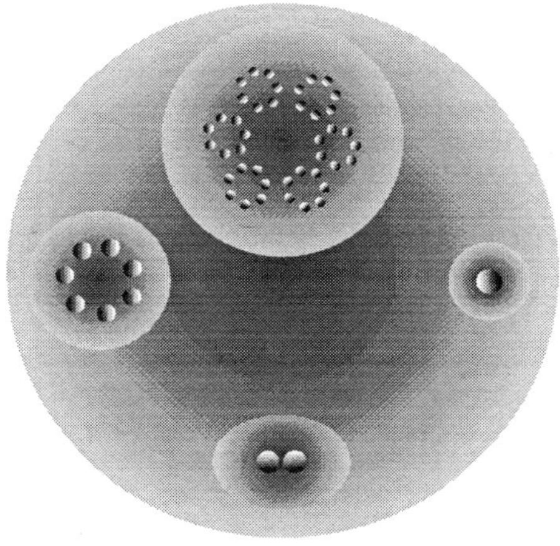

Personal fields are linked to other personal team or shared fields; any change to the larger field has a corresponding effect on the personal fields of all participants.

Change the Field at Your Own Peril

My team at the Venture Centre has been gifted with a number of opportunities to work with diversity-rich organizations. I have worked extensively in El Paso with Mexican-Americans and on Indian reservations with a number of Native American tribes.

As a result, I have had ample opportunities to walk into offices, work spaces, and training rooms peopled by folks different from me. In each case, assumptions, unspoken agreements, and fields existed between us. In some cases, the fields facilitated our work together. In other situations, the fields inhibited the realization of our goals.

Over time, I developed tools to change the fields and create an environment where we could work together to build a new field that helped all participants fulfill their needs.

Ironically, one of the more challenging fields I have encountered was with a group largely comprised of people whose skin tones, age, language, and gender were identical with mine. However, the dominant majority in this international group was not North Americans, but white South Africans. And their reactions to the challenges, simulations, and activities which I use to help teams see themselves (and their fields) were perceived as personally threatening. In one situation, I had a middle-aged man standing at the back of the room, veins bulging on his neck , screaming, "You, liar! You, liar!"

The workshop was uncomfortable for everyone, but it was successful because it revealed a lack of trust and a clash of cultures. The team got a good look at itself.

the behavior of individuals within the field. And they have virtually no influence on members of the larger organizational field.

Fields are so resilient, they are very difficult to change. Since personal fields are linked to other personal team or shared fields, any change to the larger field has a corresponding effect on the personal fields of all participants. Put more simply, if my girlfriend wants to change our interpersonal field, it forces me to examine not only our relationship, but myself—and it is likely to feel very threatening. To some degree, the same situation can occur when the office (team-field) is disrupted by something as trivial as the boss swapping out the water cooler. It is not about the water cooler, but the disruption of the team-field threatens the integrity of my personal field. It may feel like a threat to my very being!

How Fields Resist Change

Fields have a resilient, highly adaptable, change-resistant architecture. At the core of every personal , interpersonal, team- or organizational-field is an unspoken agreement to maintain the status quo. This way, people are spared the inconvenience of continuously reassessing themselves and having an identity crisis every time they meet a new person or someone disagrees with them. People routinely remain in relationships, on teams, and in organizations that are uncomfortable—even painful—because the alternative is unclear and might be worse.

Fields are change resistant because, like the tar baby, their self-adjusting mechanisms maintain field integrity in spite of dramatic shifts within the field or imposed from outside. Although in most organizations control is the favorite means of bringing about change, it may be the least effective strategy. Here is why.

Let's look at a typical scenario: An organization has an unmotivated staff and low morale. Management's reaction is to reorganize.

Managers usually choose between two opposing strategies. One tightens up the *system,* placing greater responsibility on individuals, while increasing accountability through revamped reporting systems. The other focuses on *people,* rewarding those with more motivation and removing or demoting those who do not demonstrate the desired commitment. By nearly any measure, either initiative will result in dramatic alterations to the organization. Yet, as anybody who has tried either method knows, lasting, profound changes are not likely to materialize.

The reason is: *neither strategy is likely to alter the shared-field.* If the shared-field remains intact, the newly enhanced system will gradually return to its original state. Likewise, new faces in new places are quick to take up the features of the previous and existing organizational-field—resulting in the "same old, same old."

How does this happen? In this scenario, managers used "command and control" to bring about change. But what if too much control and lack of autonomy for staff caused low participation in the first place? If the mechanisms which maintain the organizational field are a "command and control" management style, how can more of it lead to a change in the field?

The only way to change the organizational field is by changing the critical components of the field. People make up one component, but there are many others: management style, access to information, values, organizational models, accountability, safety, etc. The more components that can be aligned in a coherent transition plan, the greater the likelihood lasting change will occur ... and the greater chance such change will be desirable.

At the core of every personal field, interpersonal field, team-field, or organizational field is an unspoken agreement to maintain the status quo. In this way, people are spared the inconvenience of continuously reassessing themselves and having an identity crisis every time they meet a new person or someone disagrees with them. People routinely remain in relationships, on teams, and in organizations that are uncomfortable—even painful—because the alternative is unclear and might be worse.

Chapter Three

Making Lasting Change

Making Lasting Changes

Before moving on to explore how fields change, let's review the nature of fields from the previous chapter:

Field Theory Review

1. It is commonly believed that change is difficult to initiate and people are resistant. Actually, change is a fundamental quality of nature and people readily adapt. However, they routinely resist having change imposed upon them by others.

2. A wide variety of natural systems maintain their homeostasis through a process of continuous change. On the surface, these changes appear random. Yet they are self-generated, self-organized, and self-enhancing examples of adaptability.

3. Social groups demonstrate many of the same characteristics found in other naturally occurring complex systems, including the ability to self-reorganize.

4. When complex systems are forced to change as a result of external control mechanisms, changes are only temporary. In order to maintain the changes, control must continue to be exerted.

5. People are more than minds and bodies. They are complex systems involving thoughts, emotions, values, attitudes, histories, and agendas. The aggregate radiates outwardly, similar to a magnetic field.

6. The character and quality of the fields shared with others increases in complexity from personal to interpersonal to team and, ultimately, organizational fields generated within organizations.

7. A field responds to change efforts by incorporating change agents into the field. A relationship that is fundamentally control- or fear-based, for example, cannot be changed using control or fear because real change would necessitate the elimination of fear and control.

The truth is really an ambition which is beyond us.
—Peter Ustinov

The Technology of Change

The following three steps outline key processes and introduce several methodologies to *perceive, disrupt,* and *change* the fields within organizations.

PERCEIVE: Making the Invisible Visible

Perceiving the Personal Field

The most powerful tool to help individuals change themselves and participate in changes within the organization is personal awareness. There appears to be a correlation between organizations which prohibit the blending of workers' work and personal lives, and the organization's failure to foster participation and buy-in from the workforce.

The most effective tool for developing self-awareness is relationship. The more we reveal—the more we let others know about us—the more we learn about ourselves.

In addition to informal self-disclosure, structured dialogue guided by a counselor has become a popular tool for personal development—psychotherapy is no longer just for emotional disturbance. Many people expand their insight through faith, prayer, and meditation. I also find that time in the wilderness soothes my soul and stimulates deep introspection.

One of the primary reasons our wilderness workshops are so effective has nothing to do with the facilitators or the curriculum. It is the healing power of wildness on the troubled souls of people immersed in a world of schedules, glass, quotas, and plastic.

Perceiving the Interpersonal Field

The challenge of initiating, maintaining, and ending relationships is so universal, it's the essence of art, history, and literature. Ultimately, relationships are at the core of the human experience. No university could create a classroom to afford greater opportunities for self-awareness and learning than the relationships each of us is immersed in every day. Every relationship is an opportunity to learn and improve; it makes no matter with whom: God, family, children, co-workers, adversaries, lovers, strangers, even the earth.

Personal Styles Instruments

Human Resources professionals, consultants, and psychologists have used personality tests to categorize working, sales, decision-making, and leadership styles. Probably the most widely used is the Myers-Briggs scale—but there is a raft of others ranging from elaborate psychological models to simple self-scoring inventories. Some purport to measure core personality traits; a few define behavior styles; others focus on values. These

Humble Leadership

Last summer, we took the executive team from a division of one of the largest chemical companies in the U.S. on a high-mountain horseback adventure. We used the extraordinary scenic beauty of the Rocky Mountains outside of Aspen, Colorado, as both a relaxing getaway and the backdrop for a powerful introspective experience.

We took our "Truthful Structure" simulation which involves the construction of a complex 10-foot-high structure of PVC pipes and connectors. In this deployment, we combined the accumulation of component pieces into a wilderness orienteering activity. Instead of just dumping dozens of pipes on the ground, we hid them in bundles all around the camp, and gave members of the executive team compasses and bearings to find the pieces.

Before leaving, the executives reported a heightened awareness of team processes and an acute understanding of the importance of trust among team members. Amazingly, one of the most significant events was when the CEO, an avid horseman, fell off his horse into a mud puddle. As I got off my horse to offer assistance, I was thinking, "Great, first two miles, first day, and the boss is in the mud." Exhibiting the qualities of a real leader, he smiled and said, "Well, let's look on the bright side. Everyone who was nervous about falling off or looking foolish will feel better now that the boss has done it!"

No university could create a classroom to afford greater opportunities for self-awareness and learning than the relationships each of us is immersed in every day.

personality assessment instruments can be very enlightening. For most, it is like looking in a mirror; people are fascinated by the unusual perspective of their inner self. Anything that expands personal awareness will have a corresponding influence on performance. Yet there is a down side to these instruments. More precisely, the down side is in how the information is used. In many situations, the result is a profile that effectively "brands" workers with simplistic and often unflattering labels. Indeed, the real problem is the possibility that a worker may feel both labeled and constrained from self-improvement. To justify their own validity, many instruments are made to sound not only accurate, but a reflection of such deep personal reality that results seem etched in stone. The other problem is the prevailing practice of sharing results in private, thus reinforcing the notion that what is being revealed is deeply profound.

I find it ironic that when these instruments are accurate, the only people surprised by results are occasionally the test subjects themselves. Co-workers, friends, family, members, and associates already know how we behave. They know our values through our work—though sometimes we ourselves live in denial.

While I believe personal awareness can be enhanced with these instruments, it is vital that the information is presented in a context to support introspection. I prefer sharing as much information as possible and distributing it as widely as possible. Lastly, I prefer that once information is shared, team members are given the time and tools to explore ways to use the information to enhance interpersonal communication.

One of the ways I achieve all three outcomes is with a simple personal-style model I created a few years ago. I describe four personal styles that most people find familiar and comfortable: *Thinkers, Doers, Friend,* and *Visionary*. I give each member of the team five ballots. I instruct them to write their name on four cards and give the cards to selected members of the team. Next, I ask them to use the remaining card to rank themselves. Which personal style is the most dominant, second most, third, and least? At the same time, the other team members use the cards they were given to rate the person whose name is on the card they

When a Team is NOT a Team

Many intact teams are not ready to openly and honestly share information—especially when it is about the contribution of individuals on the team.

I worked with a management team that had been intact for a number of years. They were looking forward to a retreat where teambuilding would consist of golf, reviewing the year's results, and a few trips to the lounge.

I was asked to shake things up a little. So, I asked each person to complete a questionnaire called the "Learning Team Composite Profile." I adapted it from material developed by Peggy MacKay of the Glen Douglas Group in Colorado Springs, Colorado. The profile consists of a booklet with five worksheets: communication, leadership, productivity, interpersonal, teamwork. Each worksheet has five assertions with six boxes to be checked off: always, usually, often, sometimes, rarely, and never. Each member of the team was asked to distribute a booklet to five different members of the team. Each would then be collected anonymously by the facilitator for scoring and tabulation. This is similar to the popular 360-degree surveys which invite feedback from co-workers, subordinates, and supervisors—but this was from just co-workers on the same team!

The completion of the exercise was to furnish each team member with the tabulated results. They included a graphic that compared the person's results with the averaged results for the whole team. One team member would then get in front of the group and discuss the results, explaining what team members were proud of and ideas to improve areas which needed work.

The team got together in the bar and decided the exercise was just too uncomfortable. They chose not to participate. They understood that there were no secrets; that any information revealed would not be a surprise, but it was just too personal! Their concession was to acknowledge they needed a lot of work to develop real teamwork!

The Rest of The Story ... In The Manager's Own Words

On the way to the off-site, I reviewed the current state of affairs in our office. I was taking my management team to our first team-building workshop with Ward Flynn. We all felt as though we were a team. We communicated with each other. We basically got along well, and we were meeting our primary business goals—growing and making a profit.

After the first day of Ward's experiential training exercises, it became increasingly clear that we knew nothing about what it takes to be a high-performing team. There was a lot of anger building, and by that evening, the managers got together and decided they had had enough!

By the following morning, we had a mutiny on our hands. Ward received the brunt of their anger, but he handled it very well. Unlike me, he had a lot of experience with this type of reaction. As their boss, I was feeling both left out and embarrassed. Driving home, I was very concerned about the future and whether I would ever get this group of managers to function as a team. Furthermore, how was I going to fit on that team as their GM?

Continued next page ...

The Manager's Story

continued from previosu page

That Monday morning, I met with the managers individually to ask how they were feeling after the weekend. Some were embarrassed about how the group had behaved, but some were still very angry. I waited a few more days, then brought the group together in the conference room. After everyone had shared his or her thoughts, I posed the bottom-line question, "Do we shoot the messenger or do we recognize that we have a lot of work to do?" I left it up to them.

Fortunately, we decided, as a group, to commit to learning how to become a high-performing "truth" team. Over the next nine months, we experienced many more "moments of truth," but because of the team's strong commitment, we have reached ever more effective plateaus of success. We have been acknowledged by the highest level of leadership in our multi-national organization and have earned for ourselves a reputation as leaders.

—Manager, 1994

received (each person may have a number of ballots received from other people). When completed, each is returned to the person whose name is on the card. After the original four ballots are collected, the data is averaged together with the person's own ballot. Once the data is tabulated, the results often stimulate a gush of self-awareness. Why do people see me the way they do? Why does everyone see me differently? Why does everyone see me one way, and I see me differently? What can I do to be seen in a different way? Can I improve my behavior?

In addition, because the data is unscientific, it is not taken too seriously. Even when the information seems unflattering, people are willing to hear it and consider behavior changes. I often encourage people to place a color coded "flag" on their name badge for the rest of the workshop. Then, to encourage people to try alternate behaviors, I ask them to switch "flags" during particularly challenging activities. In this way, the whole notion of personal style is removed from an indelible label to a set of behavioral habits that CAN be modified if they no longer serve the person.

One of the most innovative and entertaining instruments I use is called the Preferential Shapes Test, developed by Angeles Arrien, author of *Signs of Life*. I have used this process with individuals and groups. People look at five graphic shapes and rank them in order of preference. These shapes are the cross, circle, triangle, spiral, and square. Each has a rich anthropolcgical and mythic history reflecting deep archetypal significance in cultures as disparate as Native American, Celtic, Chinese, and Egyptian. Ranking each shape means number one is the figure the person prefers most, while number five is the least preferred shape. Then by simply decoding these preferences according to Ms. Arrien's research, it is possible to gain fascinating insights into a person's personality and current situation.

My work with shapes has been well received and led to a great deal of dialogue among individuals and teams. I try to facilitate a review of options available to the group to improve communication, trust, and understanding.

Sometimes it is desirable to work with a group on specific interpersonal conflicts. In such cases, a more concrete model of interpersonal behavior is required. I have found no model easier to understand and use than a '70s flashback to Transactional Analysis or TA. You may have read the popular book by Dr. Thomas Harris, *I'm Ok—You're Ok*.

Personal Style Instrument On-Line

At the Truth Zone web site, there is a hot link to the Kiersey Temperament Sorter, an on-line, instant personality profiler. It is inspired by but not, according to many Myers-Briggs aficianados,nearly as sophisticated as the Myers-Briggs scale. Select a couple dozen multiple choice answers and, voilà, your very own personal profile rolls off your printer. Connect with the Truth Zone web site via the world wide web at:

http://www.truthzone.com

States of Being: Parent - Child - Adult

The TA model describes three primary "states" of being available to all of us and played out in our behaviors each day. As a psychological tool, the TA model also describes deviant (far from normal) behaviors where one of the three aspects of self is partially or completely blocked. Although seriously dysfunctional people *do* show up at work, as champions of change, our attention should be focused on the great majority of us who may be somewhat neurotic, but are generally normal. Harris points out that TA's founder, Dr.

Eric Berne, did not consider the three "states" abstract ideas like "id," "ego," "superego," but "phenomenological realities" created by the playback of past *real* experiences.

Remember that while all of us have a favored state of being, even the most parental people occasionally function from their "child" or "adult" state. We all have the capacity to instantaneously flip from one "state" to another—indeed these flips are largely unconscious—triggered by a variety of stimuli.

The Parent at Work

Bosses need to tell their subordinates how they are doing. Workers need to ask.

"I want everything complete and on my desk before anyone goes home tonight ... I will accept no excuses ... this is not negotiable ... case closed." These "bossy" words characterize the parent at work. A real pain—but without the parent, work may never get done. Innovation can go so far afield that projects never yield products, and the bottom line may fall off through the floor.

The Child at Work

"I've gotta work late again ... nobody ever listens to me ... those engineers screwed up so we have to stay late again ... this TQM stuff will never work here ... I'll show them; they can make me stay late, but they can't make me efficient. " When the child comes to work, the result can be cynicism, blaming, undermining, and victimization. On the other hand, without it, there is no fun, humor, or spontaneity—stress has no outlet.

The Adult at Work

"We have a problem ... if we do not get this report in the mail tonight, we will lose the Johnson account ... Whatta ya' say we get some Pizza in and all work together so no one has to stay too late tonight?" The adult balances the imperatives of the adult (we must stay late) with the whimsy of the child (let's get pizza and make it fun) so as many of the team's needs are met as possible. The adult neither orders nor shames people. It does not fall into the habit of blaming and feeling victimized. The adult gets people to cooperate in order to make things work.

We all have the capacity to instantaneously flip from one "state" to another— indeed these flips are largely unconscious— triggered by a variety of stimuli.

Parent, Child, Adult Dynamics at Work

The complex, unspoken dynamics of interpersonal fields can be illustrated and better understood using TA. Here is how a conversation can seek to realign the field, even while the other person tries to shift it:

Alex: "No one ever pays attention to me."

Barb: "I hear you say that every day. And every day, I try to help you, but it never does any good. Am I missing something ... what do you need?

Alex: "I thought you were my friend. Now you sound like everyone else. You have always helped me in the past."

Barb: "I am your friend; that is why I am asking you what you need?"

Alex: "I don't need anything from you with that attitude. I am perfectly capable of helping myself ... what do you think I am, an invalid? I don't even want to ride to work together any more. I'll take a bus home this afternoon. Good bye!"

Barb: *(The adult sticking to her guns)* "I hear how upset you are. If you change your mind, I still want to be your friend, but I do not think I did anything wrong."

(or giving in - child) "I am sorry; maybe we should start over; I just feel like I am not enough for you." *(or getting angry and retaliating - parent)* "You are pathetic. Why don't you take a look at yourself in the mirror. You are not a helpless child. Get a life, and do me a favor—don't include me in it!"

Innovation can go so far afield that projects never yield products, and the bottom line may fall off through the floor.

The adult gets people to cooperate in order to make things work.

Let's face it, few people could stick to their guns in the face of such a barrage from Alex. Remember, as a co-creator of the field, Alex knows which buttons to push to get Barb out of her adult state and into either her child or parent. In this relationship, the field remains intact with either Barb's child or parent state. The one option that has any chance of actually changing the field is if Barb is able to move into the adult state.

The nice thing is, no matter where it ends up, Barb can come back the next day and start again from her adult state. Or, she can choose not to participate at all.

The beauty of TA at work is its ability to describe the subtle aspects of field theory in ways that most people will rapidly comprehend. Specifically, the dynamics linking people, even enemies, in unspoken embraces. Here is how it works: When a boss barks parent(al) orders to staff, "I want it on my desk by tonight, or else ..." even staff unaffected by the mandate will likely react to the boss's tirade with child(like) responses: "What a loud mouth ... someone should teach the boss a lesson ... I have a good mind to sabotage the whole project."

Parent behavior triggers child responses. Likewise, child behaviors trigger parent behaviors. A worker who complains and bemoans the injustices of life will trigger parent behaviors from co-workers, with comments such as, "Cut the crap. Either do the job or turn in your keys." Another type of parent behavior is care taking: "You're right. Your boss is a pain. What I would do, if I were you ... I'll talk to the boss for you ..." Even though each response is different, each perpetuates the parent-child relationship. In one, the child's victimhood is reinforced by harsh parent words. In the other, the victimhood is reinforced by someone trying to fix it for them.

You can change the dynamic (field) by being Adult. An adult response to the child-victim, above, would be something like, "How long have you felt this way ... do you feel this way about other situations or people ... what options do you have to change your present situation ... have you ever been able to turn around a similar situation in the past?" These adult questions demonstrate empathy for the person, but not sympathy. They encourage people to *own* their feelings without blaming or shaming.

NORMAL BEHAVIORS

Parent	Adult	Child
Direct	Dialogue	Obey
Bossy	Collaborate	Avoid
Intimidate	Agree	Defend
Judge	Forgive	Victim
I'm Right	Understand	I'm Wrong
Control	Team	Goof off
Blame	Learn	Shame
I did it, I win	We did it together	I don't care

Not only does *parent* "I'm right" behavior trigger *child* "I'm wrong" responses, it can actually cycle from parent to child within a single person's mind. For example, when people make a big deal about being right and then find out they are in error, their natural reaction is to feel wrong, shifting from parent to child. The *adult* state tends to get overlooked. The adult seeks understanding: "How did this happen? What can we learn?"

Perceiving the Team-Field

The participants in a field know, but usually cannot perceive or articulate, the qualities of the field. This is as true for teams, workgroups, and departments as any field.

Getting individual members of the team to see themselves offers both a technical (which instruments will effectively reveal the field?) and motivational (groups are seldom interested in seeing themselves as they are) challenge.

I tackle the motivational hurdle with activities that test the mettle of the team and—as I explain

The best way to get people to buy in is to inspire a bottom-up revolution where co-workers spontaneously evangelize each other instead of where bosses try to motivate, intimidate, or bribe subordinates. Moreover, those who do not buy in must not be punished. This is critical because those people who are unwilling to support the change must be encouraged to avoid sabotaging or undermining it. Ultimately, it does not require even a majority to bring about change, only a few people whose personal missions compel them to work toward the same shared vision.

1=Strongly Disagree 2=Mildly Disagree 3=Mildly Agree 4=Strongly Agree

1 - 2 - 3 - 4 **TEAM CLIMATE - Now**

❑ ❑ ❑ ❑ 1. Shared goals are clear to all members of the team.
❑ ❑ ❑ ❑ 2. Members express themselves, even negatively, without fear of retribution.
❑ ❑ ❑ ❑ 3. When conflicts arise, the team has skills to find resolution.
❑ ❑ ❑ ❑ 4. Responsibilities of leadership are shared by team members.
❑ ❑ ❑ ❑ 5. Team members share greater trust than with people outside the team.
❑ ❑ ❑ ❑ 6. Members have declared their personal mission and values to others.
❑ ❑ ❑ ❑ 7. The team has clearly defined roles, responsibilities, and boundaries.
❑ ❑ ❑ ❑ 8. People throughout the organization understand the team's role.
❑ ❑ ❑ ❑ 9. The team uses specific tools for problem solving AND decision making.
❑ ❑ ❑ ❑ 10. The team measures results and achieves its goals.

1 - 2 - 3 - 4 **TEAM CLIMATE - Future**

❑ ❑ ❑ ❑ 1. Shared goals are clear to all members of the team.
❑ ❑ ❑ ❑ 2. Members express themselves, even negatively, without fear of retribution.
❑ ❑ ❑ ❑ 3. When conflicts arise, the team has skills to find resolution.
❑ ❑ ❑ ❑ 4. Responsibilities of leadership are shared by team members.
❑ ❑ ❑ ❑ 5. Team members share greater trust than with people outside the team.
❑ ❑ ❑ ❑ 6. Members have declared their personal mission and values to others.
❑ ❑ ❑ ❑ 7. The team has clearly defined roles, responsibilities, and boundaries.
❑ ❑ ❑ ❑ 8. People throughout the organization understand the team's role.
❑ ❑ ❑ ❑ 9. The team uses specific tools for problem solving AND decision making.
❑ ❑ ❑ ❑ 10. The team measures results and achieves its goals.

Scoring involves determining the gap between each item. For example, if item number six receives a "1" in the NOW column and a "4" in the FUTURE column, the gap of three makes it a high priority item. Each item can be correlated with one of the Seven Steps to Building a Truthful Organization or a specific tool in the *Tools for Building the Truthful Organization.*

to team members—demonstrate the team's baseline behavior. If a team is unable to achieve an objective members feel is within their grasp, they want to delve deeper into the dynamics of the team's field.

Activities such as the Blind Polygon and others give a team a great deal of information about the existing field. However, to clarify the specifics of the field, a simple inventory instrument works well.

One instrument assesses where the team is along a continuum between "authoritarian control" at one extreme, and "leaderless collaboration" at the other. It is important to know both where team members feel the team is NOW, and where they think it should be in the FUTURE. If there is no gap—the team is where it should be—no work needs to be done. Those areas where the gap is largest indicate where work should begin. To assess the NOW vs. FUTURE gap, the instrument must be administered twice.

Each participant needs to respond to each assertion twice. However, they should respond to all 10 in the NOW column first, then go back and do it again responding to all FUTURE items. The scores represent the participant's level of agreement with the assertion:

Other instruments and processes can yield similar results. The most appropriate strategy is to design an instrument that reflects the vision and intention of the team in question. These questions are critical: what is going on now, and how do we want things to be in the future?

No matter what instrument—anecdotal or statistical data—the data must not be allowed to stand on their own.unchallenged. It's best to use them as subjects for dialogue, introspection, and analysis.

Perceiving the Organizational Field

The instrument we use at the Venture Centre is a 28-item inventory in the model (Future—Now) of the Team Climate instrument described above. It is called the Truth Quotient™ or T/Q. These items represent data points at the intersection of the *Seven Steps to Building the Truthful Organization* and the *Four Levels of an Organization*.

These items generate a wealth of information about individuals, teams, and organizations. Not only does each item reveal how an individual feels about it, but correlations emerge which identify areas where the organization may be

Team Challenge

A popular team challenge is called the Blind Polygon. In this initiative, the team is given room to move around and form a large circle. Each member puts on a blindfold while instructions are explained.

They are told this is a team activity and should involve everyone. They have to find a length of rope which is in the room (taking care to keep participants away from obstructions such as furniture). Then they are told the entire group should grasp the rope and form it into a polygon. (the facilitator specifies one: square, perfect circle, triangle, etc.) They are reminded that everyone should be holding the rope.

How the team manages this is very revealing. Chaos quickly emerges. People argue about the rules. Suggestions are tendered. People raise their hands, waiting to be acknowledged. Others jockey for control. Voices rise. Some begin to check out, their body language expressing frustration, disgust, anger, etc.

Most groups come to a conclusion. The quality of their output is not nearly as important as the information the team gains about itself. With a carefully facilitated debriefing, the team's field can be perceived by most participants.

—Adapted from *The adVENTURE Kit, High Performance Team Initiatives* manual, by William D. Baker, Ed.D., Gale Arnold, and Ward Flynn

Truth Quotient™ Assertions:

1. My actions are based on my vision, values, and goals.
2. My "feelings" are at least as important as my "thoughts."
3. An important way I add value comes from my knowledge and/or training.
4. I regularly engage in activities to help clarify my "truth" and understand myself better.
5. I am more committed to learning from mistakes than looking good and being right.
6. My choice to work in this organization is part of my greater "personal mission."
7. When I feel like I am not adding value, I let others know and take action to get back in the game.
8. I do not allow others to undermine my self-confidence.
9. My need to be liked does not interfere with my ability to express my true feelings.
10. I recognize mastery in others and expect others to acknowledge mine.
11. I think people get along better when everyone respects each other's right to be "true to himself."
12. When I am involved in an interpersonal conflict, I look for what can be learned.
13. When I am unhappy with someone, I try to work it out, even if I have done no wrong.
14. I understand that relationships sometimes require speaking my personal truth, even though it may be uncomfortable for others to hear.
15. My team checks in with each other to make sure we all know how everyone feels about what we are doing and where we are going.
16. The people I work with deal with each other as the complex "people" we are, not just as a "worker."
17. When things are going badly, my team expects me to say so—to help us get back on track.
18. Teams are most effective when people are encouraged to fully participate in their own unique ways.
19. My team celebrates what has been learned when mistakes are made.
20. I put aside my personal agenda in order to better serve the goals of the team.
21. As a team, we create "truth zones" to help us build trust and safety into the team process.
22. The "walk and talk" of my company's leadership accurately reflects the vision/values and purpose of the organization.
23. My organization has policies and takes actions to support workers in the pursuit of living a healthy, happy, balanced life.
24. My organization acknowledges my unique contribution to the organization.
25. Everyone is expected to take a truthful stand even if it goes against prevailing "wisdom."
26. My organization supports my growth and rewards my increasing knowledge and experience.
27. My organization has helped me fully comprehend its vision, values, and goals.
28. My organization acknowledges and rewards those who make individual contributions to building a more truthful organization.

out of alignment. For example, individuals (personal, interpersonal fields) may demonstrate alignment about trust. However, at the team and organizational field level, there may be little commitment to building trust. This lack of alignment represents an aspect of the organizational field that should be addressed.

The 28-item Truth Quotient, shown here, can be downloaded from the Truth Zone web site at "http://www.truthzone.com". Participants are asked to determine to what degree these assertions are true.

The kind of data available from the Truth Quotient helps determine whether the personal, interpersonal, team, or organizational levels need attention. Every individual determines the "standard" by establishing an ideal or goal profile. Then, each individual determines the present situation and compares the difference, if any. Because the instrument has been used for several years in many locales, quantities of data are emerging to establish norms.

Another key feature of the instrument is its measure of commitment to change. It is not unusual for participants to demonstrate a large gap between what *is* and what's *desirable*. However, the instrument indicates that their commitment to *change themselves* may be significantly less than their expectation that *others* change.

Readiness for Organizational Learning

Another powerful measurement tool which can help reveal the quality of the organizational field is the one developed by Calhoun Wick, author of the *The Learning Edge*. I became acquainted with the man and his work through a series of serendipitous events.

Completely unbeknownst to me, Wick & Company, of Wilmington, Delaware, along with the University of Michigan School of Business, was conducting a careful study of a regional office in which I was conducting a Truthful Organization intervention. In a profession generally considered "soft" on data, an objective "blind" analysis of work like mine is extremely rare. But it gets better. Not only was my work at the regional office studied, it was compared with a control group—a similar regional office deemed "typical" at the headquarters of the company. The control group had not been exposed to the Truthful Organization material.

A Small Group of Committed Individuals ...

I often illustrate the idea that it does not take a majority to move a large organization. Even a small group of committed people working in unison can shift a larger group of unfocused people.

Imagine a large gymnasium with a shiny wood floor. In the middle of the court stands a large grand piano on rollers. Surrounding the piano are 200 people standing a discreet distance away. A booming PA system instructs the group to "move the piano."

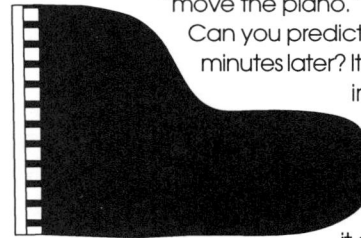

Can you predict where the piano will be five minutes later? It is most likely that it will remain in roughly the same place because, without an explicit direction (vision), each of the 200 people will have an idea about where it should go. Even if a specific direction were given, it is not certain that the whole group will agree.

Now consider a slightly different scenario. Imagine that, prior to the first direction, 25 people agreed (personal mission) to move the piano to the North West corner. Can you predict where the piano will end up?

It is very likely that 25 people working in concert could counteract the un-coordinated chaos of the other 175. But they must be personally motivated and share a common vision.

Companies Participating in Wick & Company Research Project:

3M
Arthur Andersen
Boeing
Champion International
Chevron
Chubb & Sons
Ciba-Geigy
General Electric
Hewlett-Packard
IDG
Lincoln National Insurance
Motorola
Pioneer Hi-Bred
Public Service Gas & Electric
Rensselaer Polytechnic Institute
Sears
Smith, Kline, Beecham
Trinova

The Seven "Fast-Factors" Identified by Wick & Company

Wick & Company has identified seven traits which correlate with what Wick calls "fast organizations;" they are companies best able to respond to change and learn rapidly. As Wick points out, the ability to learn and adapt rapidly is critical in today's highly competitive global marketplace.

Constant Future Focus

Organization is open minded.
Company acknowledges fresh ideas.
Organizations seek new ways to work.
Risk-taking is not punished.
Mistakes are opportunities to learn.
Leaders enjoy learning.

Rapid Learning

Fast learning is part of the business strategy.
Culture and rewards support rapid learning.
Learning quickly spreads across organization.

Change Happens Fast

Expectations are high.
People are challenged to shape the future.
New ideas are sought before old ones are implemented.
Change champions are strong.
Milestones exist to track progress

Competencies: Strong, Right, and New

Company has the right competencies.
Teams and individuals are encouraged to evolve new competencies.
Company is good at anticipating the future.
Company has a bold, clear, energizing sense of purpose.

Customer Focused Experts

Customers trust the operation.

Experts learn ideas that add value to the customer.

Company works to master what it does; to be the best.

Company has confidence in meeting future challenges.

Communication: No Borders/No Barriers

Cross-functional teams are in place.

Upper management encourages information sharing.

All levels communicate about business goals.

Everyone is informed about important decisions.

Commitment to Flawless Performance

Organization seeks flawless execution of work.

Company upgrades systems until work is done right.

Work is organized around business processes.

Reviews and upgrades processes are used to learn.

The Wick Research Design

Each company identified two organizations within its ranks—one fast, the other typical of the organization as a whole. Then 50 questionnaires were distributed to members of each organization and returned for tabulation. Follow-up telephone interviews were conducted with five members of each organization. The data were tabulated and interpreted to provide comparisons between pairs of organizations within the same company, as well as any organization across the entire array.

Results are presented to the client in statistical and graphic form along with interpretive and anecdotal (consisting of quotes from interviews) comments.

Conclusions from Wick & Company Study

Let me note that the following conclusions are mine, based on results reported by Wick & Company. Wick was as unaware of the Truthful Organization process as we were of his research project. Therefore, his interpretation did not specifically address the Truthful Organization. However, in an anecdotal conclusion, Wick interpreters made this recommendation to the decision makers of the organization in which I was working. (The company name is withheld)

> *"It would be useful for [the company] as an enterprise if the [truthful region] found ways to communicate its successes across the corporation. From the corporation's perspective, [truthful region] should be considered a 'laboratory' that tests undertaking significant improvements while still having a diligence for detail. With major industry changes on the horizon, the industry is next on the list to encounter the upheaval other attention-to-detail industries are facing ... the question for [the company] is how can the [truthful region] make the transformation from 'maverick' to becoming the norm. Their willingness to change will insure survival in the ... industry of the future."*

As expected, the selected organization, referred to as the 'truthful region' because it was deploying the Truthful Organization, qualified for its selection as a "fast" company by corporate headquarters. Its scores were superior to its "typical" counterpart in the same company. For example, the truthful or "fast" organization's score is at the 62nd percentile, while its "typical" counterpart is at the 47th percentile.

Other correlations are equally intriguing. Of the seven "fast-factors" identified by Wick, little work was done at the time the research data were collected in the area of customer-focus. Moreover, at the time the study was conducted, the headquarters of this international firm was vacillating on whether work on the Truthful Organization should proceed. (An e-mail from headquarters advised some regions to discontinue all facilitation efforts until told otherwise.)

Parallels between Seven Steps to Building The Truthful Organization and Wick's Seven "Fast Factors."

Seven Steps to Building The Truthful Organization	Calhoun Wick's Fast Factors
Step One *Declare and live out your personal mission.*	Competencies: Strong, Right, New
Step Two *Accept responsibility for your own safety and happiness.*	Commitment to Flawless Performance
Step Three *Acknowledge conflict as natural.*	Change Happens Fast
Step Four *Model truthful behavior by creating "truth zones" within the the organization.*	Communication: No borders/barriers
Step Five *Seek continuous learning for yourself and the organization.*	Rapid Learning
Step Six *Claim a personal stake in the viability of the enterprise and live out the vision/values of the organization.*	Customer Focused Experts
Step Seven *Champion truthfulness in the organization; be a leader in architecting a truthful environment.*	Constant Future Focus

The truth is not simply what you think it is; it is also the circumstances in which it is said, and to whom, why, and how it is said.

—*Václav Havel*

Of the seven scores, all were at or above average "fast" (defined as the mean scores) while two were slightly below average "fast." The below average scores were in the "Customer Focus" and "Communication" categories. Were the lowered scores due to headquarters' sword-rattling e-mail? We cannot be certain.

It is possible that the "fast" organization was fast before they even embraced the Truthful Organization material. The only way to know would be with a before-and-after study, in some future organization. In the meantime, the results are very intriguing.

Cal Wick's work represents an important step in the development of yet another tool which may be useful for revealing the character of an organization's unseen field. Further, when before-and-after testing is coupled with a control group, a powerful baseline and tracking methodology emerges. While organizational development has traditionally been a world of touchy-feely, "soft" measures, Wick's work could be viewed as a breakthrough offering a more objective family of measures.

Approximately one quarter of the group is all for the change to TQM. Another quarter strongly resists. The other half vacillates between obligation to go along and the hope that TQM will go away and die a quiet death. Ultimately, the field does not support TQM and, not surprisingly, another TQM program bites the dust.

In a Truthful Organization, the ability to measure change is a critical component for all participants to know where we are, how far we have come, and how far we have to go.

DISRUPTING FIELDS: Making Waves

Before Fields Can Be Changed, They Must Be Disrupted

Emergencies generate big waves! Any time a crisis arises, fields are disrupted. More than one manager has been tempted to threaten a crisis just to motivate employees. Emergency situations involve real or perceived jeopardy—physical danger, fiscal peril, layoffs, legal entanglements, loss of revenue, liability claims, etc.

Another less dramatic sure-fire way to disrupt a field is to set up feedback mechanisms which mirror field activity to all participants within the field. Examples of feedback mechanisms include performance reviews, audits, year-end review (profit or loss), etc.

The third way to disrupt a field is with a facilitator's intervention. At the Venture Centre, we use a method called *Managed Perturbation.* We create activities for the team and its membership to experience "perceived jeopardy." At the same time, we set up "feedback mechanisms." As a result, the team sees how it functions (perceives its field) in the midst of perceived jeopardy.

Emergency Fields - Crisis Management

At times of crisis, people are at their worst and their best. One of the greatest crises in recent history was World War II. At the time, millions of people's lives were totally transformed. Never since have so many people pulled together, so unselfishly, for such a long period of time. More recently, lesser catastrophes have provided fresh examples of people pulling together to overcome incredible odds.

It takes two to speak the truth—one to speak and another to hear.
—Henry David Thoreau

Many managers have had the experience of delivering bad news to the team: impending layoffs, loss of market share, impending dissolution, etc. When these crises occur, people pull together. Productivity soars, motivation goes through the roof, etc. The problem is, it does not last. Either the crisis passes, (or is resolved because of the improved performance) or people lose the fire due to a sense of habit. More than one manager has been tempted to proclaim a disaster just to rally the troops. But people are not dumb. They know the sky cannot fall every day. And as people become habituated, they no longer respond to the threat of impending crisis.

Emergencies are painful, unpredictable, and impossible to "control." In the event of a real emergency, there is no guarantee the team or company will adapt and learn quickly enough to assure success. The company can fail. While some managers do try to manage by crisis, the Wharton School of Business is unlikely to include crisis management in its curriculum.

Emergencies offer insights into the nature of the field. When an emergency occurs, members of the team dramatically move to a perspective which affords the team an opportunity to "see" its own field. Consider Monday morning quarterbacking; after the fact, dissection of a crisis affords observers 20/20 hindsight.

The truth is a snare: you cannot have it, without being caught. You cannot have the truth in such a way that you catch it, but only in such a way that it catches you.
—Søren Kierkegaard

Feedback Mechanisms — Developing self-awareness

Feedback is anything that accurately reflects the current situation to participants. In a world of three 360 degree feedback instruments, computer-based tracking systems, psychological assessments, e-mail, etc., the most powerful mechanism for feedback is conversation—among co-workers and between supervisors and workers. Yet it is possible to find departments that never have meetings, and workers whose only conversation with their bosses involves listening to instructions. Bosses need to tell subordinates how they are doing. Workers need to ask how they are doing.

In addition to (but not in place of) conversation, regular performance evaluations as part of a comprehensive employee development program will provide staff with objectives, signposts, and progress reports.

One reason Open Book Management described by Jack Stack in his book, *The Great Game of Business*, has attracted much attention is because of his commonsense approach to developing a score card for the entire organization. By itself, a score card may not be so unusual. But at Stack's Springfield Manufacturing, score cards are the company's financial reports revealing not only the bottom line, but every aspect of the company's performance ... for all to see. And he makes sure everyone is trained to understand the documents and how an individual contribution shows up.

Managed Perturbation

Managed Perturbation involves an activity or environment made for the purpose of creating the *perception* of jeopardy, or even danger, while carefully guarding the actual safety of all participants. While the experience can perturb anyone, it is carefully managed to prevent going overboard. At the Venture Centre, Managed Perturbation means we combine elements of both the *crisis* experience and *feedback* mechanisms. The core of our training programs is augmented with carefully structured activities, games, and simulations. Each activity creates the perception of risk and offers participants detailed feedback on both team and individual performance.

In the "Blind Polygon" activity described earlier, a series of constraints (blindfolds, extraneous noise, vague instructions, confusion about outcomes, desire to succeed, etc.) put pressure on the participants—creating the perception of jeopardy. During and after the activity, Venture Centre facilitators are trained to help participants understand *how* they involve themselves in the action, or whether they participate at all. A careful debriefing of the experience offers feedback to the team. Participants note the difference between work-related behaviors and those that might be unique to the activity. In this way, team members are able to transfer what they learn to the workplace.

When we believe ourselves in possession of the only truth, we are likely to be indifferent to common everyday truths.
—Eric Hoffer

CHANGE:
Changing the Field

Changing Fields

A field can be changed in at least two ways. In one, participants within the field are guided toward a carefully crafted new field. In the other method, the organization is immersed in a self-reorganization process without a pre-designed master plan and collaboratively constructs a new field. At the Venture Centre, we use both processes.

If we review the previous steps, first the field must be perceived. Usually, this means that someone (or perhaps an entire group) concludes that the field needs to be changed—often as a result of a crisis. Next, the field is disrupted due to a natural crisis, a feedback mechanism, or Managed Perturbation. At this point, a field in disarray, if left alone, will return to a close approximation of its previous state. It is to be expected that no matter how uncomfortable the pre-existing field, some people will be dedicated to its restoration. To bring about lasting change, members of the team need to develop a heightened awareness of the field, including its history and options for changing it.

Introducing a New Pattern

Reorganization will occur. There is likely to be tension, if not an outright struggle, between those who wish to restore the field and those who want change. Most change initiatives fail because of what happens at this point. Those people, usually a quarter of the group, who want to go back are offset by a group of equal size who share a vision of what "could be." The rest of the group, about half, is noncommittal—moving first one way and then another.

There is no such source of error as the pursuit of absolute truth.
—Samuel Butler

Let's look at an organization in which TQM is being deployed and what goes on with the fields. Approximately one quarter of the group is all for the change to TQM. Another quarter strongly resists. The other half vacillates between obligation to go along and the hope that TQM will go away and die a quiet death. Ultimately, the field does not support TQM and, not surprisingly, another TQM program bites the dust.

Reorganizing the field to be more supportive of TQM requires providing enough information and training to get more people to agree that the field must change. This is more than merely convincing people; it is getting them to make a *personal decision* to let go of the past and embrace a new field that will support TQM. The best way to get people to buy in is to inspire a bottom-up revolution where co-workers spontaneously evangelize each other instead of where bosses try to motivate, intimidate, or bribe subordinates. Moreover, those who do not buy in must not be punished. This is critical because those people who are unwilling to support the change must be encouraged to avoid sabotaging or undermining it. Ultimately, it does not require even a majority to bring about change, only a few people whose personal missions compel them to work toward the same shared vision.

Self-reorganization

Self-reorganization takes a different direction. At the point the team perceives its own field and experiences its disruption, the tension is maintained. As described earlier, pressure to embrace a particular resolution tends to divide the group—but none is offered or permitted to take hold. Instead, the team stays in this chaotic state as long as possible. To help the team remain in this much discomfort involves the skills of an effective facilitator.

Eventually, the team gets to know itself well. The team learns what it can and cannot do. It learns its strengths and weaknesses. Most importantly, it determines what its future CAN be and the steps necessary to bring it about. Even if a few people do not fully agree, as described earlier, it is ok; as long as they agree to "get out of the way" by not getting in the way! This team creates its new field from the inside out. Buy-in is NEVER a problem!

A field in disarray, if left alone, will return to a close approximation of its previous state. It is to be expected that no matter how uncomfortable the pre-existing field, some people will be dedicated to its restoration.

Unfortunately, the existing infrastructure may feel threatened. Even if they support the process, they may not agree with the outcome. To what ever degree is possible, all stakeholders need to be involved in this kind of reinvention.

Change-resistant Fields

The most change-resistant, highly concentrated field is addiction. Most recovering addicts know the phenomenon of addiction substitution:

"I quit smoking ... now I can't stop eating."

"The hours I cut back at work ... I now spend at the gym."

"Ok, I'll stop smoking pot ... but don't ask me to stop drinking."

When Chris, the workaholic, cuts back unhealthy overtime to work out at the gym, it would appear a positive change has occurred. Chris for one, would certainly have us subscribe to that conclusion. But has the field really changed? Not if Chris has switched addictions from workaholism to exercise addiction. Whether he has broken through the field of addiction or found a new way to feed the emptiness that gnaws at the soul, is Chris' business. But he may not be certain, and others will find it difficult to determine because working out is so different from overworking. It is tempting to focus on the details instead of the field. But to do so leaves people in the dark about the fields in which they live and, even worse, leaves them ill equipped to delete or change fields that no longer support them.

Addictions may seem to exist only in a personal field. However, the phenomenon known as co-dependency, which has come to public awareness in recent years, describes an addictive, interpersonal field. Both team- and organizational fields can also have addictive components.

Truth must be the foundation stone, the cement to solidify the entire social edifice.
—Pope John Paul II

It is not unusual for organizations in trouble to waste precious time and resources doing the same old thing. And it is common for addictive organizations on the verge of catastrophe to borrow money, make false promises to vendors and customers, mistreat staff, and behave in an untruthful manner.

The Personal Commitment to Change

Einstein defined insanity as doing the same thing over and over, expecting different results. While most people instantly comprehend the wisdom of Einstein's words, few of us have enough awareness of our own fields to know whether we are making progress or merely doing the same thing over and over. In the final analysis, making lasting changes requires a conscious choice and a commitment to action on our part. It cannot happen without us.

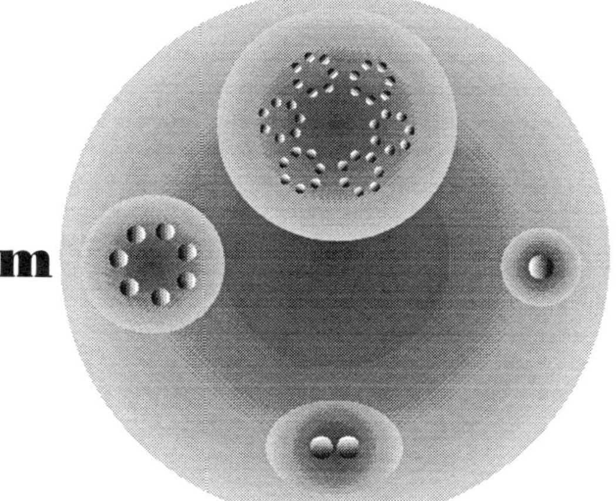

Section Two

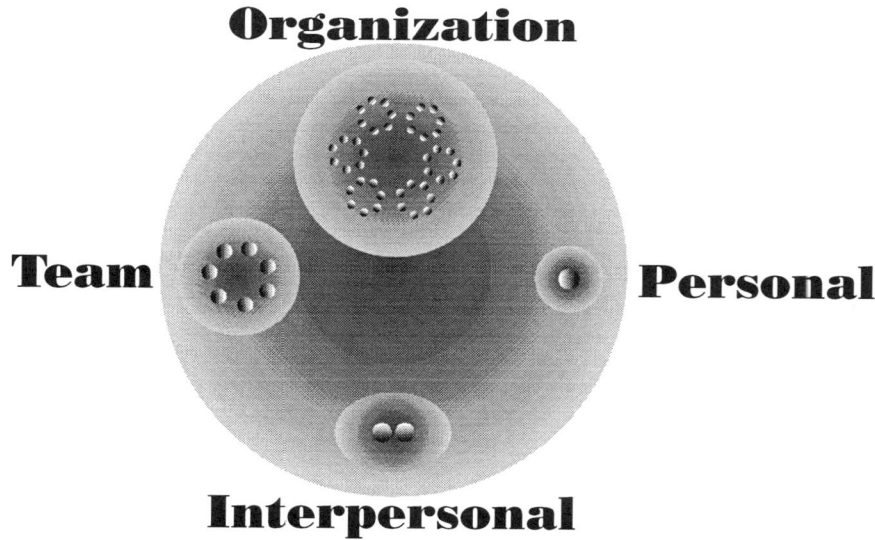

Building The Truthful Organization

Building a Truthful Organization

Building a Truthful Organization requires the resolve to make changes. While most of us are motivated to change others or the 'system,' most of the changes must ultimately be our own. The *Seven Steps to Building the Truthful Organization* which form the organizing principle of this section can be your road map to lasting changes, improving your life and making a more significant contribution at your workplace.

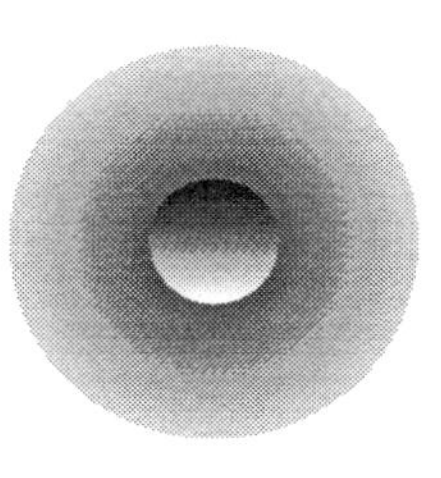

Chapter Four

PERSONAL: Participation Gets The Job Done

PERSONAL: Participation Gets The Job Done

STEPS TRUTH 7

1. Declare and live out your personal mission.

Far and away, the most common problem facing organizations of all types is lack of agreement or alignment among participants. These participants, sometimes called stakeholders, include: workers, managers, unions, owners, investors, customers, vendors, and others in the greater community.

Two forces have conspired to create widespread confusion, diminished productivity, and a nearly universal malaise in organizations of all sizes.

First is the longstanding belief that the workplace should be unencumbered by human emotion, leading to the admonition "leave your personal life at home."

Second is the general belief that when everyone on the team has the same understanding of where the company is going (a shared vision), each person will make appropriate contributions to arrive at the same outcome.

Open, interpersonal communication facilitates rapid transitions from fear- and control-based behavior states to adult-appropriate behaviors. This fosters greater interdependence among team members.

Each of us is a free agent; our relationship with the company is based on our ability to add value—not sentimentality, loyalty, politics, or tenure. Our value is based solely on our ability to contribute.

The Problem with Leaving Your Personal Life at Home

The things managers desire most from employees are skill, motivation, loyalty, passion, enthusiasm, initiative, integrity, commitment, and cooperation. All but technical skills are derived from a person's inner, personal life—an inner life complicated (to one degree or another) by emotions. Unfortunately, many people are so uncomfortable and unskilled to handle emotions that any hint of a personal life at work is prohibited. Some companies go so far as to ban plants, artwork, pictures of family, and other personal objects from the workplace. Consequently, the very characteristics managers have been seeking for generations are barred every time they say "Leave your personal life at home." Many business people are genuinely terrified of emotions. Some actually believe happy people are not businesslike. Angry people are dangerous. Sad people are shut down. Compassionate people cannot be trusted, and so on.

Most managers, like the rest of us, were never taught how to deal with emotion. What is not understood is generally feared.

The reality is, that people only show up for work because of their personal life. Few people's last words are ... "If only I had spent more time at work." Motivation comes from deep inside. All managers want workers to be motivated, but when people show up with the rest of their emotional baggage, some of them freak out.

Most managers, like the rest of us, were never taught how to deal with emotion. What is not understood is generally feared. Until recently, the prevailing emotional strategy at work has been a systematic elimination of feelings from the workplace. Some in business are beginning to see a connection between the exclusion of a worker's personal life and the malaise described above. When a worker's personal life is precluded in order to rid emotions from the job, is it reasonable to expect motivation and enthusiasm to remain? Besides, when emotions are suppressed, they do not go away. They only go underground and get locked in a drawer for eight hours.

Fear-based people give away their personal "power" and diminish their capability. Control-based people rob others on the team of their "power" by taking control and responsibility from teammates. The goal of the Truthful Organization is ADULT-appropriate behavior in which people behave in a way that supports everyone on the team to do his or her best.

No one has escaped the "nothing personal" phenomenon. A few years ago, I underwent an outpatient biopsy. I returned to work for the remainder of that day and the next before receiving the results. My productivity was compromised by my inability to concentrate. I was petrified by the possibility of cancer. To avoid feeling my fears, I tried to stay busy; the fact that I was less than 100% effective was of little consequence to me. Thank God, my trial had a happy ending. How many similar situations do people face every day? Some may be less painful, others are even more traumatic with unhappy endings, but every challenge takes it toll and has its effect on the quality and quantity of work performed.

Ironically when these *personal* aspects of life are forced underground, it means people are prohibited from talking about what may be bothering them. This line of reasoning assumes talking about personal problems will prolong or exaggerate a problem. The fear is that ill feelings may extend beyond the affected person and involve others—thereby diminishing productivity on a grander scale.

If workers feel compelled to come to work when they know they are in a diminished state, does it not make more sense to let others know about the situation so the team can more appropriately respond to a problem which affects the whole team?

The challenge has less to do with people's personal problems than with caretaking by others. Caretaking is when one person takes on another person's problem as if it was his or her own. Caretaking is not adult behavior—it is parental. Yet only small children and the very old or severely disabled need caretaking. The rest of us only need understanding, encouragement, and assistance when requested. Knowing the difference between support and caretaking is critical to adult behavior.

There is no way to show up for work without a personal life. When people work in an environment that forces them to behave as if they have no personal life, they do not receive the support they need. Moreover, the team is forced to ignore a whole class of issues that do affect team performance. As it turns out, management's effort to suppress issues often backfires. When personal problems arise, the manager is deliberately kept in the dark, while the team rallies around the worker. Caretaking in the face of organizational indifference is just one more example of the hidden organization.

Every worker is a whole human being. Instead of forcing people to disown parts of themselves, it makes more sense to provide them with the necessary skills to participate in an adult work environment where each worker has feelings and thoughts; a personal life as well as a work life. When "whole workers" are the norm, work is not interrupted by intrusions from home—the work field barely fluctuates!

The challenge has less to do with people's personal problems than with caretaking by others. Caretaking is when one person takes on another person's problem as if it was his or her own. Caretaking is not adult behavior—it is parental. Yet only small children and the very old or severely disabled need caretaking. The rest of us only need understanding, encouragement, and assistance when requested. Knowing the difference between support and caretaking is critical to adult behavior.

Every worker is a whole human being. Instead of forcing people to disown parts of themselves, it makes more sense to provide them with the necessary skills to participate in an adult work environment where each worker has feelings and thoughts; a personal life as well as a work life. When "whole workers" are the norm, work is not interrupted by intrusions from home—the work field barely fluctuates!

To be true to your personal mission, values, and purpose, it is first necessary to define and declare them, then commit to living them.

The most effective method is to encourage people to be true to their personal mission, values, and purpose. But first it is necessary to define, declare, and then commit to living out a personal mission. Instead of living out a personal mission, most people live in a reactive mode—responding to the actions of people and events around them. They live paycheck to paycheck, crisis to crisis, opportunity to opportunity, holiday to holiday, etc.

Our Personal Filter - The Internal Program

Something in each of us makes it possible to respond to external occurrences in a fairly consistent manner. Inside each of us is something like a filter. Some describe it as a computer program. Others think of it as a set of values. Whatever its nature, everyone has it. And beyond making us who and what we are, it permits people to make choices and respond to situations relatively quickly and efficiently. For most people, this aspect of themselves is unknown. It becomes apparent when our choices are called into question: "Why do you like blue? What's wrong with a rainy day? Is chocolate really better than vanilla?" and so on.

People who achieve great things are nearly unanimous in their belief that the most important difference between excellence and the ordinary is getting in touch with that internal program. Nearly every book on personal motivation offers a new twist on this old theme. When people get in touch with their internal programs, their lives become richer and more productive. When they learn to reprogram themselves, focusing on specific goals and a long-range vision, the potential for achievement is unlimited.

By taking time to do the inner work necessary to get in touch with their personal program, people see life differently. Suddenly, it is no longer a journey to endure, but a quest driven by a mission full of adventure, learning, and growth. The first dividend is passion. When people take the time to define their mission and declare their intention to live it out, they come to work renewed and invigorated like entrepreneurs in search of their pot of gold.

Shared Vision Is Not Enough

The notion that having a clear understanding of where the company is going will assure success is incomplete. Workers also need a personal mission. A company vision is a poor substitute for a personal mission. People uncertain about their personal missions are usually willing to sign on to the company vision for several reasons: Doing so may appear to ensure their continued employment. The vision promises them a more specific target. The workers are not sufficiently in touch with their own missions (or values) to be compromised by subscribing to the company vision. Ultimately, sign-on has little real meaning. Even groups who have spent days debating and tens of thousands of dollars on retreats have participated only at an intellectual level. The proof is the absence of lasting passion and influence reported by managers in every field.

By contrast, when workers who have clarified and declared their personal missions are presented with a company vision, they cannot take it lightly. If the vision presented goes further than their personal missions, they must decide whether they are up to the challenge. If it does not go far enough, they must do everything in their power to influence its enhancement. To do less is to work in an environment that offers little or no challenge. The vision may contradict their personal missions in some way. Then people feel compelled to change the company vision or rewrite their own missions. When neither is possible, staying with the company means certain pain and continual suffering. They will usually choose to leave.

Nearly every book on personal motivation offers a new twist on this old theme. When people get in touch with their internal programs, their lives become richer and more productive. When they learn to reprogram themselves, focusing on specific goals and a long-range vision, the potential for achievement is unlimited.

Alignment - A True Course

Look at the results when a worker's personal mission is aligned with the vision of the company. In such cases, the worker's deepest motivators become the driving force behind their job and every task. The result is a committed, highly motivated worker, dedicated to the shared vision of the company. The untold millions of dollars spent each year trying to motivate and, more recently, empower workers is putting the cart before the horse. Empowerment, like motivation, comes from the inside ... from home!

The work force whose members find joy in their work are capable of greater, sustained productivity.

Contrary to comfortable old beliefs, no one can empower another person. Many managers talk about "empowering" their workers, but only we can empower ourselves.

Contrary to comfortable old beliefs, no one can empower another person. Many managers talk about "empowering" their workers, but only we can empower ourselves. Managers who try to empower workers not only fail, but invariably miss the irony of their own paternalism.

Whether it's called empowerment, alignment, commitment, or motivation, most managers are confused about how to make it happen. They do, however, know it when they see it. It is most often found in entrepreneurial settings. Unfortunately, it seldom exists in established organizations and is downright scarce in bureaucracies.

What would happen if an organization, even a big one, was peopled by employee-entrepreneurs? Until recently, it was a commonly held belief that entrepreneurs represent a distinct personality type. That was until Lloyd E. Shefsky wrote *Entrepreneurs Are Made, Not Born*. In this fascinating book full of case studies, Shefsky makes his argument. In the final analysis, the difference between entrepreneurs and the rest of the population is *passion*.

The more closely a person's mission is aligned with his or her work, the more passion a person brings to the job.

If people do not have passion for their work, motivation will always be a struggle. Put more positively, the more closely a person's mission is aligned with his or her work, the more passion a person brings to the job.

A Mission Statement

A mission statement reflects a person's deepest reasons for being while simultaneously defining his or her highest intentions. A mission statement represents a genuine commitment to live out your dreams and take responsibility for your life.

A mission statement represents a genuine commitment to live out your dreams and take responsibility for your life.

In our culture, people learn to direct their energies outwardly, and the message is clear. What is important is what we do, who and what we know, what we own, where we live, what we wear—even what we drive—rarely *who we are*.

Without a willingness to look inside and do some introspection, people may find it difficult to craft a meaningful mission statement. And because inner work is an ongoing process, over time, a person's mission evolves, reflecting the expanding boundaries of maturity and growing personal awareness.

The fact that vast numbers of people have little motivation to know themselves, let alone craft a mission for themselves, must not deter those who seek more than the status quo. There is a vast difference between people who seek inner knowledge and a "place" in the scheme of things and those who do not. No one has captured the tension between these two groups better than Daniel Quinn, in his haunting novel, *Ishmael*. Quinn makes an amazing assertion about how some of the most vital components of our culture—including, science, technology, rationalism, etc.—contribute to our cultural discontent.

According to the late Joseph Campbell, who wrote *The Hero With a Thousand Faces* and many other books, coming of age in a culture without roots and with little regard for the inner landscape sets in motion the seeds of its own dissolution. Campbell wrote volumes about mythical and work-a-day heroes. Heroic or not, the driving forces behind grand personal achievements are inner knowledge, vision, and planning. Without inner awareness people are doomed to live out the Chinese proverb, "If you are not sure where you are going, any road will take you there."

What motivation experts have been saying for years is true! It <u>is</u> possible to live life like a champion. People can add depth to it by transforming their lives and impacting the lives of others. The process begins with the script. Unfortunately, most of us don't have one—we live life one day and one paycheck at a time.

Personal Passion in the Print Shop

About 20 years ago I was beginning my consulting practice. I was young, undercapitalized, and struggling. I took a night job in a printing plant. It was a wonderful dichotomy. Blue-collar graphic artist at night and white-collar consultant by day. But a curious thing happened. My passion for my new business carried over to the night job. I developed an interesting relationship with co-workers who were a little wary of me; they knew I did not fit in. I was not interested in gossiping or complaining about the boss. Instead, I asked, "What do you think we can we do to help Dave?" People liked me, but were suspicious of anyone they could not "enmesh" into their drama. Because I could see from the perspective of a part-time worker AND through the eyes of an owner, I could not be enmeshed. Were there problems? Yes. Did Dave have problems dealing with his employees? Yes. But my perspective was dramatically different than my co-workers. About six months later, Dave offered me a full partnership in the operation and management of a new plant. All I had done was let my passion show and behave like an owner!

A lifelong entrepreneur, I turned Dave down and went on to build my own firm. My experience with Dave, and the subsequent years of building my own business, have helped me appreciate the power of personal passion.

Mission Planner

Because I am convinced of the importance of creating a personal mission, I have made arrangements with my publisher to make available FREE OF CHARGE, (with the exception of a $1.00 handling fee) a step-by-step, MISSION PLANNER workbook to help you with this critical process. There is no charge for this important tool if it is used by you personally. Additional copies may be purchased for $6.50 each, plus handling. You may receive your mission planner by mail (call us at 800-748-1103 - one per person, please) or download the document directly from the world wide web at http://www.truthzone.com. Attention consultants, managers, and trainers: quantity discounts for purchasing the MISSION PLANNER may be arranged.

When we take the time to define our mission or write a so-called script, we run into another wall. There it is right in front of us, bigger than life. WHAT IF WE FAIL? At least with no specified plan, we are not accountable. As long as the plan remains in our head, it is a dream and nothing more. Enticing, yes, but not a yardstick to be measured against. Anything resembling a yardstick causes most of us to run away posthaste. It is a fear of accountability which causes us to dismiss the idea of sitting down and writing a personal mission statement.

Personally, I resisted the idea for years. I did not want to be tied down. If I focused in this direction, I would immediately think of all the other directions I was closing the doors to. I had already discovered, as a child, that it never paid to tell people about "my big ideas." If I failed to reach a goal, I not only had to deal with my own disappointment, but the jeers of others who seemed to delight in my failure. And therein I discovered a subtle but vital clue that led to the resolution of my resistance to writing a personal mission statement.

A mission statement is not a goal. Goals are but signposts on the journey toward the realization of your mission. A mission involves two components. It is an *outcome* or vision of your most optimistic and ideal future (a step beyond the attainable) as well as the *intentions* and behaviors that will define the character of the quest. For example, a mission many people espouse sounds like this:

Through my day-to-day actions,
I wish to make this world a better place.

Notice there is a specific, although difficult to measure, *outcome*—the world will be a better place, or it won't. And there is an *intention* to contribute to the outcome through small day-to-day acts, rather than one large achievement.

A mission is not a goal. A goal may be to plan a specific good deed for a week from next Thursday. You may or may not achieve that goal. You may lament your failure or celebrate your success, it is up to you—but that one deed does not define your mission!

When I realized the distinction between measurable goals and a well-crafted mission statement, I made the leap.

It will take many years to determine how well I fulfill my mission. I appreciate now, more than ever, how important it is that my mission always be "one or two steps beyond my reach." When I begin to close in on it, I stretch it out—just beyond grasp.

Now I can even set goals! Carol Ann (Wilson) Folmer, entrepreneur par excellénce and my mentor regarding goals, worked with me for years. However, it was not until I set a mission for myself that I was able to commit to short-term and then long-term goals. Some work out, others don't. But now I set my inner barometer to fulfilling my mission, not to achieving a specific goal. And that is the breakthrough about goals. Goals are mere blips on the journey toward fulfillment of a mission. Instead of signposts, think of goals as steps on a very long journey. Any one step is relatively insignificant. Some steps move us forward; sometimes we have to detour around obstacles. If we must go back and retrace our steps, is that really a setback? Detours are part of life. They may be bumpy, or full of new opportunities. Either way, we move onward toward fulfillment of our mission.

A mission is not a goal.

The Worker as Free Agent

A key aspect of writing a mission is seeing beyond the obvious—seeing the field that binds our fears, desires, goals, and assumptions into the fabric of life. As long as people define themselves by what they do, they are bound to continue doing it. As long as we define ourselves by our toolbox, we are unlikely to seek additional tools. The doctor must see beyond medicine, the lawyer beyond law, and the worker beyond the job. Workers who see their jobs as a safety net live a disempowering lie. No job offers security. And what looks like a safety net today may be a sticky web that traps and holds people back. Every worker must look beyond the job and find meaning, purpose, and value beyond work. Most importantly, workers must know both their intrinsic, internal value and their worth in the marketplace.

No job offers security. And what looks like a safety net today may be a sticky web that traps and holds people back. Every worker must look beyond the job and find meaning, purpose, and value beyond work. Most importantly, workers must know both their intrinsic, internal value and their worth in the marketplace.

Your Job is a Gift

Liza was recently promoted to a new position. Her boss was also new and had little to do with the placement of Liza. She was feeling good about her promotion and new duties when her boss told her the only reason Liza got the job was because there was nowhere else to put her in the organization. Her boss said her skills did not really merit the promotion, and she did not have the skills to do the job outside of this organization.

Liza was hurt and lost a lot of sleep. She had worked hard to get into the new position, but now she was told she was underqualified and, most importantly, that she was now dependent on the organization.

Liza needs to talk straight with her boss and convince her she cannot do the job under the present circumstances. Maybe she did not have the formal training, but what will the organization do to remedy that? Liza needs to reclaim her status as a free agent, or else she will be depleted and exhausted trying to prove herself.

If it is true that she is unqualified, the decision makers made a mistake. They need to correct that mistake in one of two ways: If they think it is not likely Liza will succeed and add value, they need to admit the mistake and find a more suitable position for her. If they think Liza can do the job, she needs to be supported with classes, coaching, and perhaps a mentor so she can grow into the position .

Declaring the Mission

Once defined, the mission needs to be declared. It does not have to be in front of a large group or published in a newsletter, but at least a few people need to be the recipient of your mission. If the idea is threatening, consider finding a partner or coach with whom you are willing to share your inner world.

Making a declaration adds life to people's intention by incorporating it into their personal field. Moreover, psychologists have known for years that when people disclose facets of their personality to others, those aspects of personality are awakened. This kind of self-disclosure, among trusted relationships, is the most reliable way people use to develop their personalities. Yet it is a step which cannot be completed alone; it is essential that at least one other person significant to you participate in this disclosure.

This is not to say that the workplace should become an encounter group. Work is not the appropriate place for therapy. Nevertheless, the more familiar people become with their inner landscape, the easier it is to identify, craft, articulate, and declare a personal mission. That mission will soon become a standard by which all sorts of decisions are made, as well as the foundation for personal empowerment.

Those in power need to be encouraged to create an environment in which introspection is supported as a vital part of employee development for the whole company. On the other hand, organizations must be diligent to discourage amateur psychologists anxious to analyze, counsel, and "caretake" their fellow employees.

This is not psychotherapy. As we strive to respect all people and honor their participation, in whatever form they choose, we do not try to change people. As leaders, it is important that we set an example of personal respect for all members of the team.

Personal Mission: The Anchor in a Storm

People with clear personal missions are better able to deal with change. This is true whether the changes are organizational, technological, or personal.

People undergoing change or stress need something constant to hold onto while the environment shifts. When people define themselves by what the environment reflects, then every change in the surroundings has a corresponding effect on each person. When bad things happen "out there," we feel badly "in here." On the other hand, when people define who they are by what is inside at the core—even deeper than feelings—then when the environment shifts, they are not so easily overwhelmed. It is possible to feel feelings, empathize with others, and respond to the surroundings without losing balance. Such a person is able to navigate even the most turbulent whitewater.

While a personal mission may be valuable, when most people look inside, they do not find their mission chiseled on stone tablets. In fact, sometimes it is quite difficult to get clear about what is really going on inside. This is because there is another factor. Most call it self-talk. Nearly everyone reports an inner "voice" that speaks in his or her head. Some people report a chorus of comments. Little of what is said is useful. It is often painful, usually confusing, and nearly always critical.

The Truthful Participant

I was taught as a child and trained myself as an adult to live by the principles of integrity, fairness, tolerance, excellence, and a strong work ethic. We were taught to never sell out on our principles; that they would get us by when all else seemed to fail. We learned living this way was not easy. Often we would have to stand alone while others disagreed with us. We were told we might not always be liked, but respect was the greater choice. The truth, however unpopular, was not negotiable.

As a single parent of two young children, no college degree, and little experience, I was interviewed for a position at a television station. I had few of the listed qualifications required for the job, but I got it. Nine months later, I put in my resume for the management position I now hold at the station.

I told the hiring committee there were certain principles by which I live and work that were not negotiable: they do not change. I recommended that after I shared with the committee, if they felt they could not live with them as presented, not to hire me. Those principles were:

1. I do not lie. Integrity is the foundation of how I live and work. When I or my staff make a mistake, we own it 100%, look for solutions, and move on. We do not blame, make excuses, or pass the buck.
2. By the same token, we do not take the heat for anything we have not done, no matter how politically advantageous it may be. That means that if something has gone awry, and someone else does not wish to own the error, I will never stand by passively and allow myself

continued on next page ...

Truthful Participation
continued from previous page

or my staff to receive blame or responsibility ... no matter who the individual is. (This would come to challenge my values in later years in a situation with my boss. I did not relent. It was a painful time. We worked it through. There has never since been a question of where I stand or how far I will go in living by my principles.)

3. While there may be some people I do not like or enjoy, they will likely never know it. I work as hard and with the same excellence for all. I sabotage no project or person.

4. While I will always stand up for myself or my staff, I will never be vindictive to someone who has been that way to me. I never pay people back for their unkindness. As long as I live according to my principles, eventually someone else will come along to do the job. I never have to expend the negative energy or hatefulness for pay-back.

5. I never take credit for other people's work. I make certain they put their ideas in writing to document their contributions.

For a station not always courageous in the early days of hiring strong managers, that committee accepted my rules. In the history of the station, no one ever stayed longer than 2 1/2 years in my position as director of communications. It was always considered a political job and one in which the manager was either beaten up or disregarded. After 15 years as the director of communications, I know I have affected positively the integrity, enthusiasm, and standards of excellence of the station and staff over the years.

Through the years, all the people on that committee did test my tenets. And, certainly they did not always like that I stood firm. But congruency was something they have always been able to count on with me and my department.

— Name Withheld

This voice tends to express our doubts, impose unrealistic expectations, and generally criticize our behavior. Some describe this voice as an ever-present "parent." Others call it the saboteur, gremlin, or dragon. Whatever name it goes by, everyone reports one thing—nothing is ever good enough to please the voice.

Dealing with the voice is an important reason to develop a personal mission. If we take the time to develop a clear picture of what is important to us, we can rely upon it instead of living at the mercy of the voice. As described above, a personal mission doesn't just come to you. It requires focused work. Even more importantly, it has to be written down. Writing it down forces you to take it seriously. From then on, the voice has a formidable opponent. If the voice says "no" but the mission says "yes" ... you can trust the mission.

When people have a firm handle on their own mission and values, self-confidence is difficult to erode. Using their personal mission as a tool, people can empower themselves and, if they desire, develop leadership skills for the good of others and the organization as a whole.

STEPS TRUTH

2. Accept responsibility for your own safety and happiness.

A reward that comes from having a personal life-mission is an enhanced sense of personal responsibility. Not responsibility as in obligation or guilt—it's more like authorship. People with a mission accept responsibility for themselves—their health, their behavior, and most especially, their feelings and moods!

Change does not mean life is suddenly transformed into a bowl of cherries. Rather, when an obstacle or conflict is encountered, people with a mission are more intentional and direct in dealing with the problem. People with clear missions avoid getting bogged down in blame and fault finding. Perhaps because they are so focused on the mission, they just don't waste time nitpicking. Instead of asking "Who did this?", their questions tend to be: "What happened? What needs to be done? What can we learn? How can I help? How are we doing?"

The general question "How are we doing?" is a critical one. It originates with an understanding that health, happiness, and safety are important for everyone involved. When a person is unhappy, their participation is compromised. When a person's health is unsound, their performance lacks lustre. When a person's safety is threatened, fear causes them to keep their guard up.

It was not until I set a mission for myself that I was able to commit to short-term and then long-term goals.

Goals are mere blips on the journey toward fulfillment of a mission. Instead of signposts, think of goals as steps on a very long journey.

What is Balance?

In Arthur Miller's award-winning play *Death of a Salesman*, Willy Loman recounts his years of sacrifice providing for his family. However, the value of his long hours, business trips, and near total preoccupation with work is challenged by his family—the very people he thought he was serving. One of the sad messages from the play is how easy it is to lose touch with what is really important.

In the previous chapter, much was made of the entrepreneurial model. When employees act more like owners with a stake in the business, many motivational and quality issues are

Vision Quest

While working with an organization on an Indian reservation, I ran into a unique set of circumstances regarding the declaration of personal mission.

For one thing, many Native Americans (in this case, the Lakota people) actively pursue a personal vision through ritual and prayer. A key aspect of their way of life is a four-day, four-night ordeal called a Humbleché in which a person goes on a hill, alone in the wilderness, to "cry for a vision." This spiritual vision is not discussed with others. With the possible exception of an elder or medicine teacher, it remains a central motivator in life, but is not discussed out loud.

Asking some Lakota people to talk about their personal mission required that a careful distinction be made between a personal mission and the underlying spiritual *vision* that generates it. With this understanding, the Lakota and non-Indian people could participate fully in this activity.

In one exceptional case, a non-Lakota participant stood up and made a big deal about how he was a private person. He had no intention of sharing himself with his co-workers. He stated in no uncertain terms that it was not about trust, since he had complete trust in his co-workers and supervisors.

In a later discussion, he mentioned that he liked to hear other people talk about themselves, so he could "better understand whether to trust these people or not." I pointed out that I thought his approach seemed unbalanced by keeping everyone wondering about him while they revealed themselves to him. He just smiled a canary smile.

Over time, it was he who was unable to be trusted by his co-workers or supervisors.

resolved. Like any model, there are limitations. For example, the problem with the entrepreneurial model is the lives of some entrepreneurs lack balance and seem unhealthy.

- Some are poor role models.
- Entrepreneurs have a tendency to become workaholics.
- Many are driven, not by a personal mission or dream, but neurotic compulsion to be busy—and avoid introspection.
- Some seek only to prove their worth—by building a successful business.
- Many try to fill the emptiness in their life—by accumulating wealth.
- Others struggle to overcome feelings of inferiority—by having power over others.

WARNING: Getting in touch with your mission may unleash such passion that you may choose to work at the expense of other important aspects that balance your life! Do so at your own peril.

Work may not always be healthy, fun, and perfectly balanced. But if balance and health are not your conscious intention, whose intention is it? Who is watching out for you? Who will tell you when you are going overboard?

Whose voice will you listen to when it says: "Don't work so much! Stop smoking! Don't sweat the small stuff! Play a little! Stop drinking! You need more exercise! Stop raging! Reduce the fat in your diet! Lighten up!"—certainly not the surgeon general, not your mother, or your spouse, not your children, not your boss, or your doctor ... when are you going to say these things to yourself? When will you listen?

If you are unwilling to be personally responsible for your own (and your family's) health, happiness, and quality of life, how can you contemplate changing the environment in which you work? People don't need to be perfect, or become health nuts. But those who live in denial of their own lifestyle can hardly be considered truthful. Be careful here ... leading the revolution from a place of personal denial will get you in trouble. Likewise, waiting until your house is in order to make changes in your environment is a perfect excuse for cancelling the revolution. Find the middle road ...

1. **Begin with introspection**
   - Who are you?
   - What do you stand for?
   - What matters to you?
2. **Clarify your intention**
   - What do you want to accomplish?
   - How do you wish to proceed?
3. **Craft a personal mission**
   - What are you really passionate about?
   - Who are you willing to share it with?
4. **Develop a step-by-step plan**
   - Identify specific goals.
   - What is first, second, third?
   - How will you measure progress?

When you have begun your journey toward balance and health, consider exploring your role in the revolution! Even though you may be committed to living in a new way, others may not share your interest. But that doesn't mean you can't have an important role in moving the organization in a positive direction.

More and more firms are supporting this process with "wellness" plans to encourage lifestyle improvement through education, incentive programs, and regular checkups. But most organizations are far behind those few who lead the way.

Ironically, companies routinely manage their capital equipment and vehicle fleets with more aggressive preventative maintenance programs than are generally available to workers.

I Can See Forever

Steve Gerrior is a young man who works on our Challenge Course and guides some of our Whitewater Experiences. In his senior year of pre-med training at the University of Colorado, he has come a long way toward fulfilling his mission to be a healer-physician. His road is long. His tests, each class, and every manuscript are goals and then steps. He believes he will achieve the physician part of his mission. But to be a healer, not just a medical technician, is far beyond any medical school's credo. Because he is a spiritual person, he knows his mission will always be just out of reach!

The Boner Award

I had the opportunity to work with an organization that acknowledged the importance of learning from mistakes by presenting a special "Boner Award" at its annual awards and recognition banquet.

This company had initiated a quality improvement program and wanted to eliminate fear of making mistakes in order to increase productivity. The president came up with a creative incentive to promote employee risk taking. One year, at the conclusion of the traditional awards ceremony,he placed a $100 bill in plain view. He then surprised the gathering by telling them about the biggest mistake HE had made in the previous year. Immediately following his story, the president challenged his employees to win the $100 by telling the crowd about a mistake they had made at work. It had to be bigger, and more significant than his own.

As with most new initiatives, the "Boner Award" was at first met with skepticism. However, after a few brave souls stepped forward and told their tales of error, the company's employees embraced the award and the goal it was intended to accomplish.

In only its second year, the "Boner Award," became the most anticipated part of the annual banquet. The president looks back and marvels at the training value this $100 award buys. Not only do his employees understand his commitment to supporting them to take risks, he has been surprised at how often the sharing of the mistake stories taught other employees about paths not to take in their search for creative solutions.

—William D. Baker, Ed.D.
Partner
Venture Centre

Beyond lifestyle issues, there is the matter of safety. Many businesses display posters that proclaim: "Safety is everybody's business." But in our culture, we can get so caught up in fault finding, we forget that safety is, first and foremost, our own responsibility.

The challenge for individuals who wish to live a more truthful life is to balance the needs of the workplace with the very real needs of self and our families. We may not be able to control everyone in the organization. But with good intentions and by our own example, we can enlist the support of others and impact the organization as a whole. The degree of impact cannot be predicted, but, in the process, we take back responsibility for our own lives—and experience real empowerment!

Look Into The Abyss

People say life is precious. Yet most of us live it as if we had all the time in the world. That is how we are able to postpone dieting, exercise, and taking proactive steps toward health. In my work, I have found it helpful for people to get in touch with their own mortality. Not by jumping out of airplanes—although many feel our Challenge Course is a close cousin—but by putting people in the face of powers greater than themselves. We have all had such experiences, but when was the last time you looked into the abyss?

To help people prepare for writing their personal mission, I ask them to write their own eulogy. A eulogy helps people explore what is really important. Did we walk our talk? Did we reach for our dreams or merely fall into line on our lifelong march to the grave?

When employees act more like owners with a stake in the business, many motivational and quality issues are resolved.

Another tool suggested by Gail Hoag, a partner in the Venture Centre, is to write letters to your grandchildren to be opened on their 21st birthdays. What would you tell them about:

1. Your intentions
2. Your accomplishments
3. How you lived your life
4. The wisdom you have accumulated

I want my clients to get in touch with their mortality not only to remind them of their uniqueness, but also to recognize the very limited time we have to apply that uniqueness. The notion that workers have a unique contribution to make flies in the face of past wisdom which said workers were nothing more than living machines—one pretty much the same as the other.

As long as people define themselves by what they do, they are bound to continue doing it. As long as we define ourselves by our toolbox, we are unlikely to seek additional tools.

In the Truthful Organization, each individual is a part of the organization, not by happenstance, but because of a unique qualification that makes him or her special. For some people, it is their physical ability and willingness to do the job. For others, it is technical ability. But for many it is the "soft stuff" such as commitment, passion, curiosity, integrity, focus—the list goes on. The unique qualities that make one person's personality more suited to one task than another is more important today than ever before. As workers are left to themselves with less guidance and more responsibility, it is these intangible qualities that make one worker successful where another falters.

Who is Responsible?

According to the 1990 U.S. Census figures, nearly a million people die each year from preventable causes. The leading killers are: tobacco (400,000 per year), diet, inactivity (300,000 per year), and alcohol (100,000 per year). Stress, toxins, illicit drugs, firearms, AIDS, motor vehicles, and untreated microbial infections round out the list.

As we strive to respect all people and honor their participation, in whatever form they choose, we do not try to change people.

Unfortunately, in many organizations, technical skill is so critical, there is little room for feelings. Yet, psychologists, teachers, and personality experts agree we must learn to balance feelings with intellect. Whether we admit it or not, all of us have feelings about everything, all the time.

Well-rounded employees are able to talk about feelings as well as thoughts with peers, subordinates, and supervisors. Leaders in the Truthful Organization never admonish employees for taking feelings into account. People in the Truthful Organization are not afraid to express feelings in a constructive way, even if it means others feel uncomfortable. In this way, people can interact with each other as complex, multifaceted personalities—not living machines defined simply by their job, skill, or duty.

No One To Blame

When we accept responsibility for our own happiness and safety, we may ask for help and support. We won't rely upon the caretaking of others and won't feel resentful if it is not offered. Neither will we seek to take care of another otherwise independent person. When requested, we will offer assistance, advice, and support unless it undermines a person's own resourcefulness. There is no one to blame for our misfortunes. No person can take (or should be given) responsibility for our success. Other than fate and unseen forces greater than us, our happiness and safety is in our own hands. Each of us is a free agent; our relationship with the company is based on our ability to add value—not sentimentality, loyalty, politics, or tenure. Our value is based solely on our ability to contribute. Improving technical and people skills is a way to increase value. Even so, when the relationship stops working, you may need to go elsewhere— carrying with you your personal mission, experience, skills, and training. People who have planned their career responsibly will have eschewed the seduction of the "golden handcuffs" to remain free. Instead they plan how to make retirement, insurance, and other benefits as transferrable as possible.

A fundamental aspect of being in the Truthful Organization is accepting responsibility for personal safety and happiness. Every compromise to personal truth upsets, to one degree or another, the delicate interdependence between all members of the team.

Fear- and Control- Based Behaviors

The upset may manifest as *fear-based behaviors* generated from a person's CHILD state:

- Playing "poor me"
- Feeling shame or self-hate
- Being the procrastinator
- Being cynical

Or, the upset may show up as *control-based behaviors* generated from the person's PARENT state, including:

- Acting bossy or intimidating
- Blaming others or the system
- Being judgmental
- Having a self-righteous attitude

We may not be able to control everyone in the organization. But with good intentions and by our own example, we can enlist the support of others and impact the organization as a whole. The degree of impact cannot be predicted, but, in the process, we take back responsibility for our own lives—and experience real empowerment!

When people are in the grips of fear- or control-based behavior, they isolate themselves from the rest of the team. Fear-based people give away their personal "power" and diminish their capability. Control-based people rob others on the team of their "power" by taking control and responsibility from teammates. The goal of the Truthful Organization is ADULT-appropriate behavior in which people behave in a way that supports everyone on the team to do his or her best.

Those in power need to be encouraged to create an environment in which introspection is supported as a vital part of employee development for the whole company.

Anything other than adult-appropriate behavior undermines individual and team performance—yet we live in a challenging world that knocks us off balance sometimes. No one can be adult-appropriate at all times; even if we could—how boring life would be. In pursuit of more effective relationships, members of Truthful Organizations talk openly

Attitude Adjustment

Last spring in Colorado, we had a late heavy winter and the rivers were gorged with boiling torrents. On one occasion, I climbed down an embankment to stand next to the run-off from Barker Dam, on Boulder Creek. Being on a ledge a few feet from this intense gush of water had a strange effect on me. No fence separated me from this prodigious cascade. Nothing could save me if I fell. Nothing could protect me if, for some reason, the flow surged in my direction. It was both awesome and frightening. I felt puny and insignificant. My insides felt mushy. And as I walked away, the feeling remained; I was shifted in some subtle way that remains with me today. Later in the summer, clients and I had opportunities to share similar experiences on some of our wilderness and whitewater trips. Always the results are the same. We come away invigorated, yet inwardly calm and more alive. In such a state, the best of me and the best of my work comes through!

and honestly about their own *and* others' fear-based (child state) or control-based (parent state) behaviors.

Open, interpersonal communication facilitates rapid transitions from fear- and control-based behavior states to adult-appropriate behaviors. This fosters greater interdependence among team members. However, rapid transitions and open communication are not enough. We must adopt a less judgmental attitude about our own behaviors. We must be willing to accept the fruits of our behavior, even when it is a bitter harvest.

Accepting responsibility for our own safety has singular implications. There are no guarantees. If we are cognizant of that and diligent in maintaining our safety, scapegoats disappear.

My partners and I have gone to considerable effort at our Challenge Course to make the arrangement of poles, walls, cables, and turnbuckles as safe as possible. In fact, safety is our primary, number one, bottom-line, absolute concern! Yet, when participants ask me (and they always do) "Is it safe?", I am always tempted to say: "No!"

I want everyone to understand there are risks in everything. There are no guarantees. I could tell them they are statistically safer here than on the drive up, but if I tell them it is safe, my fear is they will let down their guard and expect us to be responsible for them. In reality, we must all work together to make the experience as safe as possible.

This message of personal responsibility is growing rare in our culture. It is not just a rush to litigation, but an even more pervasive attitude we encounter in countless subtle ways every day. The subliminal message sounds like: *"I have a right to be safe. If I am injured, it must be someone else's fault. I can expect the responsible party to compensate me for both my recuperation and suffering."* Clearly, there are situations in which others may be at fault, but we must be willing to honestly assess and declare our own culpability when it exists.

In the Truthful Organization, we are proactively diligent for our own and others' safety. On the challenge course or whitewater trips, everyone looks out for each other—after all, umpteen pairs of eyes are better than one. When we designate others to be liable for our safety, we abrogate our personal responsibility and give over our power. This does not mean the organization can wash its hands. It must continue every effort to make the work environment as safe as possible for everyone. In the Truthful Organization, however, everyone shares this responsibility.

Let's not forget about happiness. Creating happiness may not be the primary responsibility of the company. Moreover, it is not the responsibility of individuals to make teammates happy. However, just because happiness is a personal issue does not mean it is not important to the organization. The work force whose people find joy in their work are capable of greater, sustained productivity.

So if you are unhappy, what to do? If you wait for someone else to fix you, you may stay unhappy for a long time. For example, if you believe your boss is a &%$#@, you are going to be unhappy. But your boss is unaffected by your assessment; he or she may not even know what you think, much less care. First, you need to understand, *the problem is yours!* When you own the problem, you stop being a victim. Now you can

It's Not My Fault

I am reminded of the elderly woman who won a judgment against McDonald's restaurants. She scalded herself after spilling hot coffee in her lap while pulling away from the drive-through window. Her son was the driver. McDonald's defended itself with a commonsense argument: Coffee is hot. The movement of an automobile is unpredictable and often results in spills. How can anyone live to an advanced age and not exercise reasonable precautions?

The defense claimed the coffee was excessively hot and its client had not been warned about the possible dangers inherent in purchasing hot coffee from a drive-through window. The last time I went through a drive-through at McDonald's, I noticed a small sign that says something like: Coffee is extremely hot; be careful not to spill it on yourself.

I am sure she had a horrible experience and suffered enormous pain. I cringe when I think about it, but every time our legal system resolves a case in this way, we remove more and more responsibility from people and bolster the illusion that personal safety can be guaranteed. There are **no** guarantees!

Life is not safe; it is terminal. The more active we are, the more people we come in contact with, the greater the jeopardy. Work puts us at greater risk than staying home. We never know when we may be exposed to untold unfriendly agents from commuting traffic to asbestos, from maniacal co-workers to AK-47-toting co-workers. And if mad bombers don't get us, there is always the next round of downsizing.

Someone once said, "Every day, you must decide for yourself ... are you going to be a statue or a bird?" When we see ourselves in danger and living at the mercy of a cruel and heartless world, we are little more than a statue—powerless, immobile, defenseless. Each individual has the capacity to free the shackles of powerlessness by empowering themselves. The first step in that process of empowerment is to accept responsibility for our own feelings and forego the temptation to blame others.

As long as people hold others responsible for the quality of their lives, they live as victims and martyrs. When people accept responsibility for their own happiness, they stop blaming others and become a full participant in their own life.

make changes. You can change your point of view, consider alternative ways of working with your boss, explore a transfer, even investigate leaving the job.

To be responsible for your own happiness means having the intention to be happy and being proactive about anything that interferes, by causing you discomfort or pain. Others who make your life difficult are seldom aware of the effects of their actions. Even well-intentioned people can inadvertently cause you pain. Some people are difficult to work with and could care less about your pain. In all cases, it is appropriate to offer feedback about how others are affecting you as a good faith effort to craft a relationship that works for all parties. As long as people hold others responsible for the quality of their lives, they live as victims and martyrs. When people accept responsibility for their own happiness, they stop blaming others and become a full participant in their own life.

Chapter Five

INTERPERSONAL: Relationships Are All There Is

INTERPERSONAL: Relationships Are All There Is

An organization is more than a group of people. The degree to which people cooperate, coordinate, and support each other's individual efforts largely determines the overall effectiveness of an organization.

The degree to which people cooperate, coordinate, and support each other's individual efforts largely determines the overall effectiveness of an organization.

Historically, organizations have focused on the technical rather than the social aspects of workers and their work. Even today, managers are often selected because of their technical credentials rather than their people and leadership skills. The mistaken notion that a manager's primary responsibility is to supervise the technical performance of workers lingers. Recruitment and hiring practices follow the same vein; finding the best candidates usually means those with the best technical track record. Training, too, is habitually focused on technical instruction. This preoccupation with the technical, or direct service, aspects of the organization is giving way to a more balanced management approach.

STEPS TRUTH 7

3. Acknowledge the value of conflict.

Things Are Different Today

Nearly every job is different today than it was just a few years ago. Some of this change has come about because of emerging technologies, but most has to do with how companies have (re)organized themselves.

New concerns have emerged. Global competition—the quest for continuously improving quality, world-class service, and healthier equity and earnings ratios—have stimulated unprecedented transformations in nearly every business sector. Many

In the absence of managers, individual workers have more responsibility and greater autonomy to manage themselves than ever before. Add to this the new emphasis on teamwork, and today's work environment bears little resemblance to the workscape with which all but the youngest employees became used to.

companies have responded to new challenges by downsizing or choosing not to hire additional middle managers and supervisors. In the absence of managers, individual workers have more responsibility and greater autonomy to manage themselves than ever before. Add to this the new emphasis on teamwork, and today's work environment bears little resemblance to the workscape with which all but the youngest employees became used to. Unfortunately, most workers were schooled to function in the old setting; few are prepared for the reality of today's work environment.

When work was regarded as a set of repetitive (usually manual) tasks, people were organized according to those tasks. A team used to mean a group of specialists that provided comprehensive service under the careful orchestration of a manager. The manager assembled the team, defined the problem, established priorities, allocated resources, and coordinated the work of each individual. Finally, the manager was responsible for evaluating quality, determining the level of success (or failure), and meting out rewards (and punishments).

Today's teams include fewer specialists, more cross-trained staff, and even some generalists. A manager, if one exists, takes on more of a coaching role rather than one of control. The manager serves as facilitator, both among team members and between other teams and external resources. The manager's focus is less on the technical aspects of the team (workers are expected to be technically proficient or report their need for assistance or training) and more on the effectiveness of team interactions, including communication, cooperation, conflict management, problem solving, decision making, and other interpersonal issues.

This is not to say the job of the manager is social director—responsible for making people happy! At risk of bursting some people's bubbles, research indicates happy workers are technically no more productive than unhappy ones. That is not to say there is no benefit to fostering worker satisfaction. Before managers pull the plug on the summer picnic, day-care center, and free coffee, a reality check is in order. There are sound reasons for encouraging worker satisfaction. According to D. W. Organ, in his book, *Organizational Citizenship Behavior,* workers who enjoy a high degree of job satisfaction bring better "citizenship" to the job. Historically, citizenship held a distant back seat to individual productivity because jobs were carefully compartmentalized and micro-managed from above.

In today's team environments, most organizations seek more than technical competence from staff. They want people to be able to work together to deliver improved team productivity. So beyond technical expertise, workers today need emotional maturity, optimism, cooperation, collaboration, open-honest communication, and enthusiasm. In other words, better citizenship!

While it was difficult to make a case for creating congenial work places in the past, today it has become vital and the case compelling. When people are forced to manage themselves while working more intimately with others, all participants need citizenship skills! Job satisfaction, quality of work life, and personal commitment are no longer the wish list of touchy-feely human resource types. These are the building blocks of today's high-performing, self-managed work teams.

When people are forced to manage themselves while working more intimately with others, all participants need citizenship skills! Job satisfaction, quality of work life, and personal commitment are no longer the wish list of touchy-feely human resource types. These are the building blocks of today's high-performing, self-managed work teams.

Citizenship is Relationship

How people behave in a social setting has more to do with the quality of their work relationships than the rules, manners, or social etiquette to which they have been exposed.

When people care about others, they are naturally more sensitive to the effects their own behavior has on them. When people do not care about each other, or are prohibited from building relationships with each other, working together becomes problematic. Even people who profess no concern for others do have emotions—and sometimes those emotions get in the way! When people work in an environment where feelings are suppressed and "people are not in relationship," they lose the ability to talk about feelings, deal with hard truths, and resolve interpersonal conflicts.

Relationships Anyone?

I have often used an icebreaker event that begins with people standing in a large circle, holding each other's hands in order to successfully complete the task. On one such occasion, I was amazed to see people holding back. I am used to a few nervous comments (that's why it is a good icebreaker), but on this occasion, the men were outright homophobic. Since there were not enough women to arrange themselves boy/girl, boy/girl, the men would not hold each other's hands.

Then I really put my foot in my mouth. I said, "How can we build relationships if we cannot even hold each other's hands?"

"We don't have relationships with each other; we just work together," was angrily hurled back at me.

This is just one example of the many times I have overestimated people's ability to distinguish between romantic and other kinds of relationships. People have completely non-romantic relationships with mothers, fathers, brothers, sisters, cousins, teachers, pets, cars, children, coffees, favorite restaurants, etc. Why not co-workers?

What other word can describe the range of feelings from anger to ambivalence to admiration that exists between most co-workers? Even if I ignore someone, I am focusing attention on them in my mind ... that is a relationship. If we do not use the word relationship, what is it called?

The idea that emotions are contrary to business and "nothing is personal" is a traditional pillar of business history. The dearth of feelings in the workplace probably has more to do with the dominance of males in management positions than with any aesthetic rationale. If a male manager is uncomfortable with his own emotions and those of others, it follows that feelings will be avoided, denied, and eventually outlawed. Over time, the absence of emotions becomes institutionalized and self-validating; there *are* no emotions, therefore there *should be* no emotions. Men *are not* in touch with their feelings, therefore men *should not* be in touch with their feelings. No one *is* in relationship, therefore no one *should be* in relationship.

This all changes in the Truthful Organization. Everyone understands that relationships are critical. The organization cannot afford for anyone NOT to be in relationship. That does not mean everyone must be friends ...

- It does not mean everyone gets along all the time.
- It does not mean people always agree or have no conflict.
- It does not mean everyone is happy or polite.

It DOES mean that people choose to be truthful about their reality. Everyone acknowledges that as co-workers they ARE in relationship—it is unavoidable.

Even when people ignore one another, they are still in relationship! In the Truthful Organization, relationships are considered so important that when problems interfere with the team's ability to cooperate, coordinate, or commit, participants take proactive steps to improve the relationship, even if it appears to take precedence over the technical task at hand. At first, this may seem like some kind of left-wing, humanistic exaltation of people above the objectives of the business. On the contrary, it is a recognition that problems are solved by people. When people work together, those problems are solved smarter, faster, and better. So job 'one' is not quality (to borrow a phrase) but *the people who produce the quality!*

When people work in an environment where feelings are suppressed and "people are not in relationship," they lose the ability to talk about feelings, deal with hard truths, and resolve interpersonal conflicts.

Recalling the discussion of the "fields" in which each person's field of energy, perspective, experience, and assumptions merge with another's, I notice that teams and organizations quickly focus on the technical aspects of a problem with little or no regard to the influence of the shared field—the system within which the problem exists. Even though Einstein said, "The significant problems we face cannot be solved at the same level of thinking we were at when we created them," I see leaders of organizations make valiant, if misguided, attempts to prove this statement wrong.

In the Truthful Organization, relationships are considered so important that when problems interfere with the team's ability to cooperate, coordinate, or commit, participants take proactive steps to improve the relationship, even if it appears to take precedence over the technical task at hand.

In the workshops I lead, I use experiential activities that re-create real business issues facing an organization. I help the team observe its own behavior and see the formerly hidden agreements which constitute its own field. One of the most difficult hurdles to overcome is getting a team to take time to get ready. I used to describe this shoot-from-the-hip style as READY ... FIRE ... AIM ... I now believe it is more accurate to describe typical team problem solving as FIRE ... AIM ... READY ... The very last priority of most organizations is getting "ready." Getting *ready* means working out the bugs in the way people work together—in other words, developing the relationships within the shared field. The second, least favorite process is "aiming." Teams have a strong aversion to exploring alternative solutions, strategic planning, and systems design. What people like to do is "fire" at the target and hope for positive results.

However, with the use of business simulations, teams can learn that performance is dramatically improved when they invest the necessary time up-front to learn how to work together. In that time, a team can establish operating agreements, set up a decision-making apparatus, and build solid working relationships.

I use experiential activities that re-create real business issues facing an organization. I help the team observe its own behavior and see the formerly hidden agreements which constitute its own field.

A critical test of an organization's commitment to its people comes when circumstances force the leaders to choose between improving the quality of relationships and a short-term performance objective. The Truthful Organization and its people understand that productivity improves when the quality of relationships is enhanced. That does not mean the workplace becomes a "lovefest" without structure, accountability, or boundaries. On the contrary, relationships in the Truthful Organization are based on truth and trust. People are respectful, both openly and behind the boss's back. When a premium is placed on relationships, it becomes difficult to pointlessly pull rank or engage in scapegoating or backstabbing behaviors. When someone's behavior does get in the way, there is a commitment to improve the situation by working on the relationship. The motive for relationship building is the improvement of the organization.

Teams can learn to dramatically improve performance by investing the necessary time up-front to learn how to work together.

Those individuals who thrived in the old-style organizations tend to fear an organization based on relationships. They imagine it to be devoid of order and out of control. To some degree their assessment is accurate, but as organizations which have made the leap have learned—when external control is diminished, personal responsibility flourishes. Moreover, a notable quality of Truthful Organizations is the respect people show each other—regardless of title, race, seniority, gender, or education. People begin to care about each other. However, even well-intentioned people occasionally come into conflict with one another.

The Truthful Organization and its people understand that productivity improves when the quality of relationships is enhanced.

Conflict Happens!

When people are clear about their mission and committed to its realization, their passion inevitably leads to conflict with others because other people's priorities are different.

Conflict is unavoidable. Even though it affords the organization powerful opportunities for improvement, most people fear it. The Chinese word for conflict combines two characters: danger and opportunity. Conflict can go either way.

When people are unskilled at dealing with conflict, they and their organizations fear it. People who fear conflict have no way to manage it. Usually they try to avoid it. They drive it underground, outlaw emotions, cover up with politeness, and make it difficult for anyone to rattle the lid.

When conflict is not dealt with openly and directly, there is a strong likelihood any positive opportunities it may have generated will pass, only to be replaced by either of two dangerous versions of conflict: violence or covert conflict. Either can destroy an organization.

Relationships in the Truthful Organization, are based on truth and trust. People are respectful, both openly and behind the boss's back. When a premium is placed on relationships, it becomes difficult to pointlessly pull rank or engage in scapegoating or backstabbing behaviors. When someone's behavior does get in the way, there is a commitment to improve the situation by working on the relationship. The motive for relationship building is the improvement of the organization.

Before Conflict is Conversation

While conflict management skills are valuable assets, it is more important to develop the ability to build working, truthful relationships up-front, using open, honest, and direct communication.

The workplace is full of opportunities to use communication to improve relationships. Work assignments, teamwork, and special projects afford participants the opportunity to build better working relationships through conversation.

Few people are accustomed to relationship building in the workplace. Most approach a work assignment as if it were an order. People have learned:

- not to ask questions ...
- not to express personal reservations ...
- never, never, ever refuse an assignment ...

When external control is diminished, personal responsibility flourishes.

Instead, people resort to the fire, aim, ready habit. Most people believe the "right" response to an assignment is to appear enthusiastic, skilled, and ready. Sometimes people earn points for starting even before the instructions are complete. Never mind that, in

The Polite Truth

I worked with a major international financial giant who, for the purpose of this story, will be called VAST Company. VAST Company was struggling to implement a concurrent quality and reengineering effort using a top-down deployment approach. It was an old, traditionally hierarchical organization with enormous disparities between various levels of the organization. While it was obvious to the outsider there was a great deal of conflict hidden within the organization, many within the company reported it was well managed because everyone got along so well.

No wonder. There was something called "VAST POLITE," an institutionalized double-speak. Only good things are said, and a spade is rarely called a spade.

To my eye, there was no mystery about why one of the greatest challenges facing the organization was buy-in. The president landed in the corporate jet to give the troops a pep talk about cutting expenses and embracing change. Even after an impassioned speech, he seemed powerless to create an atmosphere of permission that allowed the staff to question his commitment to either change or austerity.

I met with great resistance within the organization because I challenged VAST POLITE behaviors. However, I became an anathema when I asked people to talk about their true feelings. I even suggested that a regional management team evaluate one another's performance in an open meeting. Everyone agreed there were no secrets; after all, everyone's performance was visible to the rest of the team. But it would be impossible to talk openly about each other in this way. Rather than say or hear something unpleasant, team members chose not to participate. In their words, "We know we are a good team because we occasionally get together after work for cocktails."

some circles, this is called "jumping the gun" or "going off half-cocked."

On one hand, people run off after hearing only half the instructions. On the other hand, some people hold critical conversations in elevators, hallways, or in passing. This non-chalant attitude toward conversation is contrary to *truth*. Everyone understands that at the core of all action are ideas—ideas first manifested as words. This is why conversation is considered sacred in the Truthful Organization. It matters *how* things are said, *where* they are said, with *what intention* they are spoken, as well as how they are *received* and *interpreted*. Both sides of the conversation are equally important.

Building Working Relationships Through Conversation

Instead of half-baked, haphazard conversations in the hallway, it is important that co-workers practice the craft of relationship building while also requesting assistance.

TOBACCO contains seven steps that when used as a conversational guideline, dramatically improve the likelihood that the quality of both work and relationships are enhanced.

TOBACCO AGREEMENTS

(See Sidebar Story)

1. T*alk straight.*
   Establish rapport. Communicate your intention to be in relationship—work together—and be of service.
2. *Old business.*
   Clear up any old business that may affect the relationship and the ability for either party to fully participate in the task at hand.
3. B*e clear on the details.*
   Seek a deep and thorough understanding of the details available to the other person. This person is your customer—be proactive in seeking information.
4. *Accurately reflect back what you understand.*
   Repeating the details before beginning the task assures both parties that everything which has been communicated was complete and understood.
5. *Conditions for your participation.*
   Before jumping into the task at hand, consider your ability to fulfill the request. Can you do it? Do you have needs? Do you have the authority, information, tools, time, and support necessary to do what is being requested? Make certain your needs are heard and understood.
6. *Communicating the hard truths.*
   Do you have the right to refuse the task? Can you tell the other person (whether it is your boss or a co-worker) how that person's performance affects the project? Likewise, will you get honest, ongoing feedback about your own performance?
7. *Overview of the agreement and relationship.*
   Conclude the meeting with a summary. It spells out the details of the agreement for both parties and ends with an acknowledgement of the current state of the relationship.

Tobacco Story

I have been privileged to spend time with a number of notable and unsung elders of the Lakota (Sioux) people. On a visit to the Pine Ridge Reservation in South Dakota, I was "put on the hill" for a traditional vision quest or Humbleché to "cry for a vision."

The experience culminated a full year of preparation, including coaching and counseling by my Lakota benefactors. Many people warned me anything I learned would have no relevance to my modern life, that nothing Indians could teach would have any value—especially in my worklife. They could not have been more wrong.

Not only has my life been enriched by my involvement with Native American cultures, I have been inspired to apply what I have learned in the context of my work. One important example is a simple ceremony that is part of every workshop I conduct.

Continued on next page ...

Tobacco Story

Continued from previous page ...

Unlike modern culture where communication is haphazardly conducted amid a wide variety of contexts, straight-talk is highly revered among the Lakota people. One can imagine that 120 years ago when they were still a self-sufficient society of independent, nomadic bands, straight-talk meant the difference between life and death.

For example, when a hunt was planned, lives depended upon its success. Choosing the right people, sifting through the information supplied by scouts, and determining the best strategy were all critical conversations not to be taken lightly.

A long-standing tradition among the Lakota assures a person's full attention. It signals to all concerned that what is to be discussed is vital and requires honest, heartful attention. That signal is a simple gift of tobacco.

To the Lakota, tobacco has a special significance because it is ceremonially smoked in the Chanupah or sacred pipe. To the Lakota, the pipe, a sacred gift from spirit in the form of White Buffalo Calf Women, represents a special covenant between Great Spirit and the People. It represents, through the visible ascension of smoke, the prayers of the people rising to Great Spirit. So tobacco is a symbol which represents both the pipe and prayer—the most sacred (wakan) form of communication.

When someone gives me tobacco, I know the conversation requested needs to be open, honest, and direct. It must come from the place in my heart where prayers come from.

It is unfortunate there is no corollary to this simple ceremonial gesture in our modern culture. However, by sharing this story with co-workers it becomes a part of every Truth Zone and, to some degree, a part of the culture in every organization in which I work.

Note: As a non-Lakota, I can only approximate with imperfect words the richness of an experience that is probably beyond my full comprehension. If I have in any way misrepresented the ideas here, I humbly ask indulgence.

Hard Truths

The most challenging of the seven steps is also the most helpful in averting conflicts and building relationships. Unfortunately, it goes against the way most people were brought up. They were taught to "let sleeping dogs lie." Children are routinely told, "If you have nothing nice to say, don't say anything at all." It is difficult to avoid the lesson: *protecting other people's feelings is paramount.* Consequently, talking about difficult issues at the beginning of a project or early in a relationship goes completely against the grain. Hard truth, if it comes at all, is reserved for those ticklish occasions when the project is in danger of imminent failure or the relationship is already rocky.

Choosing NOT to talk about issues up-front means one or both parties risk the possibility that unspoken issues may arise—potentially undermining the job. It is important that parties to an agreement (whether between supervisor and subordinate, or co-worker to co-worker) proactively discuss the current state of their relationship. Is there any old business that might get in the way of the task at hand? Is either person carrying old baggage, assumptions, or biases that might undermine the pending work?

In the process of defining the agreement, more difficult subjects must be raised. What if either party does anything to impair progress? Can either person discuss the other's participation without fear of retribution? Most subordinates fear saying anything critical to their boss. Yet a more difficult discussion is an open, honest, and direct conversation about the quality of a co-worker's performance. After all, "...Who are YOU to talk about MY performance. You're not my boss!"

Not Everyone Wishes To Be In Relationship

Some people are not willing to cooperate in these kinds of interpersonal conversations due to a lack of interest in being in relationship in the first place. Some have deep-seated reasons for mistrusting people. Others are uncomfortable out of habit, or because of a lack of skill. Whatever the reason, when forging a relationship becomes a one-sided operation, results are usually minimal. Even so, the TOBACCO agreements are the most useful tool available to improve the quality of work and level of cooperation at the workplace.

I speak truth, not my belly-full, but as much as I dare; and I dare the more I grow into years.
—Michel de Montaigne

It takes only one party to use the TOBACCO agreements. The other person may remain completely unaware of the specific steps, naturally assuming they have simply participated in a two-way conversation—which they have. That does not mean a typical TOBACCO agreement unfolds effortlessly.

Completely separate from the heart of the agreement are the steps themselves. While the content of the conversation could generate a wide range of reactions, the steps alone can be the source of spirited resistance. Each step brings more hidden agreements and assumptions to the surface, making the field appear visible.

Resistance to Field Disruption

Let's look at the seven TOBACCO steps as agents of change, disrupting interpersonal, team, and shared fields:

Truth is tough. It will not break, like a bubble, at a touch; nay, you may kick it about all day like a football, and it will be round and full at evening.
—Oliver Wendell Holmes, Sr.

T*alk Straight:*
Many relationships deal in a currency of superficiality and/or indirect communication. When one person disrupts the field by wanting to talk about a specific issue instead of *weather* or some other "shared" topic of interest, the other person notices a shift and may try harder to talk about weather—which has the effect of restoring the previous field. If that does not work, they may comment on the changing field, saying, "You seem different today. Are you trying to manipulate me or control the conversation... what is going on?" The person initiating "straight talk" can indicate he or she is not trying to manipulate the other, but rather wants to include discussion about the specific issue in the conversation. It is important.

O*ld business.*
As mentioned previously, it is considered bad manners to bring up old issues. A hidden agreement in most shared fields is to let by-gones be by-gones, and not hold people accountable today for past events. As my mother used to say ... "Let sleeping dogs lie."

It's better to bring up your own past issues rather than remind someone of his or her transgressions. Even so, the disruption of the field is enormous when a person suddenly escalates the level of truth telling. A person might say, "In the past, I have not always been sincere in my participation in this relationship. I would like to improve things in the future."

Instead of an appreciation for this new level of honesty, the person receiving this news is likely to take offense, feeling pressured to meet you with a similar "risky" admission. More than likely, a conciliatory, safe statement will be made. Its intent will be to defuse the situation (by reconstituting the pre-existing field) and bring things back to normal, saying, "Don't worry about it, I think we get along great ... what did you do over the weekend?" It takes effort on the part of the person desiring to clear up old business. Rather than allowing the field to return to normal, assertiveness is in order. Respond to resistance by showing desire to create a new level of honesty in the communication.

Be clear on the details.

When most people are asked to do something, they jump to it. People believe the best way to demonstrate competence and commitment is to get started on tasks as quickly as possible ... "get them done right the first time."

Not getting started right away and asking questions for clarification disrupts the field by acting in a way that may seem lazy, confused, dumb, unmotivated, disruptive, insubordinate, etc.

The other person may try to mend the field by snapping back: "Just do it!" or "Enough with the questions already ... If you can't get on this, I'll find someone who can ... If I knew it was going to be this complicated, I would have done it myself."

State questions clearly to save time and effort later on. This communicates a sincere desire to cooperate and add value.

I maintain that Truth is a pathless land, and you cannot approach it by any path whatsoever, by any religion, by any sect.
—Jiddu Krishnamurti

Accurately reflect back what you understand.

If it disrupts the field to ask questions and get clear up front, taking additional time to let the other person know what you heard and how you interpreted it can push some people over the edge.

Another unspoken agreement in most fields is when someone gives you an assignment, it is no longer theirs. Hence forth, it is your responsibility. Asking questions that reflect your understanding further engages the person, keeping him or her accountable to the final outcome. While the person might ridicule you for your "slowness" or "nitpickiness," he or she is more likely frustrated because the field has been disrupted, leaving them uncertain and insecure.

Man can embody truth but he cannot know it.
—W. B. Yeats

Be clear about your accountability. The one with whom you are sharing the field will create a more productive working relationship if established early on.

Conditions for your participation.
Many people (inside and outside of organizations) operate on an unspoken agreement that when making a request of another, "no" is not really an option. Moreover, many people operate on a reciprocal agreement: when asked to do something, they should do it. "No" is not an option.

The problem is, "no" really is and should be an option. It is a well-known fact in the airline industry that most accidents are caused by human error. It is further understood that the biggest challenge in the cockpit is getting people to say no. Unfortunately, the authority of the pilot is so deeply engrained that co-pilots have, on more occasions than anyone likes to acknowledge, allowed pilots to fly planes into mountains and even swamps.

It is not because the truth is too difficult to see that we make mistakes. It may even lie on the surface; but we make mistakes because the easiest and most comfortable course for us is to seek insight where it accords with our emotions especially selfish ones.
—Alexander Solzhenitsyn

Disrupting the field before take-off is still difficult and could, in certain circumstances, put a person's career on the line. But once the mountain looms ahead, disrupting the field can be excruciatingly painful.

Communicating the hard truths.

The shared field includes an understanding that no one likes to be wrong. Even fewer people like having others point it out. Yet, for the good of the organization, someone must have the courage to speak up.

In most organizations, supervisors always want their subordinates to tell them the hard truths. Yet, they themselves are reluctant to tell their own supervisors. The shared field in most organizations seems to have the following agreement in place: "I can handle the hard truths, but my boss cannot." But if this person's subordinate subscribes to the same agreement, no one tells anyone the hard truth.

Overview of the agreement and relationship.

Something as simple as restating and summarizing a meeting can meet with resistance. This disrupts the agreement that says, "Once people are assigned a task, it is all theirs." A summary holds all parties accountable to the nuances of the shared understanding. At its core, summarizing a meeting disrupts the "assumed agreements" of the field, replacing them with situational, reality-based agreements.

Resistance might sound like, "All right, already ... enough; let's get to work. If we aren't clear about everything by now, we never will be ..." A response of "I just want to be clear that we understand our agreements on this assignment" can save a lot of time and confusion later on.

But remember, even with a healthy relationship, conflicts will arise.

Conflict is NOT Aggression, Rage, or Violence

There are books, video tapes, workshops, and advice of every description to help people resolve interpersonal conflicts. Conflict resolution techniques attempt to mend a fracture in the field so that aggression does not prevent work from continuing. It is ironic that many organizations have simultaneous programs operating at crossed purposes—while change initiatives are designed to disrupt the existing field, conflict resolution programs are busy trying to mend it.

Mistakes are, after all, the foundations of truth, and if a man does not know what a thing is, it is at least an increase in knowledge if he knows what it is not.
—Carl Jung

Conflict is not the problem most people think it is. The real concern should be about behaviors resulting from conflict such as aggression, violence, and rage. While aggression is not the ultimate and inevitable outcome of conflict, most (but not all) aggression begins as a simple conflict. Nevertheless, most conflicts are never mediated, resolved, or even acknowledged—and very, very few result in aggressive or violent, behavior!

Separating conflict from aggression is an important step in building more truthful interpersonal relationships. Conflict is a vital and inevitable part of all relationships. On the other hand, aggression, rage, and violence—while natural to the species—serve no purpose in civilized relationships.

Organizations must be proactively creating a field that acknowledges the value of conflict while never condoning rage, aggression, or violent behavior of any kind.

Conflict: Resolution vs. Realization

In the Truthful Organization, conflict cannot be resolved or fixed. Instead, it needs to be acknowledged as a natural, even vital aspect of all interpersonal relationships. Conflict comes from tension which is often the genesis of new ideas, fresh points of view, and innovative thinking.

On another level, conflict represents a shift in the field. When the first reaction to conflict is to resolve it and restore the field, an opportunity to dramatically improve the quality of the field—and the relationship—may be lost. The challenge is to realize the nature of the conflict and then, together, agree to live with it for a time while exploring its effect on the larger field.

With this kind of realization, conflict runs its course out in the open. When people begin working through conflicts without relying on resolution techniques, mediation, or silent compromises, they have stepped into an entirely new level of relationship honesty.

Disrupting The Field and Moving Through Conflict

No matter how hard one person works at building better working relationships with co-workers, others will not always be willing to go along. As discussed earlier, even using the TOBACCO steps may lead to resistance and defensive behavior.

Much defensive behavior has little or nothing to do with the subject at hand or the steps. It usually shows up as either Parental, or Child behaviors:

Defensive Parental Behaviors	***Defensive Childlike Behaviors***
Bossing	Surrendering
Intimidating	Being a victim
Controlling	By-standing
Judging	Whining
Blaming	Being in denial
Raging and yelling	Procrastinating

Fields include unspoken defensive agreements. For example, an unspoken agreement exists between an intimidator and a victim. If the victim stops feeling victimized, it disrupts the field and forces the intimidator to reassess. Breaking through these defensive behaviors usually involves some form of personal confrontation.

Supervisors always want their subordinates to tell them the hard truths. Yet they themselves are often reluctant to tell their own supervisors similar truths.

Typically, the dynamic involves one-upmanship: You blame me; I deny it. You blame more; I deny more; and so on. As long as we agree to this relationship, we are locked in. There is, however, a way to break through—personal confrontation. If, when you blame me, instead of going into my denial routine, I say, *"I hear your frustration, but I am not willing to accept all of the responsibility for what has happened. I feel like we could move through this a lot better if we could look at what we can learn instead of who should be blamed."* Personal confrontation often only shifts the roles. For example, in the above scenario, my attack eliminates my denial, but I have replaced it with an accusation. What will your defensive behavior be in response?

Another form of confrontation is easier to hear than a personal attack. Instead of simply labeling your behavior, if I were to describe the field as I see it, focusing on both sets of behavior in the context of the organization, it will be easier for me to speak and easier for you to hear. *"I see that things are not working very well between us. I am willing to accept responsibility for my actions which I have denied up to this point, but your constant blaming is difficult to take. I suggest we both choose new positions before proceeding—I want to work together."* Both forms of confrontation will disrupt the field, but the latter is more likely to engage both parties in a lasting change effort.

Fear of Conflict and Courage of Conviction

When people are afraid of confrontation, they are unable to speak the kind of hard truths every organization needs.

BREAKDOWN: Moments of Truth

One of the most difficult challenges is knowing what to do when things do not go well. When a team faces obstacles, it may go into "breakdown." Breakdown occurs when the team bogs down and things stop working. Progress slows, cooperation disintegrates, and emotions get in the way.

Change initiatives are designed to disrupt the existing field. Conflict resolution programs attempt to mend the field.

Breakdown is often the result of someone taking a stand that goes against the grain. The moment people take a stand, they are immediately in conflict with anyone holding a different view. Conflict does not mean hostility, arguing, or even fighting. Conflict only means people holding different positions. Many people are so uncomfortable with hostility, they avoid even mild conflict at all costs—even acquiescing on points they hold to be true.

Separating conflict from aggression is an important step in building more truthful interpersonal relationships. Conflict is a vital and inevitable part of all relationships. On the other hand, aggression, rage, and violence—while natural to the species—serve no purpose in civilized relationships.

As if dealing with a breakdown were not difficult enough, what happens when you are the only one on your team who sees a problem? Or has the answer? My associates and I believe in an experiential approach. We use business simulations and challenging games to help our clients get a hands-on experience with these kinds of problems. This approach gives participants an opportunity to explore team behaviors, trying out interpersonal and team skills in the process.

The first time I went through a simulated "survival" game, five of us had to determine the best strategy for survival after a small plane crash. First, we each devised our own plans. Then we came together to collaborate on a team strategy. There was one woman in the group who seemed shy and nonassertive. We kept trying to get her to share her ideas, but to no avail. When the results of the game were tabulated, our team strategy would have caused our deaths. When the individual scores were posted, hers was nearly perfect! She had the information necessary to save our lives, but her shyness made it impossible for her to share, resulting in our collective demise.

Building the kind of trust that permits individuals to take an unpopular stand requires a proactive effort by leaders of the organization. In the Truthful Organization, trust is encouraged, supported, and acknowledged.

Beware of Dysfunctional Fields

The "battered spouse" syndrome which has only recently come to the nation's awareness is an extreme example of this kind of dysfunctional relationship. We would be very naive to think that such dysfunction does not show up in the workplace as both the victim and the perpetrator recreate parallel relationships with co-workers. Some workers get so used to being controlled and even abused by their bosses that when the perpetrator and the perpetrator's control system is eliminated, some workers actually resent it. Can we permit fear and hostility to thrive, even if it is accepted by some? The resolution of such problems can be found in the shared vision statement of the organization. That vision statement can be used to adjudicate the appropriateness of any contemplated intervention. What do we want to stand for? What means are we willing to employ to achieve our end?

The ability to deal with conflict openly, directly, and without hostility for the good of the organization is a powerful breakthrough idea. It means we clear the air of problems that have always been in the workplace, but were traditionally off-limits for discussion. The old parental organization's attitude is "ignore the problem, it will go away." Thus the admonition: "Leave your personal life at the door." Everyone knows that has never been possible. All that it did was drive feelings and conflict underground.

Everyone occasionally has a moment of truth. These are situations when the participants in a field experience the feeling that either there are no choices available to them or the choices that do exist are unacceptable. It seems as if there is no choice for the course of action. Most often, these moments are brought on by some perturbing effect which disrupts the field and makes it visible.

Empowerment and Interpersonal Communication

The clearer people get about who they are and what their mission is, the more important it becomes to develop effective interpersonal communication skills. The reasons are two-fold:

One, as people get clearer and more focused on what they wish to accomplish, they naturally empower themselves. I call this "entrepreneurial empowerment," because it is the same self-generated, high-energy empowerment many entrepreneurs exhibit. Entrepreneurial empowerment can be found anywhere—start-ups, mom and pop ventures, and even large corporations. An empowered entrepreneurial field is as powerful as a

I Told You So

One of the nation's largest aerospace contractors was shipping a large component to Cape Canaveral for a date-certain launch. A team of engineers watched their "baby" carefully lifted onto the bed of a flat-bed trailer. Each monitored the transfer with an eye to detail. When the truck driver asked about a loose corner of the tarpaulin, he was told to keep his input to himself, to worry about the trip ahead and what route would guarantee his timely arrival at the Cape. A storm followed the truck and its multi-million dollar cargo all the way to Florida. Upon arrival, it was discovered that the tarpaulin had allowed water to damage an expensive mylar laminate. The cost of ignoring the truck driver's warning was more than a million dollars, mostly from overtime to meet the deadline.

volcano and as focused as a laser beam. When others encounter it, they are often intimidated and put off. The cantankerous, distracted, absent-minded professor-inventor-entrepreneur has become cliché, but serves to illustrate the situation. It is so often difficult for others to penetrate the entrepreneur's field that the responsibility to communicate beyond the field must rest with the empowered person.

Two, as people move forward in the process of self empowerment, they usually wish to do more—and move faster. A terrific national magazine has come onto the scene focused on this demographic. It is called *Fast Company*. To make real headway and increase productivity, companies in the fast lane must learn to enlist others into the entrepreneurial field. It is amazing how many otherwise effective individuals and large organizations have failed to develop these skills and struggle to foster participation. The process of empowerment must be supported with a new organizational structure that acknowledges both the visible and hidden aspects of the organization. When both aspects of the organization are brought into view, the structure which exists is the truthful structure.

An important discovery of recent years is that, contrary to popular assumptions, entrepreneurial empowerment can be fostered in any organization. It is found anywhere a person has aligned his or her personal mission with a larger vision or cause. When that happens, dedication, passion, and zeal appear. It is this force that starts and drives the entrepreneurial business. But it can just as easily drive an individual, workgroup, or department in even the largest conglomerate. However, running the business and producing a product or service over the long haul takes enormous energy and staying power. Unfortunately, as organizations grow in size, there are bureaucratic forces which thwart the process. Rules, regulations, social norms, goals, lines of authority, and accountability develop and become institutionalized. A delicate balance is struck between the geometric architecture and the unstructured organic components of the organization.

Fear of loss

Loss of a competitive edge—loss of control—conspire to squelch the entrepreneurial spirit. The most powerful factor inhibiting the entrepreneurial spirit of participation is a systematic destruction of the organic and spontaneous quality of the team or organizational field.

When rules (written or implied) dictate who may talk to whom, the structure of the organization becomes brittle. This happens when the team-fields comprising the organizational field of the organization lose resiliency, and become hardened and rigid. When that happens, a subtle shift changes the relationship between the fields of individuals and the organizational field. If the organizational field—formerly an aggregate comprised of individual and team fields—reflects the collective character of the individual fields, now the rigid structure of the organizational field exerts influences back on individual fields. It shapes and changes the character of each to reflect qualities of the organizational field—individuals now feel compelled to *go along* with the influence of the majority. Where once the organization and its systems were put in place to support the individual efforts of staff members, they now feel their responsibility is to support the organization. The power shift from individual contribution to the will of the group is the fundamental difference between entrepreneurial enterprises and bureaucratic firms.

The most powerful, and perhaps the only, way to rekindle a spirit of entrepreneurism in a company lacking zest is to so radically shift the organizational field that it becomes necessary for people to reinvent the interpersonal relationships in the company, from the bottom up.

Unfortunately, the downward spiral of individual and team energy is nearly inevitable in most organizations. Empowered entrepreneurs are the least likely to dedicate resources to help others empower themselves. They are generally too focused on the technical aspects of the job. It is a rare entrepreneur who can start, build, and mature an organization. Cashing out the founding entrepreneur is usually the best thing for the company. Moreover,

A Moment of Truth about "Moments of Tuth"

The *Moments of Truth* model is adapted from material presented in a public workshop, entitled "Business and You," offered by David Neenan (co-author with Dudley Lynch of *Evergreen*). "Business and You" is a current iteration of a workshop originally developed by Marshall Thurber, entitled, "Money and You." The actual term "Moments of Truth" is a figure of speech in many languages. In 1987, a book by that title was written by Jan Carlzon, President of Scandinavian Airlines.

since the entrepreneurs' empowerment is a byproduct of the zeal they have for their technical expertise, they rarely know how to help others empower themselves.

Most entrepreneurs feel getting the product right or the customer satisfied takes precedence over anything to do with employees. Many would avoid staff all together, if they could do everything themselves. At the very least, the entrepreneur typically carries the vision for the company, the passion for the mission and, in smaller organizations, many of the technical skills. Employees often feel there is plenty of work, but no real opportunity for them in the organization. Others are forced to work "around" the entrepreneur.

It is so often difficult for others to penetrate the entrepreneur's field that the responsibility to communicate beyond the field must rest with the empowered person.

If resources for empowerment and motivation are scarce, there is even less time devoted to communication and relationship building. Conflict resolution, creative problem solving, strategic planning, group decision making, and leadership, all tend to be driven by the entrepreneur instead of the team.

If larger organizations must disrupt the field in entrepreneurial settings, the entrepreneur must be willing to get out of the way or expect to be challenged. If the challenge is met with an overpowering imposition of authority and control, the organization's *moment of truth* will pass with little or no real change.

Moments of Truth

Everyone occasionally has a moment of truth. These are situations when the participants in a field experience the feeling that either there are no choices available to them or the choices that do exist are unacceptable. It seems as if there is no choice for the course of action. Most often, these moments are brought on by some perturbing effect which disrupts the field and makes it visible. Unfortunately, most perturbing effects are uncomfortable and often downright painful, involving lay-offs, reorganization, financial reversals, conflicts, etc.

At the moment of truth, a person will feel in some way inhibited or otherwise trapped. Some people describe it as a fly on flypaper. Suddenly, there you are, asking "How do you work this thing?" "How did I get myself into this?" "What do I do now?" Interpersonally, you may wonder what you are doing in this relationship. These are questions which herald a *moment of truth.*

In reality, when a person has a moment of truth there are always four options:

1. Change Self

Changing one's self changes the personal field. People change their personal fields to participate in a team or organizational-field. For example, if a person disagrees with a team decision, the resulting field is one of resistance. The resistance may be so uncomfortable that a *moment of truth* ensues. The choice to change self means giving up the resistance and choosing to embrace the team's decision. When that occurs, the field changes from one of resistance to one of agreement and cooperation.

It is amazing how many otherwise effective individuals and large organizations have failed to develop these skills and struggle to foster participation.

Unfortunately, some fields are so intense and have become so rigid that the individual participants are forced to change themselves on a regular basis. In such cases, the field is not one of cooperation, but a field where individuals are expected to go along. This is a field of personal acquiescence. In such situations, a *moment of truth* causes people to disrupt the field by taking a personal stand—and simply not going along.

2. Change the Situation

Some fields can be disrupted and reorganized directly. The most obvious manner is through negotiation. When a worker is asked to complete a given project by a specific date with a defined set of resources, he or she may feel trapped by unrealistic expectations. The team or organizational field may be described as authoritarian; people are told what to do and expected to do it.

The worker disrupts the field by asking questions, clarifying expectations, and negotiating the outcomes.

3. Get Out

Some fields are so rigid that people feel they have changed themselves all they can, to no avail. In some fields, people have tried negotiating, only to be continually rebuffed. When people can no longer change themselves or negotiate, a *moment of truth* must make them consider getting completely out of the situation.

Getting out should not be viewed as quitting. It is realistically ending a period of prolonged suffering when everything that could be done was done. On the other hand, getting out physically or emotionally before trying to change one's self and the situation demonstrates either a lack of commitment or poor interpersonal skills.

Sometimes, the decision to get out disrupts the field so dramatically that getting out becomes unnecessary, as others become willing to dialogue. This is not to say, however, that a person should threaten others for the purpose of disrupting a field. Not only could it backfire, it is not honest!

Getting out should not be viewed as quitting. It is realistically ending a period of prolonged suffering when everything that could be done was done. On the other hand, getting out physically or emotionally before trying to change one's self and the situation demonstrates either a lack of commitment or poor interpersonal skills.

4. Stay and Suffer

The least desirable option is the option to stay and suffer. People who stay and suffer are numerous. They are prone to cynicism, complaining, and a general lack of commitment. They are completely checked out. The only time they check in is to complain and criticize.

The most powerful, and perhaps the only, way to re-kindle a spirit of entrepreneurism in a company lacking zest is to so radically shift the organizational field that it becomes necessary for people to reinvent the interpersonal relationships in the company, from the bottom up.

Their cynicism is understandable. After all, people who choose to stay and suffer are killing themselves. The choice to live in pain and under continual stress cannot possibly be adding years to their life.

The tragic irony is that most of the people who choose to stay and suffer usually report they are doing so for someone else's sake: spouse, children, parents. Unfortunately, these people rarely appreciate the self-sacrificing efforts of the martyr; they would prefer less martyrdom and more quality time and good spirits. The dangerous part of martyrdom is how easily the field expands to include a person's entire life: "I am not appreciated enough at work for people to take me seriously; I only stay for the sake of my family. And when I get home, all I get is why don't you get another job ... it seems like no one appreciates me."

As popular as the fourth option is, the only viable options are the first three. This is not to say only the neurotic ones choose to stay and suffer. Everyone is familiar with all four options—on any given day, most people experience all of them, but spend most of their time in one of the four.

If you are in a place of staying and suffering, it is time to change the field. Check in with your team before you check out!

Checking in

Shortly before, or during, a moment of truth, people get an inkling that things are not right. Most people suppress these inklings and behave as if nothing was going on. People in Truthful Organizations make another choice. They choose to check in, before they check out.

There are two ways to perform a check-in. One is to let the rest of your team know how you are doing. The other is to take a brief time-out to find out how others are doing.

One of the most interesting observations about our business simulations is when a quiet person has a powerful, innovative, break-through idea, but is not listened to, or is completely ignored. The result is a worst-case team scenario: The quiet participant, although physically present, goes away in every other way. In addition, the team is deprived of a "breakthrough" idea and may not achieve its goal.

In almost every situation, someone on the team heard the quiet person's idea and noticed he or she was no longer participating. In this scenario, either the people who go away could make themselves heard, or any other team member could have dealt with the situation.

Check-ins work because they disrupt the field. When a check-in is met with trust and acceptance, the team can quickly move through *moments of truth* for the good of all team members.

Quality Check In

As a member of the Venture Centre's extended faculty, I recently worked with Ward Flynn and Bill Baker, Venture Centre partners, to deliver a program to the American Society for Quality Control (ASQC). We observed that it was challenging for the technical and engineering participants to "check in," telling someone either about how they were feeling or about how others were feeling. Our solution to this dilemma was to create red and green laminated cards which we gave each of the participants. Having a "tool" to communicate whether they were *checked-in* seemed to motivate them to raise a flag when they had concerns to be addressed. The anonymity of the colored props allowed the group to support each other in taking the risk of expressing their feelings, even when they felt uncomfortable.

—Edina Preucel

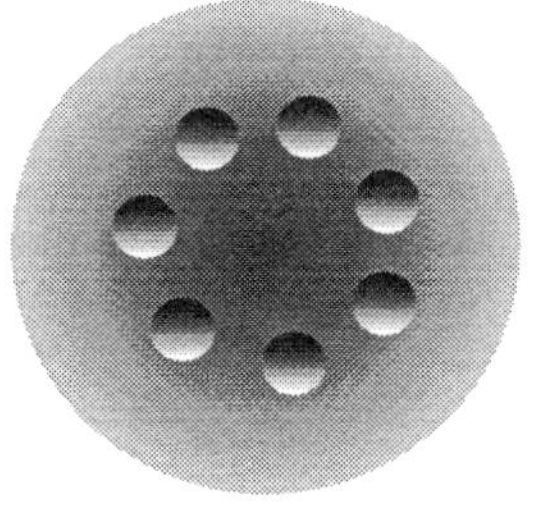

Chapter Six

TEAM: Tools To Work Together

TEAM: Tools To Work Together

A lot of people talk about team building. But bringing about team*work* requires a much greater commitment of time, energy, and courage. Individuals must be willing to work through the first three steps, described in earlier chapters. To review, they are:

1. Declare and live out your personal mission.
2. Accept responsibility for your own safety and happiness.
3. Acknowledge the value of conflict.

People who are unable to define and articulate a personal mission for themselves will remain vague and uncommitted to other team members. Those who are unwilling to accept personal responsibilities for themselves will tend to blame other team members, thus disrupting the team-field. Team members who are unable to question others or be questioned cannot meet other members on an equal footing, and thereby weaken the team-field.

If a team member withholds vital information about his or her participation, it undermines the team's effort. Not everyone needs to lead. Not everyone must follow. But everyone must be willing to "get out of the way" for the good of the team.

If all members of the team embrace these steps, the team is ready to enhance the field. If some members are unwilling or unable to embrace each one, at the very least, their positions must be known to the group. It is not acceptable for one member of the team to approach the leader and say, "I am really committed to this project and I like the other team members, but I have always been unable to assert myself. Please do not embarrass me by telling the other team members."

It is possible for a team to function without full participation or buy-in from all members. But it is essential that the level of participation of all members be a subject of dialogue among them. Ultimately, the team must decide how to work with (or around) each individual team member. If a team member withholds vital information about his or her participation, it undermines the team's effort. Not everyone needs to lead. Not everyone must follow. But everyone must be willing to "get out of the way" for the good of the team.

When a team has clarified the level of participation of its members, it has made a critical advance toward step #4 of the *Seven Steps to Championing Truth in the Organization.*

4. Model truthful behavior by creating Truth Zones within the organization.

A team that has the ability and willingness to talk about the performance of individual team members models the first three steps while overcoming an obstacle to future growth. As long as performance is discussed only generally among the group and specifically only behind closed doors, the team will never break through to a level of high performance.

In a high-performing team, it is critical that any member be able to point out problems, ask for explanations, and make specific suggestions to improve the performance of any other individual member of the team.

While a Truth Zone field will be qualitatively different from the rest of the organization, it is critical that participants are not made to feel better than, or above, others in the organization.

To talk this openly and honestly with each other, a great deal of trust should be built among team members. People must be willing to give and receive communication that may be critical, but always delivered truthfully. That is, trust is developed with compassion, in context, and through constructive delivery of the message. Thus the formula: TRUST = C^3. *Compassion* means communicating with heart and sensitivity for how what is being said will be heard and felt. *Context* refers to making the right comment to the right person. Can this person do anything about the issue? For example, the team representative from customer service may not be the appropriate member to discuss sensitive financial issues. Likewise, the team member from finance may not be able to do anything about the delay in the engineering project. *Constructive* means, "How can you say what needs to be said in a manner that will add value?" Is this something the person has control over? Is it fixable? If not, your comments are only whining!

Building a Truth Zone

In addition to embodying the first three steps and trusting enough to talk openly and honestly about team performance in front of the rest of the team, a Truth Zone needs to be declared and posted.

It is not enough that a team live out the first three steps and talk openly and honestly with each other. It is important that other teams know your team has designated itself a Truth Zone. In doing so, you put them on notice that your team has specific operating agreements and will abide by them in all dealings. It means that your team is only willing to deal with other teams or individuals outside of the Truth Zone in ways which are honest, open, and aligned with the good of the organization.

To do this powerfully, post a Truth Zone sign in the area, on correspondence, and in the e-mail system. This does not mean it is necessary to "sell" the idea. When people come into the Zone, they know what the operating agreements are. To that end, most Zones are not only posted with signs, but the operating agreements are prominently displayed as well. In this way, those from outside the Zone who choose to participate will know the rules of the game!

Curiosity is inevitable. When others ask what this Truth Zone "stuff" is all about, it is a perfect opportunity to express the importance of operating from a basis of honesty and alignment within the organization's vision.

If another workgroup asks for help setting up its own Truth Zone, members of your Zone should assist.

After a Truth Zone is established, it is important that people on the team see themselves as vital components of the larger organization. While a Truth Zone field will be qualitatively different from the rest of the organization, it is critical that participants are not made to feel better than, or above, others in the organization.

People in a Truth Zone keep their feet on the ground by seeking greater knowledge through learning. Most learning occurs as a result of taking risks and making mistakes.

Kinko's

While standing in line at my local Kinko's Copy Center, I was struck with the array of tools available to "truthful revolutionaries." It is interesting to note that until the fall of the Soviet Union, copy machines, fax machines, and personal computers were purposely in short supply in that country. The reason—the totalitarian government feared the dissemination of information. In many places around the globe, the restriction of information continues.

The equipment many of us take for granted—digital imaging, desktop publishing, video conferencing, large image blow-ups, color copying, overheads, binding and collating, not to mention high quality duplication, is available to any champion of truth in any size organization.

The next time you walk into your local copy center, look around with new eyes. Seek out the tools of empowerment and revolution. Consider how you can use them to leverage your ability for the good of your Truth Zone and your organization.

5. Seek continuous learning for myself and my organization.

STEPS
TRUTH

When people are truly committed to learning, the process of risk-taking, mistake-making, and learning becomes part of the culture. In a dynamic environment in which innovation, continuous improvement, and a personal search for excellence exists, there is no time to gloat on past accomplishments or compare one group with another.

When people fear the consequences of innovation, risk-taking, and making mistakes, an organization ceases to learn. In such situations, the field has become so strong that it no longer facilitates the individual achievements and contributions of participants. Instead, they are now expected to sustain the field, even to the detriment of supporting the shared vision of the organization.

On the other hand, organizations that don't reward risk-taking (within technical, legal, ethical, and practical limits) run the risk of losing their ability to learn, improve, and remain flexible. The expressions"Get it right the first time," and "Always first," "No tolerance for error" often communicate the wrong message. When people fear the consequences of innovation, risk-taking, and making mistakes, an organization ceases to learn. In such situations, the field has become so strong that it no longer facilitates the individual achievements and contributions of participants. Instead, they are now expected to sustain the field, even to the detriment of supporting the shared vision of the organization.

In fear-based environments, staff members waste precious time and resources covering up, justifying decisions, and seeking scapegoats to blame for problems. Petty bickering erupts between workgroups, departments, and individuals. While it is impossible to quantify the cost of such unproductive behaviors, anyone who has worked in a truthful vs. fearful organization has seen that the costs are staggering.

People Must Be Ready

Someday, when schools and universities are Truthful Organizations, students will be provided with the skills necessary for participation in a Truth Zone. Until then, the task will remain in the hands of those willing to strive for a new way of working.

Doing one's own personal development work is essential to gaining the skills needed in a Truth Zone. When people are clear about who they are and what they stand for, it is easier to work with others in a diverse group. If I am comfortable with myself and the unique aspects of my own personality, I am better equipped to deal with the differences in others. The more comfortable people are with themselves, the more comfortable they are with others.

The more comfortable people are with themselves, the more comfortable they are with others.

The opposite is also true. It is well established that racial, ethnic, and religious bigotry crosses all socioeconomic, geographic, age, and educational boundaries. The one thing all bigots have in common is low self-esteem. The lower a person's self-worth, the more difficult it is to embrace others, especially those who appear different.

When people have done some developmental work by exploring their personal mission, clarifying their values, and learning to take a stand (without falling apart or overreacting), it becomes much easier to relate to others. If everyone on the team makes similar efforts, the team will more easily move to a high-performing level. As each person learns to strengthen himself or herself, the team's ability to appreciate diversity expands. The process of individual personal development shifts the team-field and improves the team's ability to perform.

The real test comes when faced with one person who takes a stand counter to the will of the team. On an effective team, everyone is expected to take a truthful stand, even when it goes against prevailing wisdom. Truthful dissent, in service of the shared vision, is far more valuable than passive agreement.

On an effective team, everyone is expected to take a truthful stand, even when it goes against prevailing wisdom. Truthful dissention, in service of the shared vision, is by far more valuable than passive agreement.

The Phases of Team Development: *Forming*, *Storming*, *Norming*, and *Performing*

Back in 1965, B. W. Tuchman published an article in *Psychological Bulletin 63* which would forever alter the way people see team development. His model describes four stages in team development: forming, storming, norming, and performing. Even with this powerful

Teams can powerfully blend diversity with a focused cohesion. As a result, different people work toward a shared outcome.

model to serve as a guide, most companies do little beyond *forming* teams. Forming a team may involve nothing more than grouping people, often arbitrarily, as if they were putting together a sandlot ball team. Using an array of tools, including personal style indicators and communication models, outside teambuilding consultants bring more sophistication to the process. No matter how a team is formed, or how organizers try to avoid it, diversity will exist on the final team.

In the Truthful Organization, diversity is good for teams. After all, if everyone were identical, then a team would be unnecessary. Teams can powerfully blend diversity with a focused cohesion. As a result, different people work toward a shared outcome. That is why a team is capable of surpassing the performance of an individual—there are more ideas, points-of-view, prejudices, experiences, etc.

However, diversity is a double-edged sword. It is both the strength of the team as well as its bane. Inevitably, teams move into a *storming* phase—a critical period when team members are figuring out how to work together. People naturally behave in the same way they did before the team. The usual result is a group of individuals, each with a personal agenda, trying to get something done as a group. With little experience and few tools, the group (it can hardly be called a team at this point) splinters into individuals and small factions each struggling to be the one with the right answer. This is called the "storming" phase because much of the group's energy is wasted bickering over details.

A typical storming team looks like this: Out of 12 people, four or five are forceful and outspoken, some of them cooperate with each other while others jockey for control. Another four or five tend to be quiet and look "checked-out." The remaining two to four check in and out, depending on the emotional energy generated by those who want things their way. Unfortunately, much of what people learned to help themselves succeed may not serve the team. Nevertheless, over time, or with the right tools and guidance, a team can learn to function together.

The field adjusts to accommodate the qualities of individuals. It accommodates those who do not conform in a variety of ways. They may be expelled from the group or labeled "non-conformist," "not a team player," "lone wolf," "hard to get along with," etc. A team that has created a team-field and achieved a level of equilibrium is called a *norming* team.

A "norming" team feels comfortable. Roles are filled and operating agreements (though they need not have been openly discussed) are in place. The team is no longer challenged with the demands of coming together. During the norming stage, work becomes routine. Even so, this is the most challenging stage of team development because people get stuck. Many teams never explore higher performance and settle for comfort, which is usually defined as a lack of conflict. A "norming" team can work and play together, but has not yet learned to deal openly with the qualities of the team-field—some subjects are off-limits, secrets exist, trust is limited.

When I tell any truth it is not for the sake of convincing those who do not know it, but for the sake of defending those who do.
—William Blake

The "norming" stage is critical to team development because it provides a comfortable latitude to grapple with a difficult paradox: individuals want comfort, predictability, and safety, yet organizations need people to take risks, innovate, and embrace change, even though it is rarely comfortable. During the "norming" phase, it is possible to construct key interpersonal relationships, set personal boundaries, and define responsibilities to support the need for comfort, predictability, and safety. On the other hand, a team which wants to achieve a higher level of performance can build into the system a process to disrupt the field by *perturbing* (e.g., irritating, disturbing, disrupting) the state of equilibrium. Both are necessary; equilibrium without perturbation leads to stagnation and reduced productivity—perturbation without balance generates so much chaos that productivity is inhibited.

One of the most powerful agents which can perturb a group is the expectation of open, truthful communication. Not "truth or dare" games, but supporting each other to be open, honest, and committed. A "norming" team can learn to deal with difficult, even

Who Needs The Team?

A regional management team in a large multinational financial firm I have worked with illustrates the "performing" process. In about a year, the management team had moved through the first three stages of team building. They spawned a number of task forces and transformed their working environment into a model team environment. The team invited me to a one-day meeting in which they wished to re-evaluate their goals and assess their progress. To condense a four-hour discussion into two sentences, team members decided that since most of their work had been off-loaded onto other teams, there was no longer any purpose for their team to exist. They disbanded the management team! The vehicle that moved them to reinvent the office, redefine every relationship, and win accolades from the home office was unceremoniously discarded.

painful truths—directly and compassionately. When team members can see their own field and talk about how each person participates with others, they are well on their way to becoming a high-*performing* team.

A high-*performing* team delivers the best of two worlds: individual technical excellence and a team-field that brings out the best in each member. Participants on a hig- performing team can perceive and even manipulate the team-field. As a result, they are able to change the team structure to meet the demands of unforeseen challenges. The ability to change the team structure represents a pivotal distinction between a true high-"performing" team and an established "norming" team. Even though a team may have worked together so long they exhibit characteristics of high performance, only a true high-performing team is willing to change the team to cope with an obstacle. The one constant in a "norming" team is the team itself. A high-"performing" team, on the other hand, views the team structure as another tool—as easily used as discarded. A high-performing team is willing to sacrifice itself to achieve its goals.

Members of a high- performing team find stability within themselves and from some inner strength or higher power. They measure progress not by the degree to which they conform, but their ability to adapt to ever-increasing challenges further from the norm. The team rises to extraordinary challenges and adapts itself to unpredictable situations at increasingly rapid rates.

Larger scale examples of breakthroughs abound. Companies who successfully reinvent themselves are always asking critical questions intended to reveal their own field and its relationship to other stakeholders: "What business are we in?" "Who are our customers?" "What do we know how to do that people want?" Questions like these can make the difference between sustainable growth and a flash in the pan.

History is full of examples of businesses which fell by the wayside because owners could not see their own field. Take, for example, the railroads at the turn of the century. While there are some sterling examples of individual companies that remained highly profitable, as an industry, few would argue with 20/20 hindsight that the railroads blew it. A handful of railroad companies owned the U.S.! They had enormous real estate holdings; they were on the leading edge of technology; they owned banks, and steel mills; they controlled the largest communication infrastructure; and they possessed unprecedented rights of way. There were virtually no limits to their political influence. Yet they chose not to finance the fledgling automobile, trucking, communication, and aircraft industries. Why? Had they embraced any of those ideas, their future would have been very different. The implications are mind-boggling.

A high-performing team is willing to sacrifice itself to achieve its goals.

Yet as Tom Peters, co-author of *In Search of Excellence,* has described in his books and seminars, the railroads were unable to break through their own paradigm. They could not see beyond their own field (railroading) to understand they were in the transportation, shipping, real estate, and communication business.

A high-performing team must work hard to shape its field, then be equally devoted to altering or even jettisoning it if it gets in the way.

A high-performing team must work hard to shape its field, then be equally devoted to altering or even jettisoning it if it gets in the way.

Applying the "Seven Steps" to Team Building

Returning to the *Seven Steps to Championing Truth in the Organization*, the following demonstrates how to use the Seven Steps in team development.

1. ***Declare and live out my personal mission.***
   All members must discuss with the team how and to what degree their personal mission, the team mission, and the vision of the organization are interrelated or aligned.
2. ***Accept responsibility for my own safety and happiness.***
   When team members assume responsibility for their own happiness and safety (physical or emotional), they remove a primary obstacle to cooperation. Team members who hold others responsible diminish their ability to participate in the field as an equal partner. When people feel victimized and blame others, they set themselves apart and below others.

3. ***Acknowledge the value of conflict.***
   In order for a team to effectively manage conflict, it must develop operating principles and expectations that support full participation and even dissension among team members. Moreover, decision-making methods and forms of leadership must be established so that each individual is able to participate using his or her own unique style without winding up in deadlock.

4. ***Model truthful behavior by creating "Truth Zones" within the organization.***
   The roles of individual members need to be clear to everyone. Not only must each member adhere to the prior three points, but specific performance expectations should be established and integrated into a total team strategy.

Truth titillates the imagination far less than fiction.
—Marquis de Sade

5. ***Seek continuous learning for myself and my organization.***
   The team must develop or adopt a problem-solving methodology that encourages individual participation, risk-taking, and the likelihood of learning from mistakes. Further, a method must be developed to distribute information across the team to maximize individual and team learning.

6. ***Claim a stake in the viability of the organizations of which I am a part.***
   Team members must be encouraged to put his or her own agenda (expectations, methodologies, outcomes, etc.) on the table and demonstrate a willingness to put that agenda aside for the good of the team and its work. The team and individuals should be encouraged to experience natural consequences or rewards based on the outcome of the team effort.

7. ***Champion truthfulness in the organization; be a leader in designing a truthful environment.***
   The team must have a compelling shared vision that extends beyond the team and the immediate

task at hand. For example, members of the team need to understand that how their team functions is often as important as what it accomplisshes. Since every team operates in an environment that is larger than itself (department, plant, organization, industry, community), the team impacts to some degree the larger environment.

Team Tools

This section discusses tools which enhance and improve the deployment of the Truthful Organization.

I have been ever of opinion that revolutions are not to be evaded.
—Benjamin Disraeli

Team Mission

A team's mission is usually focused on a specific outcome. Some teams are intended to operate forever; others will disband after a specific outcome or date is reached. In either case, one of the first things a team should do is craft a mission statement. The statement should use few words and be posted during all meetings.

The mission statement serves as a guide for creating operating agreements, the designation of individual roles, and the resolution of decisions. When a team has a viable mission statement, each member knows how his or her role contributes to the mission.

Operating Agreements

Early in a team's development, the team should create its own operating agreements. These agreements should, at a minimum, address: meeting frequency, length of meetings, attendance, communication etiquette, conflict management, facilitation methods, and decision-making options.

In addition, the agreements might include issues which affect the environment, location of meeting, refreshments, guests, audiovisual equipment, etc.

There is the fear that we shan't prove worthy in the eyes of someone who knows us at least as well as we know ourselves. That is the fear of God. And there is the fear of Man—fear that men won't understand us and we shall be cut off from them.
—*Robert Frost*

Individual Roles and Responsibilities

Every individual on the team will have, in addition to regularly assigned duties, at least one specific role on the team. These roles may be rotated periodically, but should, at a minimum, include the following: meeting notification, logistics (room arrangements, setup, refreshments, etc.) record keeper, facilitation, and timekeepers.

Many teams assign additional tasks, including "joke meister" (politically correct humor), activity planner (a brief, fun, team activity), skill builder, ethics officer, keeper of the heart, historian, etc.

Problem-Solving Methodology

A variety of problem-solving methods exist. It is important that the team members devote time in the "forming" stage to agree on a method(s) that will most effectively allow them to solve problems. Understanding and agreeing to this process will save a lot of team time later .

A Sample Problem-Solving Method:

1. Specify the problem or situation.
2. Define resolution of problem as a specific outcome.
3. Collect alternative solutions.
4. Evaluate and prioritize the alternatives.
5. Take action on the best alternative.
6. Evaluate: Did the action bring about desired outcome?

1. Specify the problem or situation.

Teams often jump into action before everyone agrees on the definition of the problem. The leader or facilitator should write it down and poll the group to be certain everyone agrees on the definition and scope of the problem.

It is important that the group not confuse the resolution with the problem.

2. *Define resolution of problem as a specific outcome.*

Once the problem is defined, a specific outcome must be outlined. Will everyone know when it has been reached? An outcome statement should satisfy all members of the team that it is achievable and resolves the problem definition.

3. *Collect alternative solutions.*

The team should collect a variety of solutions likely to resolve the problem and satisfy any constraints which may exist. One popular method is brainstorming, introduced in 1957 by advertising executive, Alex Osborn, in *Applied Imagination*. The key is to collect input from the team without judging or evaluating the suggestions. The facilitator must keep the process moving quickly and disallow any comments which either take the team off-track or are judgments of ideas already suggested.

The highest compact we can make with our fellow is—"Let there be truth between us two forevermore."
—Ralph Waldo Emerson

Brainstorming works best if it happens fast and within rigid time constraints. If you plan 10 minutes, at eight minutes, let the group know. Some methods collect ideas until the group runs completely dry. Either way, when the collection of ideas is complete, it is time to move to the next step.

Alternatives to brainstorming include discussion, dialogue, individual analysis, or small-group study sessions with a report to the larger group. Any method that will get the widest variety of workable solutions on the table quickly is acceptable.

4. *Evaluate and prioritize the alternatives.*

Once alternative options are collected, the group must evaluate and prioritize possible solutions. The first phase usually includes consolidating similar ideas and eliminating any that are completely unworkable. Finally, the remaining solutions need to be ranked from the most to the least likely solution.

Options for ranking are many. They include: simple voting, multiple voting (where participants each have five tally marks at their disposal and can place them in any combination next to the options of their choice), a facilitated dialogue of the options, and advocacy (when each item is assigned to someone who did not generate the idea to study and present to the group). Other options include designating a leader or committee to rank the options and choose.

5. *Take action on the best alternative*

After the best choice is determined, the team implements the solution. If an implementation plan was not part of the solution, the team must create a plan that will use the team's assets effectively to arrive at the best solution in a minimal amount of time.

While an individual can usually decide faster, that does not mean others will accept it. Decisions made by individuals seldom engender buy-in from team members. Perhaps most importantly, there is research which indicates that teams make better, although somewhat riskier, decisions.

6. *Evaluate: Did the action bring about desired outcome?*

After the plan is implemented—whether the desired outcome is achieved or not—the process and outcome must be evaluated. Did it work? Was it the best solution? What worked best? What did we learn? What could we do better?

Team Decision Making

Better Decisions

The easiest way to make decisions is for one person to do it. In traditional business environments, managers were the designated decision makers. In today's changing work environment, there are often fewer managers. Workers are expected to make their own choices, or at least participate in the process. It is not possible to become a high-performing team as long as a central leader makes the important decisions for the group. While an individual can usually decide faster, that does not mean others will accept it. Decisions made by individuals seldom engender buy-in from team members. Perhaps most importantly, there is research which indicates that teams make better, although somewhat riskier, decisions [J. P. Wanous and M. A. Youtz , (1986), *Academy of Management Journal, 29,* - 1986 pp. 149-159]. If two heads are better than one, multiple heads may be even better. Unfortunately, group decision making is (far) more complex, and as the following chart indicates, takes more time.

Advantages and Disadvantages of Group Decision Making

Advantages	Disadvantages
More than one point of view Usually results in better decisions Choose from wider array of options Decision reflects group interests	Usually takes more time May result in "group think" Fast but may not be most appropriate decision Choices may be riskier May not use individual experts

Ways a Team Can Make a Decision

- Boss decides
- Boss decides after getting input
- Majority rules
- Unanimity
- Consensus with leader's constraint
- Consensus with no constraints
- Decision making is delegated to those best able to make a decision
- Non-decision

A number of specific techniques are available to teams. Among those particularly well suited to Truthful Teams are the following:

The most important quality in a leader is that of being acknowledged as such.
—André Maurois

Modified Force Field Analysis

Itemize the issues FOR and AGAINST. Next to each item, assign a number between 1 and 20 which indicates the level of support for that specific issue. Total the numbers to determine whether there is more force FOR or AGAINST.

Example: *To buy or not to buy a new computer*

Itemize Issues FOR —>		<—Itemize Issues AGAINST	
15	Prices are low	5	Prices could go lower
10	No innovations expected	5	New system could be coming
12	Improved productivity	10	Learning curve is costly
5	Compatibility with home office	2	Home may borrow system
8	Internet connectivity	5	Workers could waste time
50	Buy the computer	27	Don't buy computer

The real leader has no need to lead—he is content to point the way.
—Henry Miller

Modified Delphi Method

Once a problem is well identified, the delphi method helps the team sort through a large number of alternatives. Each member of the team writes comments and suggestions for a solution on sheets of paper. After these are turned in, they are duplicated and given to all members of the team. Then everyone takes a turn to offer feedback on each of the proposals, making it easier to prioritize or come to a consensus outcome.

Sticky-Notes (Affinity) Patterns

Transcribe suggestions to individual "sticky notes." Then place all notes on a board or flip chart. Have the group organize the suggestions in "affinity clussters." This process helps uncover previously invisible patterns. Encourage the group members to discuss the clusters and determine to what degree they move participants toward a final solution.

Multivoting

A large list of options (alternate solutions) can be posted on a large white board or multiple flip charts. Then members of the team vote (with a specified number of votes) for their choices. Next, the facilitator selects those items with the most votes and repeats the process until one, or a more manageable number, remains.

Cost (risk)—Benefit (reward)

It is possible to compare the projected benefits of a particular solution with the cost such benefits are likely to incur:

All of the great leaders have had one characteristic in common: it was the willingness to confront unequivocally the major anxiety of their people in their time. This, and not much else, is the essence of leadership.
—John Kenneth Galbraith

Proposed Solution

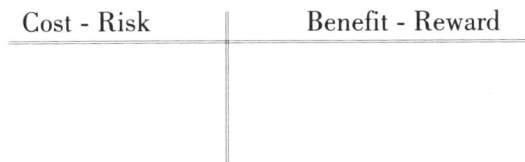

Cost - Risk	Benefit - Reward

Voting

I am not a fan of voting! While it is the backbone of our form of representative democracy, it divides teams. It creates winners and losers, and undermines individual dissent. Let's face it—voting happens when people are unable to reach consensus, team members become impatient, or they run out of time.

Power tends to corrupt, and absolute power corrupts absolutely. Great men are almost always bad men.
—*Lord Acton*

Before calling for a vote, call for a "check-in" and find out how everyone is doing. Is anyone's ego out of place? Is someone trying to force something on the team? Are some people holding a position for reasons that do not serve the team? Let's talk straight ... where does the disagreement come from? What is behind it? The inability to directly discuss difficult issues indicates people are more interested in personal safety and team stability than breaking through to new solutions.

Consensus

Consensus does not divide a group, but unifies people. It has its roots in the Quaker faith, so some of the best material on the subject can be found in their religious tradition. Consensus is often misunderstood. It is not the same as unanimity. Unanimity means everyone is in total agreement. Consensus means everyone is at least 75% comfortable with the agreement. The difference between 75% and 100% agreement is enough to avoid time-consuming, deadlock-creating unanimity.

Bryan James of Consensus Unlimited, a Denver-based consulting firm, specializes in team consensus decision making. He cites some major impediments to consensus, including:

- Competition between team members
- Lack of interest in others
- Owning (identifying with) ideas
- Suppressing feelings and conflict
- Relying upon authority
- Social prejudices
- Self-interest above team interest
- Intimidation, impatience, judgments
- Hierarchical structures impeding team function

According to James, the qualities that make such decision making work include:

- Agreement on the purpose
- Patience
- Addressing personal agendas
- Cooperation and mutual trust
- Shared ownership of ideas
- Valuing feelings and conflict
- Equalization of power
- Attention to team process and communication skills
- Willingness to persuade and be persuaded

The great secret of succeeding in conversation is to admire little, to hear much; always to distrust our own reason, and sometimes that of our friends; never to pretend to wit, but to make that of others appear as much as possibly we can; to hearken to what is said and to answer to the purpose.
—Benjamin Franklin

During the teambuilding phase, consensus work can be very time-consuming. According to James, it needs to be introduced in small steps. The team should not force "both feet" into it without prerequisite skills and foundational support.

Team Communication

Dialogue or Discussion

Most people use the words dialogue and discussion interchangeably. The difference is dramatic, according to the late physicist David Bohm, who wrote *Wholeness and the Implicate Order,* and *Thought As A System*, with others, he led a crusade to clarify the distinction and popularize dialogue in the workplace. As I understand Bohm's distinction:

Discussion is a search for truth in which participants put their ideas in front of the team for consideration. Each person's intent is to convince others that his or her idea is the best and deserves team support. This competitive approach is the common practice among most groups.

Truth Talk

As Director of Communications for a television station, I enjoy a wonderful relationship with my general manager and my immediate supervisor. We have been through some tough battles in the areas of integrity, fairness, creativity, and leadership.

My immediate supervisor, who is part of a powerful year-long community leadership group, has been sharing many lessons being taught in this group. One recent topic was moral courage in the workplace.

As he was sitting with me and one of my staff members in my office one afternoon, we had a friendly debate on some issues at the station.

I remember saying, "I certainly see your point, and while that may be true for most other people, that is not the way I would allow myself to be treated at a meeting in front of other people." This referred to a recent meeting we had had with the general manager. There I had taken a stand diametrically opposed to the GM and he had raised his voice.

My supervisor's point was that the GM has the "GM Prerogative of Divine Right" to humiliate anyone in a meeting or otherwise. His title allows it, he said. I said, "No job, no boss, no salary is worth it to me to allow someone to humiliate me in front of others needlessly. I will never be passive at those times. No one has that right. I set the boundaries of how I am to be treated."

Continued on opposite page ...

Dialogue, on the other hand, is also a search for truth. In this process, however, team members actively assist each other in a non-competitive manner. As each person speaks, other members suspend disbelief and attachment to their own point of view. In this way, each member helps the speaker uncover deeper meaning, association, and understanding. During this process, ideas are never challenged; there are no winners or losers. Whichever idea emerges as the group's highest truth—whether it was an original idea presented by a contributor, a combination of ideas, or a completely new notion—it is already owned by all. Dialogue as a formal process is new to many, but offers enormous opportunities for improving team performance.

Check-in

One tool high- performing teams need is a reality check, called a *check-in*. This is how a team takes its own temperature. Everyone is responsible for calling a time-out if things are not right. Each person speaks his or her truth and asks the question: "I am feeling __________ (fill in the blank with your truth) ... How's everyone else doing?" Notice the "I" statement reveals the person's true feelings about what is going on (sad, mad, confused, frustrated, invigorated, satisfied, etc.) At first this takes courage and trust in the group. After a while, most people discover they are putting into words the emotions others are already feeling, but may not have spoken. Even if you are the only one feeling something, now that your team knows, you can all work on it together. The power of checking in cannot be overemphasized—after a while, team members treat missed chances to check in as lost opportunities to improve. A special note of caution is in order. Normally, a check-in only takes a minute or two. Some people misconstrue check-in, using the opportunity to vent deep feelings or harangue the team. These feelings are important, but should be shared with permission, and only at appropriate times.

Leadership

In the Truthful Organization, leadership is decentralized and widely distributed. Nominal leaders encourage leaderfulness among team members by encouraging designated leaders, champions, and leadership skills among all team members.

Nominal Leaders (Bosses)

Nominal leaders are individuals selected by upper management to serve in traditional command and control positions. Nominal leaders such as managers and supervisors are often expected to lead—but leadership has never required authority to be effective. In fact, the best leaders in an organization often are not managers at all.

Many nominal leaders do not know the difference between bossing and leading. It is *possible* for a nominal leader to lead but, for most, the tendency to resort to command and control tactics is strong. Bosses who try to control the behavior of others are trapped in a *parental* field. Children are not led by their parents—they are not in choice about the relationship. True leadership exists in a completely different field—a field where a leader steps forward and others are *in choice* about their willingness to follow.

Truth Talk

Continued from opposite page ...

He said, "During the recent leadership forum presentations on moral courage, I decided you are one of the few persons in this station with moral courage. You are the only person I know who will risk losing your job and your popularity in the name of honesty, fairness, excellence, respect, and the principles by which you live. You have very high standards. You have many times inspired me.

"But (one thing I want you to know) while I support you on many of the things you fight for, I will never take the first bullet for you. You will have to take that all by yourself. There will be times, though, where I will be willing to take the second bullet."

I laughed, saying, "It is nice to know someone will be nearby to soak up the blood from the first bullet and maybe dodge the second one with me."

At the same time I also thought, what a coward's stance! What I realized later as more important, was that my supervisor had personal awareness, had drawn his own boundaries, and was kind enough to inform me where he stood philosophically and managerially. I also realized he too had moral courage. He had acknowledged me as a leader, as a person of integrity and influence, without self-consciousness, to my face and before one of my staff members. I learned a lesson from him that day.

—Name Withheld

Talking The Talk

I know of a nominal leader (department manager) in an organization of about three hundred people. The intricacies of managing a first-class establishment and keeping it profitable are extensive. Maury, the manager, is a classic workaholic. He views his contribution as absolutely vital to the overall operation. As a result, he works 60 to 90 hours a week. When hiring people, his first question is: "How many hours a week do you think you should work?" If the candidate says 40, he will not hire the person. Instead of seeing himself as facilitator, trainer, coach, and mentor, he is a judge—and nobody ever measures up to his standard. Over time, he has set up the whole department to reinforce his belief that his contribution is vital.

Workers will never be anything but second-class citizens to him. Even though his "door is always open," he brings in bagels, and he laughs with employees, he holds himself above the staff. It has even been rumored that he has, on occasion, sent staff home so he can do their jobs and save a few dollars on his budget.

To make matters worse, Maury is aware of his faults—and under pressure will acknowledge them, but there is no follow-through. His words are about empowerment, participative management, and shared decision making, but his walk lags far behind his talk.

In a Truthful Organization, leadership is decentralized and widely distributed among staff. Anyone can step forward. As long as others are willing to follow, the relationship continues.

Nominal leaders can add value to their teams; they can serve as visionaries, facilitators, and coaches.

Leader As Visionary

A nominal leader can define a mission, set priorities, and inspire the rest of the team to buy in. Even though others on the team can perform the same function, the nominal leader is in a perfect position to make certain the team's mission is aligned with the department and/or organization's vision.

Leader As Facilitator

Nominal leaders as well as others on the team can facilitate communication among team members and other teams. Good facilitators remove themselves from the details of the conversation and do not take sides in a conflict. The challenge for the nominal leader is to refrain from answering questions, but instead, ask them.

Leader As Coach

A nominal leader in the Truthful Organization is motivated by the improvement of performance of everyone on the team—not just bottom line results. The challenge for an experienced coach is to avoid jumping in to save the day. If that happens, how can people learn from their mistakes and improve their performances? In the Truthful Organization, the coach must stay on the sideline.

Champions

Teams assign *champions* to research, develop, and promote an idea, product, or cause within the team. Champions not only have the ability to influence a situation but they also possess organizational authority to bring an issue to completion. A champion may work alone or with others on a committee. Champions off-load work from the team and streamline research, planning, and execution.

A champion must, at all times, act in the best interest of the team. If the champion's agenda gets in the way by promoting or undermining the project, his or her effectiveness is lost.

In the Truthful Organization, leadership is decentralized and widely distributed. Nominal leaders encourage leaderfulness among team members by encouraging designated leaders, champions, and leadership skills among all team members.

Last Words About Truth Zones

The first Truth Zone must be shaped in the heart. Later, as people understand more and their comfort with "truthfulness" deepens, they may choose to venture out. Some include one or two co-workers; others surround themselves with a larger circle of truthful relationships. Many decide to post a Truth Zone sign in their offices or work areas. Eventually, people go on to build a truthful team or volunteer to take the lead on a project. They help build a more truthful department or plant, and even work at the organizational level.

The beauty of a bottom-up revolution is that, at each level of participation, the choice is yours. When others work along the same lines, separate Truth Zones have an increasingly influential effect on the organization's meta-field.

One of the most powerful ways to take a stand and "make a difference" is by placing the Truth Zone signs in conspicuous places within your own work area. Posting them next to the water cooler or on car bumpers is less appropriate because it would be an anonymous act. Stake out your territory and take ownership for the level of truth within that area. When truthfulness is introduced into the organization and announced in this personal manner, it carries more credibility than anything mandated from the top down. Many

It is important for everyone in a Truth Zone to remember the sign is not a badge to set them apart or above, but a flag to beckon others' participation.

Model truthful behavior by creating Truth Zones within the organization.

workplaces are decorated with propaganda posters extolling the virtues of teamwork, cooperation, safety, planning, and more. The fact that these posters are rarely, if ever, taken seriously is largely the result of their anonymity. When posters are in hallways, doorways, break-rooms, and cafeterias, it is difficult to hold people accountable for a lack of alignment between their behavior and the values illustrated in the poster.

When Truth Zone signs show up in people's offices and next to their work stations, they are not likely to be dismissed out of hand. The signs disrupt the team-field. Most people are curious; they often decide to set up a Truth Zone of their own. Occasionally, people take offense—they think the sign means others are "untruthful." It is important for everyone in a Truth Zone to remember the sign is not a badge to set them apart or above, but a flag to beckon others' participation.

This fourth step, modeling truthful behavior by creating Truth Zones within the organization, is pivotal to the overall process. While the first three steps are personal in nature, the last three are more public and visible. At step four, your truthful stand becomes visible to others. You will no longer have the luxury of anonymity because you are now visibly engaged in changing the status quo.

Whenever people champion change, no matter how modest the effort, some will resist. In the face of resistance, your greatest ally is the alignment between your personal mission and the vision of the organization. Others can say what they wish (do what they like), but you can sail a true course unfettered by their fears, jealousy, or lack of understanding. Avoid wasting energy reacting to resistance—sail the true course, walk your talk!

Everyone wishes to have truth on his side, but not everyone wishes too be on the side of truth.

—Richard Whately

If you are out to describe the truth, leave elegance to the tailor.

—Albert Einstein

It is easier to pperceive error than to find truth, for the former lies on the surface and iss eassily seen, while the latter lies in the depth, where few are willing to search for it.

—Johann Wolfgang von Goethe

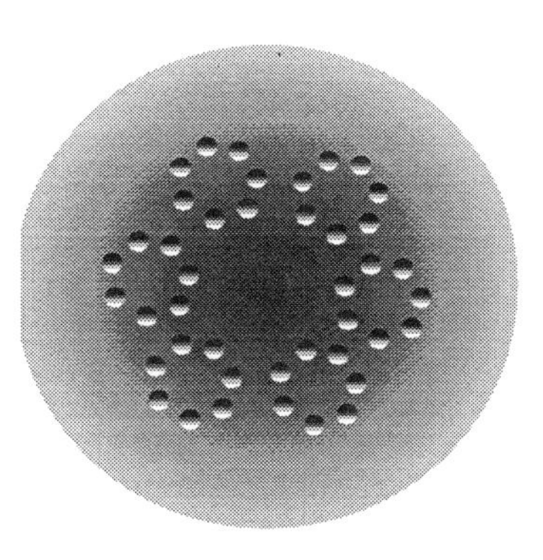

Chapter Seven

Revolutionizing The ORGANIZATION

ORGANIZATION: Alignment At Every Level

Organizational Truth

At the Venture Centre, we developed and use an instrument to assess the gap between what is happening in organizations *now*, and what is desired in the *future*. The Truth Quotient™ instrument reveals the truth 'gap.' It exists not at the personal, interpersonal, or team level, but at the organizational level in most companies. As I interpret the data, it would seem people in most companies believe its leadership talks a good line, but generates a gap in credibility by failing to put company resources and money behind *what they say*! A common example is the organization that says something like: "We value individual contributions, encourage innovators, and want staff to serve the customer at all costs." Yet the company rewards tenure with an outdated compensation plan; innovators are called troublemakers and passed over for promotions; customers only come first so long as their needs can be fulfilled within rigid guidelines of company policy.

Another issue that comes up is how executives and other individuals at higher levels of the organization hold themselves above the bureaucracy, rules, and expectations everyone else is forced to observe.

The Truthful Organization walks its talk. The organization supports truth at every level. It encourages individuals to clarify, declare, and live out their personal truths. It promotes ongoing development of interpersonal communication skills to sustain healthy working relationships, working agreements, conflict resolution, and individual responsibility. The Truthful Organization encourages teams to be high-performing, including the ability to organize themselves, set priorities, make decisions, and resolve breakdowns.

The Truthful Organization walks its talk. The organization supports truth at every level. It encourages individuals to clarify, declare, and live out their personal truths. It promotes ongoing development of interpersonal communication skills to sustain healthy working relationships, working agreements, conflict resolution, and individual responsibility. A Truthful Organization encourages teams to be high-performing, including the ability to organize themselves, set priorities, make decisions, and resolve breakdowns.

How organizations promote truthfulness:

- Develop a clear, compelling vision involving individuals from every level of the organization.
- Reward truthful behaviors—especially among change-leaders—at all levels.
- Develop an organizational structure that supports truthful alignment of all stakeholders.
- Share good, bad, and sensitive information within the organization: Technical, marketing, and financial information is shared openly and freely along with appropriate training necessary to interpret this information and make it meaningful.

Let's look at these one by one.

While many business leaders doubt the importance of a vision, few have invested the necessary effort to make it work by getting everyone's buy-in.

I. Develop a clear, compelling vision involving individuals from every level of the organization.

Many organizations have a vision or mission statement neatly printed and proudly displayed on the wall of the corporate reception area. Some companies print it on business cards, products, and posters in every office. However, few organizations do more than write and distribute the document. Most employees could not tell you what is in the vision. Even if they know, few employees attach any significance to it. Some organizations have never seriously considered generating a long-range vision. While many business leaders doubt the importance of a vision, few have invested the necessary effort to make it work by getting everyone's buy-in.

So the cycle goes on and the cynic's prophecy is fulfilled; visions get written, posted, and everyone looks at it tongue in cheek ... nothing changes. These methods are not genuine, truthful ways of implementing a company vision.

To truthfully build a vision, individuals from all levels of the organization and key stakeholders must be involved from the start. Instead of the CEO or an executive committee managing the whole process, they should join a task force with people representing every level and faction of the organization. The task force carries more credibility if its membership is well balanced by executives, managers, and staff. Equally important issues to balance are gender, tenure, and departments within the organization.

This task force determines the best process for creating, distributing, and utilizing the company vision. The process we prefer at the Venture Centre is one that uses 12 to 24 people from every level and all special interest areas of the organization. Several days are set aside for the activity which is designed to first break down communication barriers then build trust before proceeding. This *vision task force* becomes a prototype of a truthful team; it is a *de facto* role model for the rest of the organization. We move the team through the four stages of development as quickly as possible. This preliminary work pays off as the more high-performing the team, the more effective its ability to craft a vision for the rest of the organization.

Many experts believe a vision should be written to last a full century. So it is critical that no stone be left unturned as the team explores the limits of possibility. The more diverse the group, the greater the number of ideas that will emerge. Let the conversation stray. Do not be afraid of even fringe ideas!

The next step involves the team in an active process of envisioning the future. This may involve some or all of the following activities:

- *Define* the scope, history, and critical factors influencing the business
- *Research* social, economic, technical, and geo-political trends
- *Analyze* emerging ideologies and trends which may have long -range implications
- *Profile* the historical, current, and potential market; clarify existing and future customers

This foreground work is conducted and facilitated against a background of teambuilding, truthful communication, and situational leadership skill building.

Whatever method is used, it is critical that the blinders are removed during the visioning process. Many experts believe a vision should be written to last a full century.

Free Speech ...?

A conversation that strays may have interesting consequences. Working on an Indian reservation, we were using a visioning process that involved the creation of three future scenarios by the vision team. One was optimistic, one pessimistic, and the third, likely. In the midst of discussing the most pessimistic of all futures, the tribal chairman, Jay Taken Alive, walked in with an entourage of skeptical observers. They heard this:

The scenario described a time in the future when gang warfare, normally associated with big cities had come to the reservation. Not only had trust in law and order across the U.S. collapsed, but tribal government had disintegrated into armed camps with no central control. Property was in jeopardy, lives were at stake, and safety belonged to those with weapons.

Taken out of context, it looked like every crazy negative cliché about Native Americans. The chairman's face looked grim. He said, "This cannot be our future, it is our past. It is what this reservation was like just 100 years ago, when our grandparents were slaughtered here and at Wounded Knee." Even though most of the team members were Native Americans, he was not impressed. We all felt embarrassed. What could we say?

Ultimately, this scenario became part of the organization's vision statement—focusing its energy on safety and security for guests and employees. Everyone on the team got a deep visceral understanding of how important the security of guests and the safety of staff is to the overall success of the enterprise.

I learned the importance of managing access to workshops by guests, especially VIP guests. **During workshops, guests are welcome, but their observation needs to be managed and debriefed by someone who understands the nature of the workshop and the relationships between involved parties.**

So it is critical that no stone be left unturned as the team explores the limits of possibility. The more diverse the group, the greater the number of ideas that will emerge. Let the conversation stray. Do not be afraid of even fringe ideas!

The more the conversation is permitted to stray, the more important it is to have a process to gather ideas, values, and priorities from the team, weaving them into a succinct document. Since teams are generally not effective at "wordsmithing," select three volunteers to work on separate drafts. Have them come together and iron out the differences. Appoint one to write a final draft to submit to the whole team. The final result is a carefully crafted document for which each member of the task force can take ownership and passionately support.

During the next phase, pairs of task force members take the document into the organization to display as a "work in progress." Suggestions and input for improvement are solicited. A strategy should be developed to allow every member to provide input. Two questions must be asked of every person: "Is anything missing?" "Can you support and live out this vision?"

Once the input has been gathered, the task force meets again to synthesize the results and publish the final vision statement. Upon publication, and in another meeting facilitated by both a supervisor and a task force representative, every member of the organization is asked to do three things:

1. Decide whether living the organizational vision will serve his or her own personal mission. If not, each is asked to make the necessary adjustments or acknowledge this may not be the best place to work. *(This is not to say people should be put on the spot, judged, or in any way forced to leave. This is about helping people accept responsibility for their own happiness)*
2. Agree to support the vision and focus personal resources toward making the vision real.
3. Use the vision as authority for planning, decision making, and actions in the absence of conflicting specific directions.

With few exceptions, people at higher levels in the organization exhibit the most fear and offer the least trust.

II. Reward truthful behaviors, especially among change leaders, at all levels of the organization.

Within the Truthful Organization, behaviors that serve truthfulness must be acknowledged and rewarded. The greatest challenge is for managers at higher levels of the infrastructure. They have many reasons for choosing not to go along. Their commitment to truth may be as great as anyone's but, like many, they may view change as a loss. These people have worked their way up the ladder playing by the old rules. Now they are told the rules have changed. For most people, this is difficult to hear. As a result, some managers will need special guidance during implementation. With few exceptions, people at higher levels in the organization exhibit the most fear and offer the least trust.

To make truth work, everyone must know exactly how the rules have changed and what is expected. Behavioral requirements go way beyond technical skills. Each person must learn the new etiquette. Edicts are not enough; a program of training, reading, coaching, or mentoring must be instituted. Although it need not be expensive or elaborate, it must be well planned and part of a comprehensive long-term strategy to shift the existing fields.

To organize the company in a truthful manner, each individual, team, work group, and department must be mobilized to support the mission of each individual and team while moving collectively toward the organization's vision.

Finally, the organization may need to be reorganized from one that favors parental, political, command and control management systems to one that values collaboration, honesty, and direct communication. In some organizations, this involves a dramatic reevaluation of the company's structure. Systems that pit individuals against one another or force departments to compete for resources do not serve a truthful environment.

At the bottom line is compensation. Organizations get what they pay for. Individual compensation must reward technical excellence, productivity, *and* truthful behavior.

Pay for performance may be the wave of the future, but it must be seen in a wider perspective—beyond simple productivity. In addition to productivity, performance may also describe participation, learning, leadership, and attitude. Make sure performance is managed according to a comprehensive plan that supports individual, team, department, and organizational goals. Lastly, ensure that the compensation program supports the vision and values of the organization, including profitability, personal motivation, continuous improvement, and learning.

III. Develop an organizational structure that supports truthful alignment among all stakeholders.

To organize the company in a truthful manner, each individual, team, work group, and department must be mobilized to support the mission of each individual and team while moving collectively toward the organization's vision. In the Truthful Organization, there is no time for petty squabbles between the marketing and engineering department or finance and sales. Real conflicts must be dealt with openly and directly for the good of the organization. The most difficult challenge is unifying the discrete groups and individuals into a cohesive team, conflicts and all. Every iota of energy wasted with internal squabbles diminishes overall effectiveness. Yet truthfulness is much more than teambuilding; it is a redefinition of roles, responsibilities, and boundaries. Above all, it is using new tools to craft a new way of working together.

As discussed earlier, an organization is an intricate network of relationships. Each element is interrelated. The glue that binds all these components together varies from one company to another. It may be personal ambition, money, shared vision, tradition, pride, fear, duty, team spirit, or others. What is most important is the degree to which these factors contribute to a **shared vision**. In most organizations, they do not. They compete, operating simultaneously and at cross-purposes, representing the personal biases of individuals, small groups, and other factions.

Few departments willfully compete with each other. Most interdepartmental conflicts result from differing interpretations of the vision and its priorities. In other words, the vision is not actually *shared*. Every organization has some kind of vision—it may be written or informal. Unfortunately, most are so general as to be vague. The problem with vague intentions, is the lack of agreement about implementation. How one department achieves customer satisfaction may be at odds with another. This is why shared vision is so critical. All factions must agree not only on the vision, but on the means to make it real.

It is a lack of agreement about the means of achieving a vision more than disagreement on the quality of the vision which typically results in inefficiencies due to rigid boundaries, internal competition, and turf wars. Beyond shared vision, the organization must be structured in a way that supports both the vision and the strategy. This structure seldom looks like a textbook organization chart. The Truthful Organization takes proactive steps to develop a planned organizational structure. Truthful leaders know that, in the absence of an intentional structure, an extemporaneous structure evolves spontaneously—remember the trellis and the ivy!

It is a lack of agreement about the means of achieving a vision more than disagreement on the quality of the vision which typically results in inefficiencies due to rigid boundaries, internal competition, and turf wars.

The Truthful Organization takes proactive steps to develop a planned organizational structure. Truthful leaders know that, in the absence of an intentional structure, an extemporaneous structure evolves spontaneously—remember the trellis and the ivy!

IV. Share good, bad, and sensitive information: Technical, marketing, and financial information is shared openly, delivered with any training needed to interpret this information and make it meaningful.

There is no such thing as conversation. It is an illusion. There are intersecting monologues, that is all.
—Rebecca West

If relationships form the structure of the Truthful Organization, information is its lifeblood. However, people often take the saying "knowledge is power" literally by constricting the flow of information to build a personal power base.

There are many justifications for keeping information secret; few stand the test of scrutiny. The three I've heard most often are:

- The information may fall into the wrong hands.
- They won't be able to understand and may draw the wrong conclusion.
- They'll never offer to work for less, but every time we show a profit, they'll be there with open palms.

Ultimately, these justifications are fear-based. Executives fear competitors will get their hands on the information and use it against the company. They are afraid investors, creditors, or even staff may misinterpret the data. The greed of workers may deplete hard-earned margins, resulting in a need for executives to reduce the size of the workforce.

Who is there to fear?

Competitors—Information *can* be used against you. But most companies are inappropriately paranoid. After all, who knows better than the competition what it costs to do what you do? Specific financial data is easily obtained from industry sources, Dunn & Bradstreet, annual reports, and former employees. If competitors can benefit from intimate knowledge about your business, they probably already have it.

Creditors—If you owe money to someone who hasn't already asked the tough questions, I want the name and phone number! Creditors demand accurate and comprehensive information. Failing to fully disclose all pertinent information may be prosecutable as fraud!

Customers—I have heard the price of some products such as soda pop, soap, and breakfast cereal are largely due to advertising and packaging costs—not the actual product. The value of some products has less to do with raw materials and labor and more to do with marketing, distribution, and packaging.

On the surface, it makes sense. It is risky to let customers know that, of the four dollars they pay for a product, only 12 cents goes to the cost of materials while a dollar is needed for marketing and 50 cents for packaging.

However, there are many situations in which customers routinely pay prices they know do not reflect the cost of materials: fine restaurants, designer clothing, wine and spirits, specialty products, convenience stores, cigarettes, tourist services, entertainment, art, etc.

In the example above, does the manufacturer spend a dollar on marketing and 50 cents on packaging for the fun of it ... or in order to compete? If spending this money is necessary to sell a 12-cent item, then the basic cost of the item is not 12 cents, but a $1.62. Splitting the remaining $2.38 between overhead, profit, distribution, and a retailer's mark-up completes a realistic scenario. Let's say the bottom-line profit to the manufacturer for the four-dollar item is 50 centss (a generous profit margin in many businesses). That is more than 10 percent of the price of the product. How many customers would balk at such a figure?

Surveys repeatedly indicate customers believe manufacturers earn too much and take advantage of consumers. However, the same research often indicates those same customers believe manufacturers actually earn more on their products than they do. The

Who Are We Fooling?

One of my first jobs was as a stock clerk in the camera department at Halsey & Griffith, Inc., a high-end office supply and specialty store. To this day, I remember the cost code I had to inscribe on every item. Letters were substituted for numbers. This way the sales person could tell at a glance the cost of the item. The letters we used were MWSYLKBVDZ, an anagram of, "Mr. Waugh's silk BVDs" (Mr. Waugh, being the elderly owner of the store). Years later as a customer, I was still able to read the cost code, but it did not deter me from making purchases. How could I begrudge the company for generating an operating margin? Does anyone really think stores sell merchandise for the same price they pay for it?

fact is, customers have been kept in the dark and typically believe they are being ripped off. Is this the cost of secrets?

Even in retailing where the margin is typically the highest, the costs of store rent, salaries, advertising, insurance, and other expenses eat away at every penny of gross profit. There is one situation when keeping information from the customer makes sense. When (never in a Truthful Organization) the customer is being taken advantage of, that information should not be shared. How long can you expect to keep customers if they know they are being ripped off?

Data without understanding generates misinformation which can be worse than no information at all.

Unfortunately, many managers (and even entrepreneurs) are unsure how their business operates. Without the big picture and training to comprehend it, a customer, competitor, or creditor can take one fact out of context and misconstrue its significance. Consider the four-dollar product scenario. On one hand, the company is only making a small profit, but notice that the 50-cent net profit is 400 percent greater than the cost of materials. That sounds greedy when taken out of context.

How many managers and employees see only enough data to draw the wrong conclusion about their own business? If a manager believes the company is making a 400 percent profit, the executive's demand for reduced costs would seem nitpicky and misplaced. If the manager were tempted to tell the staff about costs, it would be difficult to defend the 400 percent markup—so keeping the whole thing under wraps seems preferable. Data without understanding generates misinformation which can be worse than no information at all.

Many sales people describe situations in which they "open the books" and show a customer the real costs associated with a sale. Amazingly, this maneuver often results in a sale. Customers do not want to be ripped off, but neither do they want you, their supplier, to go out of business.

In conclusion, customers have little interest in the internal workings or financial structure of your business. They are looking for value, availability, reliability, service, and a good relationship with their supplier. If they find out your costs, make sure they learn the whole picture, not a tainted part from a disgruntled and misinformed employee or competitor.

Employees—The primary argument against sharing information with employees is security. There is a fear that employees cannot be trusted to keep this information out of the hands of creditors, competitors, or customers. I find it fascinating that many defense contractors routinely share information vital to the security of the nation but still keep basic financial information under wraps.

How can a company justify allowing an employee to greet customers, handle cash, and resolve customer complaints but NOT trust them with financial information?

In the final analysis, most resistance comes from a fear of sharing power—not information. The decision to hold on to information must be weighed against the consequences.

For Managers' Eyes Only

When people are deprived of facts, it is human nature for them to make assumptions. If you, as a manager, have wondered how rumors get started and why people believe the unbelievable, you know firsthand one of the costs of controlling information. When people feel they are not trusted, they are naturally demotivated. If you, as a manager, have ever asked yourself why employees cannot get the connection between what they do and its effect on the business, you may assume the culprit is a lack of information, comprehension of that information, or both which creates the gap.

When doors are closed, whispers are heard, papers are shredded, and secrets are kept, you can expect employees will feel insecure, fearful, and even paranoid. Any worker will tell you the usual reason managers hunker down and close the doors is to keep the bad news (lay offs, downsizing, shut-down, bankruptcy, etc.) from employees so production does not plummet.

Win/Win Rescue, Tokyo Style

"Nissan gets control of troubled Fuji." This is the lead in a *New York Times* article, dated June 27, 1990. When Subaru's maker, Fuji Heavy Industries, Ltd., experienced trouble, instead of bankruptcy or a feeding frenzy by competing sharks, Subaru was not allowed to fail; that's what happens in Japan when a company the size of Fuji gets into trouble. It is potentially too disruptive to the lives of the workers and economy.

Control of Fuji was handed over to Japan' second-largest car maker, the Nissan Motor Company. The whole thing was very discreet. Great care was given to make sure no one would lose face or be embarrassed. Amazingly, not a single share of stock was part of the deal, and the Subaru brand was not jeopardized.

If your business is not going down the tubes and secrets are still rampant, consider what assumptions are being made and what rumors are floating around behind your back.

If the company is going under, consider why you are so much more capable of handling the bad news than they. More than one manager has been surprised by teams rallying to the support of the organization. In its ultimate expression, employees have successfully bought out organizations as large as United Airlines. No matter how well-intentioned, your effort to protect your employees may not be well received. People like to feel they have control over their own destinies. Managers need to ask themselves how they would feel if someone were playing such a parental role in their life.

What if the numbers are just bad?

Maybe your company is not going under, but the numbers are bad. Many managers feel bad numbers demotivate the staff. There is certainly some truth in this, but more often than not, the number shared is a single indicator: quota, margin, or expense figure. Rarely are employees given the whole picture and the instructions necessary to understand the whole picture.

Information is the oxygen of the modern age. It seeps through the walls topped by barbed wire, it wafts across the electrified borders.

—Ronald Reagan

Instead, the department gets a memo calling a stand-up meeting where they are told expenses are too high, the department is running in the red, and the old man upstairs is mad as hell. Normally, at least a few employees suspect the increased expenses are due to the selection of a new vendor for a key component. The resulting rumor sounds like, "We will be penalized because the boys upstairs selected a new vendor which drove our costs up ... there's no way to win around here." A manager who assumes that bad news results in poor morale is drawing a hasty conclusion.

If the manager really shared information, he or she would present the facts to the employees and invite everyone's participation in improving the situation. A task force could find out exactly where the cost increases are coming from and how to improve things. Notice that this scenario illustrates why information is not necessarily the problem—rather, sharing power is the manager's greatest challenge.

What can you do?

If you are not a high-placed manager or executive in your company, you may feel you have little influence on the structure of the organization. However, in the discussion of personal, interpersonal, team- and organizational fields in Chapters Two and Three, you will recall that every individual in the organization supports those fields. Every person who chooses to remain in an organization makes a tangible commitment to the status quo. Asking clarifying questions, giving feedback to the nominal leaders of the organization, and proposing alternative solutions are important ways you can bring about lasting change in a field.

This book began comparing bottom-up organizational change to a revolution. Most people will not take up the standard and invest their energy in changing the organization in which they work. But some will. If you are not willing to be the leader, search for one. No matter what level of the organization you are in, you can create a Truth Zone. You can selectively invite others to join you. We should never underestimate the impact a small group of people can have on an organization.

When Personal Mission and Organizational Vision Combine

While consulting with a firm for several months, I became aware of a disturbing trend. As long as I was there to coach and support them, they moved ahead. When I was not with them, they seemed to backslide.

Months later, I was asked to return to help them get back on track. Individual and team performance had diminished, affecting the company's financial situation. The prevailing wisdom leaned in the direction of more skill-building and greater control-based accountability. I had a different perspective. I told them team members needed to face their personal commitment, passion, and purpose.

We worked with the leadership team. We helped each individual define and declare a personal mission. Each session was heartfelt and opened deeper levels of communication, trust, and interpersonal understanding. While people were initially timid and hesitant to share personal insights, a number of "coaches" emerged;. Each modeled enthusiasm, strength, and clarity of purpose.

As a result, they acknowledged their improvement and cited the following concrete examples: personal commitment; trust increased; fun increased; creativity and clarity of purpose improved; and planning and decision making became streamlined.

—Gail Hoag,
Partner
Venture Centre

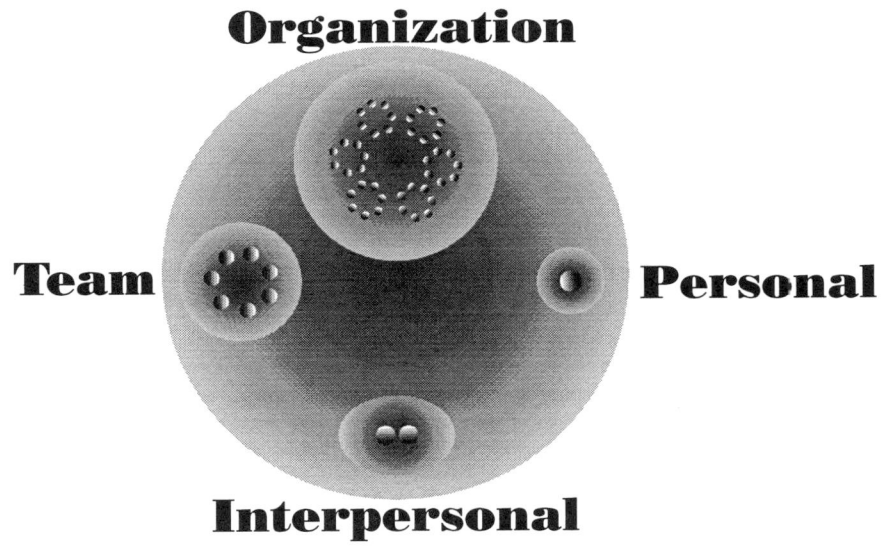

Organization

Team

Personal

Interpersonal

Section Three

Practical Applications

Section III: Practical Applications

The following chapters offer practical information to help people and teams committed to building Truth Zones and leading the revolution in the organization. Chapter Eight focuses on the roles people play and a new way of looking at leadership. Chapter Nine examines special situations in which building truth may offer special challenges. Chapter Ten moves beyond a philosophical approach to the revolution and brings it to every worker in every department. It also deals with personal and organizational accountability. Finally, Chapter Eleven offers a variety of experiential activities, building blocks and tools to help you build a more Truthful Organization.

Chapter Eight

Lead, Follow, AND Get Out Of The Way!

Lead, Follow, AND Get Out of the Way

Organizations in the last decade have increased margins in the cheapest, most unimaginative and heartless manner possible—by downsizing. This is not to say organizations had not grown fat, lazy, and unproductive; they had. But gutless, fear-driven managers by the score took the easiest route to turn around profits. The cost of these so-called turn-arounds was borne on the backs of tens of thousands of displaced families, broken hearts, and tarnished egos. Was there not another way?

In retrospect, upper management must accept responsibility in fostering untruthful, if not out-and-out dishonest, corporate cultures in which workers were implicitly told: "Trust our stewardship. We can manage the big picture; just do what you are told. If you do that, you will have a job for life." These same leaders expanded their egos while *growing* their departments—swollen with layers of superfluous managers and bureaucracy. And then, when the numbers started to look bad, how many managers took decisive, rapid action? Instead they buried their heads in the sand. Others blamed the problem on those Democrats or those Republicans or those foreigners or those damn customers. Others were so far in denial that they mortgaged their futures to pay for their mistakes—holding on to a dilapidated, top-heavy, overstaffed superstructure until there was "no choice" but to downsize.

God offers to every mind its choice between truth and repose. Take which you please; you can never have both.
—Ralph Waldo Emerson

Why was there no other choice? Why wasn't it possible to see the inevitable and detach some of the workforce to work their last year, six months, or three weeks on innovative ways to cope with the problems faced by the organization? As basic as this solution appears, most people were laid off with little or no notice. Not only were they not trusted with this critical information so they could begin planning for themselves—but tens of thousands of people were never considered a problem-solving resource.

Organizations are made up of people, not things. As long as owners consider people a liability and equipment an asset, they will continue to operate without integrity, perpetuating a lack of truth and trust in the workplace.

For many organizations, the recent downsizing is but the latest chapter in a history of expanding and contracting. Yet as they begin hiring people, they tell them the same old lies. "Don't worry about the future; we'll take care of the big picture; you just do your job. If you stick with the plan, you've got a job for life ..." No wonder so many workers are disillusioned. How can executives go through a major downsizing and then immediately begin to repeat the process? They make superficial changes, but the organizational field continues unperturbed, and therefore unchanged!

A handful of organizations faced with similar circumstances chose to be truthful. They did not try to save face by keeping the hard truths from their employees. In these organizations, staff offered to voluntarily cut back on salaries. Some workers actually purchased the company; others developed new markets for old products; still others developed new products for old markets.

Organizations are made up of people, not things. As long as owners consider people a liability and equipment an asset, they will continue to operate without integrity, perpetuating a lack of truth and trust in the workplace.

In business, like life, there are no guarantees.

Truthful Organizations must operate in as open an atmosphere as possible. They must create a full partnership with staff and not make unrealistic promises. In business, like life, there are no guarantees. Promising jobs for life or bonuses every year do staff the greatest disservice by robbing people of their self-reliance and fostering inappropriate dependency. Truthful Organizations need to help employees empower themselves. One powerful way organizations can move in this direction is to acknowledge the transience of the relationship between a given worker and an organization. Forget the retirement plan—make it mobile. Rarely do employees plan to retire from the company where they currently work. Even more importantly, build a culture in which leadership is situational; everyone (including managers) is willing to follow and anyone can take themselves out of the game for the good of the organization. In other words ... *"Lead, follow, AND get out of the way."*

I have no idea how "truthful" Chrysler was as an organization under Lee Iacocca's hand. Likewise, I have no way of knowing the context in which the words he made famous were spoken. Nevertheless, these eight words, "lead, follow, or get out of the way," could be the anthem of participants in the Truthful Organization.

To LEAD means something quite different in the Truthful Organization than it does elsewhere. For one thing, it is not exclusive; everyone must be prepared to assume a leadership role. And every leader must be willing to FOLLOW—even bosses! When it is impossible to lead or follow, it is necessary to GET OUT OF THE WAY. Either step aside while others follow through, or literally get out of the organization.

At any given moment, people in the organization will find themselves in one of these three levels of participation. It is everyone's responsibility to facilitate a natural flow of participation between all three states.

The old way of doing business was to have managers assigned the responsibility of leadership. Their job was *controlling* the actions of subordinates. Leaders led, subordinates followed, and if anyone needed to get out of the way, it was the leader's job to remove them. In Truthful Organizations, all groups must be *leaderful*. That is, everyone must be willing to assume leadership. Everyone must be willing to follow. All team members must be personally responsible for their participation and ability to add value. Moreover, *all* members of the team must monitor the ebb and flow of team participation. If someone seems to be holding back, yet has not declared themselves "out of the way," it is the responsibility of *anyone* involved to check in with that team member and facilitate participation. "You seem to be holding back ... I need to know how you are participating ... are you checked out ... would you let us know what's going on?"

All employees must work to create an atmosphere in which everyone feels safe enough to shift levels of participation. When a leader senses their efforts are losing effectiveness,

How Are We Feeling Today?

I once worked in a large non-profit community healthcare corporation. Two outside consultants were hired to design and implement a "change" program to improve quality and employee morale. They suggested that all of this be done with an employee "steering committee," selected by employees. The steering committe did not have any administrative personnel as members. Optimistic hope became cynicism and outright rebellion when this committee began meeting in secret and discussing the effectiveness of individual departments. Eventually the committee recommended changes in departments that were completely unrealistic and inappropriate. It was no wonder, there were no representatives on the committee from those departments. The total cost was in excess of $780,000. In two years it was a total failure.

—Name withheld

As long as people are frightened of losing their jobs, they cannot be full participants in the Truthful Organization.

It benefits the organization that each employee knows his or her worth—and that it's sufficient to make each person independent enough to tell the employer hard truths.

Truth never damages a cause that is just.
—Mohandas K. Gandhi

that leader must be able to step aside and follow another without losing face. At the same moment, followers must be willing to step forward to fill the leadership vacuum without self-doubt, false humility, and "are you sure you want me ... ?" or other attitudes that get in the way. People check in and out many times during any given hour. In the Truthful Organization, it is acceptable to acknowledge this natural phenomenon in others and in ourselves. So "getting out of the way" does not necessarily mean leaving the organization. It is usually a temporary situation in which a person's attention wanders or enthusiasm stumbles.

Some people permanently check out and continue to collect a paycheck. As described earlier, these people are in a painful place; their choice to *stay and suffer* keeps them "between a rock and hard place." On the one hand, they are cynical about the organization and full of resentments that make it impossible to fully participate. On the other hand, their obligations (real or imagined) outside of work keep them from choosing the healthy, honorable option to get out.

Getting out is a painful and frightening option. Most people live paycheck to paycheck. Being without a paycheck is like being adrift at sea—it can be devastating. The possibility that employees and their dependent families could be on the street is an eventuality few are willing to honestly contemplate. But contemplate it, they must!

Yet, for most people, there is nothing more empowering than learning they need not be dependent on others for their livelihood. Organizations of old fostered dependence by playing a parental role in the lives of workers. Large-scale layoffs by so many organizations represent a failure of *parental* responsibility. Ironically, unions have lost ground for the same reason—adult workers do not need parents; they need partners. Today, organizations and workers must find common ground to build working relationships based on mutual interests. For individuals to build mutual (instead of dependent) relationships, people must see themselves as a free agents. (See Chapter

Four.) The only way people can see themselves as free agents is to contemplate being unattached, unemployed, down and out ... what then?

As long as the fear of losing one's job equates with a loss of safety, health, esteem, love, and family, fear will be the dominant issue whenever a moment of truth arises. Nothing can undermine a person's integrity, alignment, and passion more than fear. As long as people are frightened of losing their jobs, they cannot be full participants in the Truthful Organization.

Removing fear is a job for the individual AND the organization. The organization needs to carefully assess and monitor the worth of each job and the specific value of each employee. That information needs to be shared openly and honestly with each employee on a regular basis. It benefits the organization that each employee know his or her worth—and that it's sufficient to make each person independent enough to tell the employer hard truths.

Beyond a careful and objective assessment system, a personal and professional development plan must be co-created with each employee to add to the value and marketability of that employee.

Supervisors — Lead, Follow, or Get...

I believe supervisors at every level get a "bum rap." People think their supervisor has unlimited power and is accountable to no one. In reality, every level of management is between another one of those "rocks and a hard place." Even the CEO presumably has a board, creditors, or at least customers to answer to. Perhaps the squeeze that managers are under accounts for the increasing levels of fear and rigidity that characterize most hierarchies.

Not withstanding Dr. Deming's certainty that the only way to get things done is by working with the TOP boss, I do not agree. I have come to believe the people at the lower levels of the organization are more eager to embrace change and, when given tools, have more power than they know.

Ya'll Come

There are two ways of looking at the staffing of an organization. One is like hosting the *party*. You decorate, put out food, and send out a guest list to the best people you know. You judge the quality of the party largely by how long people stay.

The other way of populating an organization is the *pied piper on the sidewalk* method. When you start playing the flute, some people naturally fall into step. They join the caravan and walk a while. Some join, some stay, some leave—as long as the piper plays. People make a deliberate choice to follow or leave. It is no coincidence that parties end. But as long as the piper's tune is sweet, people will follow, blending fresh ideas with the old.

As a supervisor, if you believe you are the exception instead of the rule, I challenge you to *Get Out Of The Way*. If that sounds too drastic and flies in the face of everything you know about people, your business, and your industry, you prove the rule. At this point you may feel compelled to maintain your control over all subordinates.

If, however, you are the exception, your response is probably in the form of a question ... exactly what does it mean to get out of the way? It does not mean abrogating your responsibility or being unethical. It means asking yourself how much of what you do as supervisor is really necessary. How much of your job could your subordinates do, even better? And wouldn't it be less expensive for them to do it instead of you?

The greatest obstacle to personal truth is a personal field characterized by self-doubt and cynicism. If people do not believe in themselves, they cannot believe in others or the capacity of the organization to change.

Make a Detailed List of Your Job Tasks

Leave ample room on the right and left margins next to your list. For the purposes of this activity, put company regulations and policies aside—consider only people's abilities. In the left-hand margin, put a check mark after each task a subordinate could (with some training) perform without you. In the right-hand column, place a check after each task ONLY you or your supervisor can do.

In the many situations where I have administered this activity, most supervisors admit that most tasks they perform could be performed by someone else. But they do not TRUST the quality of the work or the dedication to the total job. Supervisors have trouble trusting subordinates; unfortunately, it sets up a self-fulfilling prophecy. If you do not trust someone, they rarely disappoint you. With a little introspection, most supervisors conclude that the old system—the field in which workers need supervision—perpetuates the myth that supervisors must be smarter and more technically capable than subordinates. If the primary responsibility of a supervisor was to teach subordinates, encouraging them to be self-reliant and personally responsible, things would be different. So the question is ... *could* a subordinate perform a specific task with the right training, encouragement and support?

In every instance when the answer is yes, the responsibility of a supervisor is to provide that training, encouragement, and support.

Let's assume that there are few, if any, check marks in the "Only You" column. What would happen if you took this list to your boss, or your boss's boss? The CEO? Does the culture in your organization encourage this level of truth? Even if it does not, you can begin, in your own department, with your subordinates to set up a Truth Zone.

In the Truthful Organization, the role of supervision shifts from command and control to a range of new behaviors including: coaching, teaching, coordinating, and facilitating. Supervisors work for their subordinates. They clear the decks and get out of the way, encouraging subordinates to reach their fullest potential by adding value to the organization. These new behaviors are ways supervisors continue to add value while off-loading and delegating more responsibility to subordinates.

In the Truthful Organization, the role of supervision shifts from command and control to a range of new behaviors including: coaching, teaching, coordinating, and facilitating. Supervisors work for their subordinates. They clear the decks and get out of the way, encouraging subordinates to reach their fullest potential by adding value to the organization. These new behaviors are ways supervisors continue to add value while off-loading and delegating more responsibility to subordinates.

Non-supervisors — Lead, Follow, or Get...

In essence, this whole book is aimed at non-supervisors who see work as an opportunity to express themselves by enhancing teamwork and improving productivity in the organization. The seven steps discussed in prior chapters are the keys for personal growth and development.

The greatest obstacle to personal truth is a personal field characterized by self-doubt and cynicism. If people do not believe in themselves, they cannot believe in others or the capacity of the organization to change. On the other hand, those who do believe in themselves and have hope the organization can change have already learned important skills to facilitate building a Truth Zone in their environment. As soon as a people begin working the seven steps, they ever so slightly remove themselves from the team- and organizational field. That alteration to the team field perturbs the field and causes waves—waves that will return with force, splashing cold water in the face of anyone so bold as to step outside the norm. Becoming a change leader is a sobering and sometimes painful experience.

Be kind to supervisors.

This may be a revolution, but it is not about changing an organization against its own vision.

The best way to proceed is slowly, but always continuously. It's like getting into a cold mountain lake. Do not put one toe in and run back to the shore. Move steadily and build momentum. And most importantly, gather others to accompany you in your Truth Zone.

Get people together. Discuss this book. Practice the tools described in the companion tools workbook. Map out a strategy to guide the revolution. Don't be afraid to look beyond your immediate workgroup or even one or two levels above you. Build a team of individuals with shared values and a shared vision. Build a team-field within the organizational field of the company.

Be kind to supervisors. No supervisor has as much power as it seems—every supervisor has a supervisor. Being a supervisor is a very difficult position. It is a constant struggle to balance the interests of those above with those below while managing personal values and the ultimate interest of the organization and the customer—all at the same time. While some supervisors are willing to get out of the way, others won't. Accordingly, you and your Truth Zone must be prepared to develop a "work around" strategy. Remember, proceed carefully, thoughtfully, and with compassion. This may be a revolution, but it is not about changing an organization against its own vision.

Chapter Nine

Special Cases:

TQM, Customer Focus, Small Businesses, Large Bureaucracies, Untruthful Environments, Sales Organizations

SPECIAL CASES:
TQM, Customer-Focused Sales & Marketing, Small Businesses, Large Bureaucracies, and Untruthful Environments

There are two ways the Truthful Organization is typically deployed. One is the traditional route, at the invitation of upper management. The other, unique to the Truthful Organization, is from the bottom up—championed by one or more individuals committed to making a difference.

As may be expected, some environments are more "truth-friendly" than others. Certain environments present special challenges and opportunities.

Total Quality Management

Although Dr. W. Edwards Deming is popularly considered the father of quality, he is not quality's only proponent. Others include Dr. Walter A. Shewhart, Dr. Kaouru Ishikawa, and Dr. Joseph Juran, to name but a few. Dr. Deming's systems view of quality was unique because he elevated quality above the mundane procedure of measures and processes. His system of "profound knowledge" gave quality a broad-based conceptual framework, resulting in principles that took quality out of the exclusive hands of engineers and made it a management tool. Unfortunately, too few managers are using the tools at hand. Consequently, most quality programs do not yield measurable results for the company.

Perpetual devotion to what a man calls his business is only to be sustained by neglect of many other things.
—Robert Louis Stevenson

If the quality deployment program cannot demonstrate personal benefits for each and every member of the organization, then personal participation is compromised and the overall success of the program may be doomed.

The challenge to quality initiatives continues to be buy-in from the people. To understand this problem, we can look at two levels. On one level, it is generally understood that those people who champion quality within the organization are often "left-brain" analytical, scientific, engineering types who may not have highly developed communication and people skills. This explanation is widely accepted, but seems to lack depth.

A deeper understanding leads us back to the notion of the organizational field. When quality is introduced into a field, it naturally upsets the equilibrium. Whether it takes hold has more to do with how the upset is managed. If the waves are allowed to reverberate back and forth across the field, then everyone's personal field is affected. In other words, when quality is introduced to the whole organization in one fell swoop rather than phased in, the drama goes up. People pay attention and cannot avoid getting involved. But that involvement can take two forms: resistance or acceptance. The choice between embracing quality or resisting it is personal. If the quality deployment program cannot demonstrate personal benefits for each and every member of the organization, then personal participation is compromised and the overall success of the program may be doomed.

Unfortunately, most quality deployments are phased in to avoid disrupting productivity and workflow (mistake one - field disruption is minimal), and they are presented as a system that will improve quality for customers and ultimately increase profits (mistake two - what's in it for the worker?). What workers hear is more work for them and more profits for the owners. In between the lines, workers feel nervous with every "improvement initiative." What if my job is no longer needed?

Even if the deployment is compelling and the deployment personalized, another hurdle must still be overcome. Most organizations have a history of top-down (parental) management. When they get involved with quality, they run into cultural resistance. How can workers used to being "policed" by supervisors suddenly evaluate their own work and report their own mistakes? The cat-and-mouse game runs deep; few workers can "fess up" to a supervisor. And how many workers are ready to point out errors made by the supervisor? How does a culture that has valued the right answer and traditionally come down hard on mistakes suddenly make it safe for workers to speak their truth? What is to keep a supervisor from retaliating against a worker who speaks up? (This is why we encourage organizations to install anonymous "truth or ethics hotlines" to afford workers a greater measure of safety.)

The level of quality cannot exceed the level of truth.

In a quality organization, the level of quality cannot exceed the level of truth. As long as there is an incentive for people to be less than honest, no system of data collection is immune to the effects of compromised data. Nor can any system of measurement be both isolated from the influence of tainted data and offer meaningful information about quality and performance. Therefore, all systems are dependent, to some degree, on the integrity and intention of the people within the system.

The Truthful Organization was designed to support a quality deployment program by giving people the tools necessary to create a "quality environment."

Customer-Focused Sales and Marketing

The Truthful Organization approaches sales in a strictly win-win fashion. In the Truthful Organization, people know who their customers are (internal and external) and what they want. They know when it is not possible to give customers what they want. The organization acknowledges the shortcoming—either finding what customers want or suggesting they go elsewhere (even the competition) to fulfill their needs.

The Truthful Organization approaches sales in a strictly win-win fashion. In a Truthful Organization, people know who their customers are (internal and external) and what they want. They know when it is not possible to give customers what they want. The organization acknowledges the shortcoming—either finding what the customers want or suggesting they go elsewhere (even the competition) to fulfill their needs.

The only way to know what your customer wants is to be in relationship. My late friend and sales mentor was Bruce R. Wares. His book, *Partner $ell* is the most cogent, systematic, and truthful work on the way to build a sales organization. He goes beyond relationship by saying every customer should be a partner. While I believe Bruce could sell oil to Saudi Arabia, he says *partners* do not sell what their customer-partners do not need or want. He acknowledges that customers are not loyal. Satisfaction is not enough; he says we must promise a lot and deliver more.

When producers want to know what the public wants, they graph it as curves. When they want to tell the public what to get, they say it in curves.
—*Marshall McLuhan*

My marketing guru is Guy Kawasaki. He wrote, among other books, *The Macintosh Way, How to Drive Your Competition Crazy,* and my favorite, *Selling The Dream*. He is the marketing genius behind the Apple Macintosh. Whatever kind of computer you have, you have probably noticed how people with Macintosh computers have a special gleam in their eye when they talk about them. It's different from the way everyone else talks about computers. What if I told you that the gleam in the eye was planned and engineered by Mr. Kawasaki in his office at Apple Computer? He calls his ideology, "Evangelical Marketing." In his book, *Selling The Dream*, he explains that, as the "Mac Evangelist," it was his job to get people to buy a *dream*, not just a piece of hardware. His ideas led to putting apple decals in each box to allow people to proudly display the Apple logo on bumpers, windows, lockers, book bags, etc. And they did! How many Frigidare, IBM, Mitsubishi, Dow, or Xerox logos have you seen customers promoting? In recent years, many industry observers have said Apple seems to have lost touch with its own dream. If it has, the loss of that asset may be the greatest blow to its solvency. (It could account for speculation regarding the future of the originator of the truly personal computer.)

The challenge for sales organizations is to remain truthful in the process of selling. This represents a major challenge since one of the definitions of the word *sell* is to sell-out and mislead. For many, the essence of selling is to buy cheap and sell high. This is the ultimate, win-lose paradigm.

The Problem With "Customer First" - Don't Go Overboard

There has been a ground swell of "customer first" ideologies emerging. On the surface, this seems like a powerful reminder of who really pays our salaries and a method for keeping people focused on what is important. However, sometimes this *customer first* idea can backfire when taken to an extreme. It is not unusual that a sales clerk or customer service worker tries hard to serve a customer, but to no avail. How many supervisors have come over, without any knowledge of the situation, and berated the clerk in front of other customers?

In the Truthful Organization, there is a line. Staff are not paid to be abused—some customers are unreasonable. It is important to understand an organization is a series of relationships. If one set or class of relationships is held hostage to another class of relationships, the organization is out of balance and in need of truthful alignment.

The vision, values, and policies of the Truthful Organization assure full participation, if not perfect harmony of all concerned. External customers are not treated with any less respect; internal customers and suppliers are elevated to the same high status.

It is an interesting, and not coincidental, fact that the most inexpensive way to survey customer satisfaction is to survey internal staff! There is a direct correlation between employee satisfaction and customer satisfaction. If this evidence continues to be supported with more research, it will become more difficult to hold customers above staff.

The answer is to eliminate the lines that separate classes of stakeholders. It is not that every stakeholder should be on an even par, but each stakeholder's position should be considered. All too often, the interests of one class of stakeholder competes with the interests of others. Typically, the concerns of stockholders, board members, and executives take precedence over employees, customers, and vendors. Yet the ecology of an enterprise is as complex as any living organism. The vision, values, and policies of the Truthful Organization assure full participation, if not perfect harmony, of all concerned. External customers are not treated with any less respect; internal customers and suppliers are elevated to the same high status.

Deploying Truth in a Small Business

Things happen fast. Everyone is overworked and there is no time to put systems into place— "we'll get around to the people stuff after we get bigger." Wrong! Organizations do not substantially change over the course of their lives. If people are unimportant up-front, years later they will continue to be second-class. If there is no time to set up systems in the beginning, there will be less time later. Organizational structure will continue to be vague and ill-defined.

In many ways, introducing truthfulness into a small organization represents the greatest challenge. It is not possible to create a Truth Zone without having a noticeable and dramatic effect on the shared field. Some organizations are so small, a Truth Zone of one can perturb the field and generate big waves. Unfortunately, in small start-up organizations, there is usually a strong, charismatic leader who calls the shots. This person need not be an authoritarian *prima donna* to be an obstacle to the organization. But if systems are not in place to support the flow of information or the delineation of accountability, centralized leadership remains the *de facto* boss!

In a small organization, start at the level of personal truth and relationship building. When workers build working agreements using the TOBACCO model, they (begin to) define themselves in relation to co-workers and supervisors. A structure begins to emerge.

A reading club or series of "brown-bag" book reports can introduce ideas into the team-field at a critical stage in the development of the organization—even if time and money are in short supply.

Bureaucracies

If we did not have such a thing as an airplane today, we would probably create something the size of N.A.S.A. to make one.
—H. Ross Perot

Politics in a bureaucracy is antithetical to truth. While leaders come and go, bureaucracies maintain their integrity ... or lack of it. The meta-field in a bureaucracy is reinforced by layers of conformity supported by expectations, and spoken and unspoken rules.

Transforming a large bureaucracy from the bottom up may take years. To be realistic, it may never change. But the anonymity a large organization affords makes setting up Truth Zones much easier than it is in smaller organizations.

The key to setting realistic expectations about one person's ability to influence a bureaucracy is adjusting the scale of expectation. Assuming one person can directly transform a large cumbersome bureaucracy may be unrealistic. On the other hand, it is possible to create a Truth Zone and enroll others in it. When that happens, for all intents and purposes, your corner of the bureaucracy is changed. While the expectations must be realistic, do not be afraid to think big. If all you want is a congenial work cubicle, you may have trouble enrolling others. On the other hand, the possibility of improving the department, workgroup, or division is big enough to get the attention of others—but perhaps not so grandiose as to elicit ridicule from co-workers. Finally, ridicule or not, "... never underestimate the power of a small group of committed individuals ...".

Untruthful Environments

If only I knew then what I know now. I can recall so many situations that I should have had the courage to avoid. Clients, partnerships, relationships, customers, jobs ... in every regretful case, I was able to rationalize my participation because of some higher good ... to pay my bills, finish what I started, pay my dues.

The people always have some champion whom they set over them and nurse into greatness. . . . This and no other is the root from which a tyrant springs; when he first appears he is a protector.
—Plato

In genuinely untruthful organizations, setting up Truth Zones can be perilous. If dishonesty is part of the organizational field, imagine the impact of merely putting up a Truth Zone sign— "What is the meaning of this? What are you trying to say? Are you suggesting that we aren't truthful around here?"

If you find yourself in an untruthful environment or an immoral, unethical, or illegal enterprise ... Do something! If your company has an ethics hotline, use it. Have the courage of conviction to do what is right. If you are staying because others depend on you, make sure you are honestly acting on their behalf. Check it out. Ask your spouse, your kids, or other dependents if they want you to remain where you are, given the conditions under which you toil. Explore worst-case scenarios. Can your family (team) pull together to help you through this trial, or must you remain in a place of suffering, adrift without help? There are few stories more tragic than the marriage of assumptions never checked out. Most spouses want little more than an opportunity to support their other half. Helping is preferable to being married to a self-sufficient workhorse set on personal martyrdom.

Some people stay in untruthful organizations because of other intrinsic issues—the vision of the company, co-workers, the hope that it could get better, etc. If you choose to stay in an untruthful organization, you play a very dangerous game. Above all, you must do some worst-case scenario planning: what is the worst that could happen if the "truth"

Truth Comes To An Insurance Company

I was the principal officer responsible for customer service in the U.S. for a large multinational insurance company. I was responsible for building a couple of "truthful organizations." A well-known business writer spent several days with the people at one of my facilities recording their thoughts and feelings about working in our high-involvement environment. His notes indicated they loved their workplace and their commitment to excellence and customers. The results showed. Service unit costs dropped by more than 40% over four years; employee turnover declined each year and 96% of our customers told us that they were either delighted or satisfied with the services they received from us.

Unfortunately, the environment I created was threatening to the dominant culture and ultimately, the results we produced were irrelevant to my superiors. **I was told by my boss that I was no longer viewed by my peers as being one of the management "team" and that I had changed. He told me that I could stay and that he would work with me to "rehabilitate" me.** Work with me on my weaknesses and try to capitalize on my strengths, OK, but rehabilitation, no way.

After 27 years with the company, I cut a deal and walked away.

Interestingly, forcing me out had remarkably little impact on the way people continue to work. Front-line people have called to report that despite the reinstallation of the hierarchy, they will never go back to the old way of working. Former coaches who have been reinstated as managers report they still consider themselves senior resources for the organization—not bosses. Top management thinks everything has been restored. Not so for the people I worked with; many of the changes we put in place remain—despite my absence.

—Name withheld by request

comes out? Are you legally accountable? Even if you are not, what are the ethical and moral implications of your decision to continue participating and supporting this organization?

You need an external confidante (outside of the field) that you can talk with. These debriefing sessions are critical; they will keep you from believing your own rationalizations and losing perspective.

Personal And Organizational Accountability

Personal and Organizational Accountability

A Truthful Organizational Structure

Imagine an organization in which all workers have a genuine personal motivation to perform their daily tasks. Imagine that every worker knows what tasks are required to be performed and sees how these tasks are part of the big picture—with suppliers and customers on either side. Further imagine that they continuously measure and track the quality of their work. On a regular basis, coaches work with all workers, going over the results of their performance, to help them achieve their personal career goals and improve the quality of their participation in the organization. This is the organizational structure of the Truthful Organization.

There's nothing I'm afraid of like scared people.
— Robert Frost

After the creation of an organizational vision, there are four phases to developing a Truthful Organizational Structure:

Who dares nothing, need hope for nothing.
—Johann von Schiller

A. Each department takes ownership of the organizational vision.
B. All employees receive training to help them understand the vision, values, and mission of the organization as part of the big picture.
C. Each department and/or team establishes performance parameters, a measurement system, and a plan for continuous improvement.
D. A process is put into place that gives each worker a clear understanding of how his or her work at a task level contributes to the big picture of the organization.

Rapid and continuous feedback lets each worker assess individual performance.

A closer look reveals a systematic plan involving every individual, team, department, and relationship in the organization.

A. Each department takes ownership for the organizational vision.

In the Truthful Organization, all workers are not only encouraged to understand the technical aspects of their jobs, but also have a clear picture of how their tasks contribute to the overall operation qualitatively, and financially, and how they impact (directly and indirectly) internal and external customers.

Representatives (not just managers/supervisors) work together to take a closer look at the organizational vision. They need to have frank, open dialogue about what is included in (and what may be missing from) this vision. The most important outcome (of this process) is to clarify the department's relationship with the vision. Before completing this process, at a minimum, the following questions must be answered to all participants' satisfaction:

1. Is the achievement of the vision desirable?
2. Is the vision achievable?
3. What is the department's and/or team's role in achieving the goal? (This becomes the department's mission.)

B. All employees receive training to help them understand the vision, values, and mission of the organization as part of the big picture.

Many employees have little understanding of how a business operates. They rarely understand the relationship of income to expenses, return on investment, opportunity costs, overhead vs. cost of goods sold, inventory costs, etc. Few workers know how their tasks affect the company's bottom line.

Compartmentalization is so complete that employees routinely have little knowledge about their industry, competing products, or customers' requirements. In the Truthful Organization, all workers are not only encouraged to understand the technical aspects of their jobs, but also have a clear picture of how their tasks contribute to the overall operation qualitatively, and financially, and how they impact (directly and indirectly) internal and external customers. Moreover, as free agents, they need to understand their comparative value in both the local community and the industry as a whole. A clerk in an insurance company in Omaha should know what other clerks with similar experience earn elsewhere in Omaha and across the nation within the insurance industry.

International business may conduct its operations with scraps of paper, but the ink it uses is human blood.
—Eric Ambler

As of late, there is a great deal of interest in open-book management, popularized by Jack Stack, who wrote *The Great Game of Business,* and John Case, the author of *Open-Book Management: The Coming Business Revolution.* Both authors encourage management to "open the books" and share information traditionally reserved for upper management. The success of this style is powerfully illustrated by Stack. In open-book management, all employees, from the CEO to the janitor, use the same scorecard: income and cash flow statements, the company balance sheet, and other financial and performance measures. The intent is for everyone to think and act like owners.

The big picture must also include an understanding of how the company is organized. Relationships between divisions, departments, and individuals are mapped out and understood by every employee. Employees need to find themselves on the organizational chart and identify the supplier/customer chain in which they operate. They must understand the difference and similarity between internal and external suppliers and customers.

What's good for the country is good for General Motors, and vice versa.
—Charles Wilson

External supplier	Outside agent who provides materials information used in a task.
Internal supplier	Who gives us materials information or partially completed work required for a task.
Internal customer	Who gets the result of our work next.
External customer	Who ultimately pays for the result of our work.

Often a long chain of customer-supplier relationships link an external supplier with the end customer. In the Truthful Organization, every individual along the chain understands the way each job impacts the satisfaction of the end customer and the efficient use of every supplier's raw materials.

__In the Truthful Organization, team performance results are everyone's business. In too many organizations, critical data stops on the manager's desk and never gets in the hands of the people who really need it.__

C. Each department and/or team establishes performance parameters, a measurement system, and a plan for continuous improvement.

It is critical that the department, team, and/or work group establish achievable and measurable performance parameters. I agree with many who assert goal setting is dangerous, since goals are actually upper-limit performance boundaries. However, it seems a function of human nature to transform expectation into goals, so a goal by any other name is still a goal.

After team performance parameters are established, a means of measuring team performance must be set up. These measurements will ideally include hard and soft parameters; production levels, quality variance, budget variance, and re-work—all represent hard measures. Soft parameters include team decision making, absenteeism, conflict resolutions, safety issues, etc.

Many teams have put performance parameters in place but few go the next step. It is important that these parameters be measured and tracked with results fed back to the team in a timely manner. Quality and process engineers have a plethora of tools to measure, record, and display this kind of data. But they sometimes fall short of creating a system to disseminate (and make understandable) this information to the *whole* team. In the Truthful Organization, team performance results are everyone's business. In too many organizations, critical data stops on the manager's desk and never gets in the hands of the people who really need it.

I favor systems that display results as rapidly as possible through highly visible media: video monitors, tote boards, white boards, billboards, etc.

D. A process is put into place that gives workers a clear understanding of how their work at a task level contributes to the big picture of the organization. Rapid and continuous feedback lets each worker assess his or her own performance.

While most workers have a job description, few have task-level performance criteria or measures. Yet all jobs are performed one task at a time. If tasks are not evaluated, how do workers know how well they are doing? Unfortunately, in many organizations, effort (merely staying busy) is the primary criteria.

Finally, it must be understood by every worker that "good enough" isn't. Every worker must have an individual plan for improvement that is driven by rapid and continuous feedback. There is a correlation between feedback and improvement. If the feedback system provides sporadic updates, improvement will never be more than sporadic. If there is no feedback, any improvement will be purely by chance. The poorest (and unfortunately, the most common) form of feedback is remuneration. Alfie Kohn, the author of *Punishment by Reward* and *No Contest,* points out that compensation programs may reward the wrong things; for example, some merit systems pit one worker or department against another. Ultimately, it may *cost* a worker to help a co-worker!

There is a correlation between feedback and improvement. If the feedback system provides sporadic updates, improvement will never be more than sporadic. If there is no feedback, any improvement will be purely by chance. The poorest (and unfortunately, the most common) form of feedback is remuneration.

Quality improvement programs have demonstrated that most workers have an innate desire to improve the quality of their work. Managers who disagree with this assessment need not wonder why their workers seem to be the exception. The problem lies not with people, but with the system. It must provide each worker with specific performance expectations (a task description, performance parameters, and a plan for continuous improvement) and a rapid and continuous feedback system. Additionally, the leader must work collaboratively with the worker to find out what the worker needs to improve—and then do what is necessary to provide it. Continuously improving workers often need the following: training, assistance, people skills, coaching, access to resources, help with process redesign, and more.

Adventure is not outside a man; it is within.
—David Grayson

Alignment: Personal, Interpersonal, Team, & Organization

The Truthful Organization is characterized by a unique, personally motivated, proactive search for alignment from the bottom up. When individuals identify and declare a personal mission for themselves, their innate passion to realize that mission causes them to search for alignment with other levels of the organization. The chart below identifies the aligning factors at each level:

Organizational Level	Means of Alignment
Organization	*Shared Vision*
Team	*Performance Parameters*
Interpersonal	*Working Agreements*
Personal	*Personal Mission and Values*

Those who make peaceful revolution impossible will make violent revolution inevitable.
— John Fitzgerald Kennedy

During a transition phase when an organization seeks to become more truthful, individuals—motivated by fear of the unknown—have an unconscious need to thwart the process by withholding one or more aligning factors. For example, it is not unusual for middle-level or department managers to neglect defining performance parameters for the department. It is surprising how many organizations have operated for years without clear performance parameters. They substitute a slightly modified previous year's budget and production figures to get by. However, as people in the department begin setting up personal performance plans and creating agreements with co-workers, the need for more specific performance parameters will grow acute. Then the teams begin to ask tough questions: "What is the purpose of this team? What do we intend to do? How do we intend to focus our efforts on achieving departmental goals?" These bottom-up efforts place the manager under greater pressure to get specific.

In the Truthful Organization, each employee takes a proactive stance at every level of involvement in the organization. It is a "reality test" for each worker to be able to honestly make the following statements:

A Simple Truth Test

PERSONAL: Individual Tasks

Each individual is able to say: "It serves my personal mission to perform these tasks because I see how it contributes to the success of the organization and realization of our shared vision."

INTERPERSONAL: Shared Tasks

Each individual is able to say: "It serves my personal mission to work with you (others) in a cooperative and collaborative manner to better contribute to the success of the organization and realize our shared vision."

TEAM: Coordinated Group (Departmental) Activities

Each individual is able to say: "It serves my personal mission to fully participate with this team, including taking occasional stands that go against the majority, to better contribute to the success of the organization and realize our shared vision."

ORGANIZATION: Success and Realization of the Shared Vision

Each individual is able to say: "It serves my personal mission to contribute to the success of the organization and realize our shared vision."

Those who profess to favor freedom, and yet depreciate agitation, are men who want rain without thunder and lightning. They want the ocean without the roar of its many waters.

—Frederick Douglass

Interpretation

Whenever individuals are unable to honestly make these statements to themselves or others, they are in a personal moment of truth. To realign themselves, it becomes necessary to take proactive steps. In some cases, the lack of alignment occurs because the individual's personal mission has become vague or has even shifted. In other cases, it is a realization that others may be out of alignment. For example, as previously discussed, a manager may have withheld specific performance parameters. In such cases, it becomes impossible to feel aligned because the team or department is not defined enough to permit alignment.

In the Truthful Organization, corporate *policy* expects all people to speak up and take action to achieve clarity of purpose and alignment at every level of the organization—regardless of who may be in the way. In fact, the Truthful Organization has an official amnesty policy to facilitate this level of alignment.

I was angry with my friend:
I told my wrath, my wrath did end.
I was angry with my foe:
I told it not, my wrath did grow.
— *William Blake*

In less-than truthful or would-be truthful organizations, individuals must rely upon their own instincts to decide how proactive to become. With the help of a supportive Truth Zone team, it is sometimes possible to bring about dramatic transformations—even revolutions. But each person must remember there are no guarantees. Honesty is not always the best policy in truth-challenged organizations. Employees may want to use their moment of truth to reassess the appropriateness of their continued association with the organization.

Alignment Check-list

- o Development of a personal mission for all employees
- o Comparison of personal mission with the organizational vision
- o Familiarization of department performance parameters
- o Individual development plan
- o Job-task analysis
- o Coaching (feedback) sessions

1. *Development of a personal mission for all employees*

In a Truthful Organization, employees are understood to be motivated in ways unique and specific to themselves. These motivators may transcend monetary or traditional reward systems.

As a result, employees are strongly encouraged to explore these deep motivators and craft a personal mission statement to describe those things including, but not limited to, work that is most important to accomplish in their lifetime.

When a person's work is closely aligned with their deepest motivators, it is accomplished with more enthusiasm and greater care.

If you wish to know what a man is, place him in authority.
— Yugoslav Proverb

2. *Comparison of personal mission with the organizational vision*

A side-by-side comparison of an employee's personal mission with the vision of the organization is critical in developing true alignment. When both are aligned, a win-win relationship exists between employer-employee. The employee derives benefits from the job because specific core needs are being met; likewise, the employer benefits from the contribution of a highly motivated, loyal employee-partner.

This process is still valuable if employees see their involvement as temporary—as long as involvement with this organization contributes to the person's mission at the time. When working for this organization is primarily to earn money in order to go back to school, open a business, etc., it is critical that a time frame or dollar amount be specified. If that dollar figure and/or time limit is exceeded, it is vital that the personal mission be revisited and re-declared. Otherwise, it becomes difficult to stay aligned and motivated to do the job.

Keep cool; anger is not an argument.
— Daniel Webster

3. *Familiarization of department performance parameters*

It is assumed that each department has established specific performance parameters which support the short- and long-term objectives of the business while moving in the

__In a Truthful Organization, everyone must know how every effort, in each task, contributes to the department's success and advances the organization toward realizing its shared vision.__

__Show me a worker who does not see the big picture, and I will show you an under-utilized employee asset.__

direction of the organizational vision. If this step has not taken place, it is critical that it be completed before proceeding.

Parameters are only meaningful when employees understand how their tasks support and contribute to those parameters. In the Truthful Organization, everyone must know how every effort, in each task, contributes to the department's success and advances the organization toward realizing its shared vision. Research indicates that the single highest motivating factor for high performance and quality output is ownership of the task. Show me a worker who does not see the big picture, and I will show you an underutilized employee asset.

Each employee needs to know more than what is defined as success. Everyone must understand all performance parameters in the context of his or her own job. Specifically, the outcome of this process should be the employee's ability to describe how each task impacts team success. Then, each employee should be able to ascribe measurement indicators that can be used to assess individual contributions to the success of the department.

Even training can be deployed with the same kind of accountability. One of my Venture Centre partners, Glenn Head, has published a book entitled *Training Cost Analysis*, which helps organizations carefully measure the visible and hidden costs of training.

4. *Individual development plan*

If an organization is genuinely committed to continuous improvement, it must expect nothing less from its staff, yet continuous improvement is almost exclusively associated with products and service. In the Truthful Organization, all staff members are encouraged to embark on a program of lifelong learning and development. Acknowledging personal improvement can be accomplished in many ways: certification, gifts and prizes, matching funds for tuition, and consideration in promotions. Organizations fail to realize this valuable ideal by not integrating learning into the organizational structure. Learning, cross-training, and self-improvement must be managed at the departmental level. This is accomplished through the creation of an individual development plan. Each worker should work with a supervisor-coach to complete a plan that serves two purposes: first, it establishes a road map for realizing the employee's personal mission. And, second, it upgrades the quality of the organization's staff by effectively distributing skills across the staff while introducing new skills to the organization. Without a plan and a partnership at a departmental level, learning can easily slip to a secondary position in the organization. Without organizational commitment in the form of recognition and some financial resources, departments will tend to place their time and attention elsewhere. Learning must be integrated into the organization at all levels.

Employees need to know exactly what tasks make up their jobs. Moreover, they must understand their jobs in the context of others. They must know when the job is done, and be able to determine how well it is done. Finally, they must understand the needs of their customers, both internal and external.

5. *Job-task analysis*

Every employee needs to know exactly what tasks make up their job. Moreover, they must understand their job in the context of others. They must know when the job is done, and be able to determine how well it is done. Finally, they must understand the needs of their customers, both internal and external. Each task must be analyzed to reveal:

A. What prerequisites must exist before the task is undertaken?
B. What are the sequence and time frame for events which comprise the task?
C. What are the criteria for completion?
D. How do you measure the quality of the job?
E. Who gets your work and what are the recipient's expectations?

EXAMPLE:

Bob Helm owns a printing plant. His printer Mike does a large percentage of the printing that comes through the plant. Bob has worked with Mike to implement a task analysis:

SALES	PRODUCTION: PRE-PRESS	PRODUCTION: PRINTING	PRODUCTION: BINDERY	DELIVERY
All sales orders must be submitted to Tony whether an estimate is required or not. Tony will order paper, ink and arrange bindery services if they must be sent outside. Work order will be posted on production board as soon as order is confirmed so Mike can plan ahead.	As soon as artwork or plates are delivered, they are put into queue. All work is completed even if there is a significant lead time. This way, Mike can re-arrange and regroup jobs without waiting for pre-press to be done. When completed, the work order is noted and replaced on the production board and the press ready materials are placed in Mike's "Ready for Printing Box."	Work cannot proceed unless work order is complete, pre-press is done and paper and ink are delivered. Printing will be done only after the original customer work order and artwork is inspected. In the event something does not look right, the press person will talk to Tony or a sales person. If no one is available, call customer or artist directly. Final quality check before sending to bindery by someone other than printer.	In-house bindery work will not proceed until the job has been checked for quality. Worked to be sent out to bindery is not sent without final quality check. Bindery is instructed to call in the event a problem occurs or a job does not look right!	If job must be sent to bindery, appropriate work orders must be in attached and original work order must be noted so the job can be traced. When the job is returned, before final packaging and delivery to customer, a last quality check is made.
What could go wrong?				
Sales must specify customer's expectations! Date, samples, special delivery considerations, etc. Orders could get lost.	Some artwork is of marginal quality and the resulting film and plates may be of poor quality or require special handling. Orders could get lost.	Plates may not be right. Paper and ink may be wrong. Press could break down. Quality may not be consistent. Some artwork is of marginal quality and the resulting	Folder may run too many. Some paper will require hand scoring or folding which may delay job and add cost. Orders could get lost.	Job must be invoiced at time of delivery. Or delay in delivery or getting paid may result. Special delivery instructions? Orders could get lost.

Process Flow Analysis Worksheet

Pre-requisites: Mike gets a work order from Tony and printing plates from Jim. Paper and ink must be delivered.

Events: Mike makes sure all pre-requisites are fulfilled. Assesses the day's work flow. Sets up press: mixes ink, installs plates, stacks paper. Begins printing the job. Checks alignment, color, ink flow, coverage, and density continuously during the process.

Completion: The job is completed when the correct number of impressions have been made, meeting Mike's quality standards.

Quality: The job next moves to the bindery for cutting, folding, collating, and packaging. At each step, with a final check prior to packaging and invoicing, the job is checked by staff (other than Mike).

Recipient's expectations: Before a job can be delivered to the customer on a promised date, it must come off the press by a specific time. That time depends on how many after-press processes the job must undergo and whether it must be sent out to a subcontractor. Additionally, the job must meet every quality standard... oh, and the ink also has to be dry.

6. ***Coaching (feedback) sessions***

Even though each worker has specific measures to evaluate performance, it is still difficult to accurately self-analyze. Therefore, the primary role of managers and supervisors is to serve as coaches to individual workers. A regular series of one-on-one meetings between supervisors and staff replaces traditional assessment meetings with a collaborative coaching session. The focus of these meetings includes, at a minimum:

Coach (feedback) Session Agenda

A. What is the status of the worker's performance?
B. Are the performance measures still appropriate?
C. What resources does the worker need to improve performance?
D. Is the worker progressing on a personal development plan?
E. What should the focus of the next few months be?
F. What can the supervisor do to help the worker?

Stockholders or Stakeholders?

Categories of organizational stakeholders

1. Customers
2. Owners and Stockholders
3. Employees and Management
4. Vendors and Suppliers
5. Industry and Competitors
6. Community (neighbors, regulators, taxing districts, etc.)

Executives who see their responsibility to stockholders as increasing profit at any cost choose the interests of one class of stakeholder above others. The same is true for the business operator who places the customer's interest above all else. While not all stakeholders enjoy equal interests, an organization that pits one against another or disregards the

PRINTING - Job Task Analysis

Pre-requisites: Events Completion

Quality Issues Customer's Expectations

Typical job task analysis worksheet

Executives who see their responsibility to stockholders as increasing profit at any cost choose the interests of one class of stakeholder above others.

interests of others operates from a dangerously narrow perspective.

In Truthful Organizations, it makes sense to address all stakeholders—each has a valid (if not equal) claim for consideration. While no single stakeholder can guarantee the success of an enterprise, any one could bring about failure.

Leaders of the Truthful Organization take time to determine how the organization will manage its relationship with each category of stakeholder. The relationships of individuals, departments, and various stakeholders become the structure of the organization.

Even the assumption that stockholders care only about profit may not be as iron clad as it used to be. Investors are increasingly savvy about the nature of business and the changing business environment. Fewer stockholders expect organizations to sacrifice good customer relations for short-term profitability. With an increasing number of investment opportunities for socially responsible and ethical organizations, some investors can see the forest for the trees. The executive's lament— "I would love to do things more 'truthfully,' but my stockholders only care for one thing ... and it has nothing to do with truth,"— is a threadbare argument. More and more courageous executives are operating organizations in innovative, aligned, and truthful ways.

Some directors are choosing to proactively manage the crucial relationship between stockholders and the organization. However, breaking with the old paradigm requires carefully honed leadership skills and all that implies: courage, vision, passion, planning, and tools of persuasion.

Tying It All Together

While the components of a truthful organizational structure fit together in a well-planned alignment, the missing ingredient is a mechanism to facilitate feedback through all levels of the organization. In most organizations, communication flows smoothly from top to bottom. However, upward communication fights more than gravity. Disempowered people love to complain, but few have the skills to truthfully articulate their needs, suggestions, or concerns to management. Even empowered workers may find it difficult to say what needs to be said to the "right" people. Amazingly, some of the largest, most notoriously bureaucratic organizations in the world have a system which may offer a solution.

The system I am talking about is akin to an "ethics hotline." I first became acquainted with the one in place at Lockheed-Martin. It involves a toll-free telephone hotline that any employee can use to talk to a person skilled at facilitating the resolution of ethical dilemmas, offering advice, and even initiating an investigation. People can call anytime they feel their integrity or peace of mind is compromised. They can talk about a troublesome policy, an inappropriate request from a customer, or a supervisor who has overstepped a boundary—all while remaining completely anonymous.

Larry Tew at Lockheed-Martin explained to me that the ethics hotline is fully integrated into the structure of Lockheed-Martin. As a long-time manager with the organization, he was amazed to find out the ethics hotline was not generated within the company, but was mandated by their largest customer ... the U.S. Department of Defense (DOD).

While it would be unfair to characterize the DOD as an immoral organization, it is probably safe to assume its strong commitment to ethics has less to do with values and more to do with good business. It must be concerned about security, quality, and fair pricing—concerns not so different from organizations within the private sector.

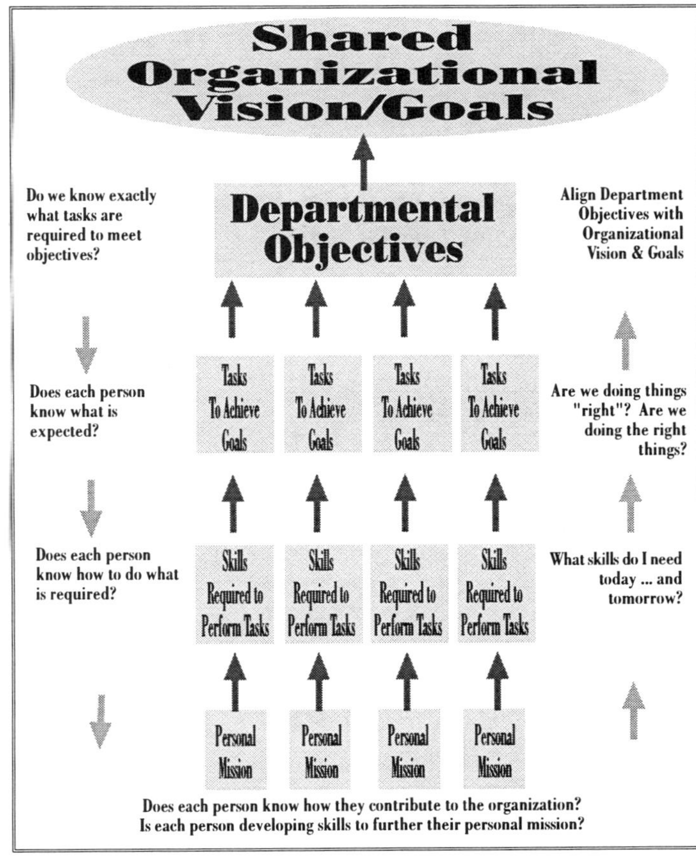

The Ecology of the Truthful Organization and Feedback Loop

A Truth Line is a powerful tool that levels the playing field. It ensures that each discrete component, department, team, and individual is always on the same page—aligned in the same way.

The Truth Line

The Truthful Organization needs more than a simple ethics hotline. The same technology (telephone, e-mail, and letters) can be used, but the mission of a "Truth Line" is more than policies, ethics, and legalities. A Truth Line is a powerful tool that levels the playing field. It ensures that each discrete component, department, team, and individual is always on the same page—aligned in the same way.

A Truth Line gives a voice for the disempowered, the intimidated, and the abused. But it also handles rumors, offers a new tool to deal with diversity, harassment, and discrimination issues, and serves as an electronic suggestion box.

The system also accumulates a great deal of data; it is an organization-wide, check-in tool. Without destroying the anonymity of the caller, the issues, challenges, and trends can be tracked. This information can be collated and distributed to the leadership of the organization and even published. In this way, everyone knows what's going on, all the time.

The Truth Line Basic Components

1. A communication infrastructure: 800-lines, e-mail, etc.
2. A trained staff (or contracted service) ready to counsel callers.
3. Staff-wide training (two to four hours) on when, how, and why to make calls.
4. A pamphlet outlining the "rules of the road" for staff.
5. A means to gather, tabulate, and report collected data (not names).
6. A newsletter, internal web page, TV broadcast, or other vehicle to distribute information, quell rumors, or address issues on a larger scale.

With the addition of a Truth Line, any organization can deploy and nurture a truthful organizational structure.

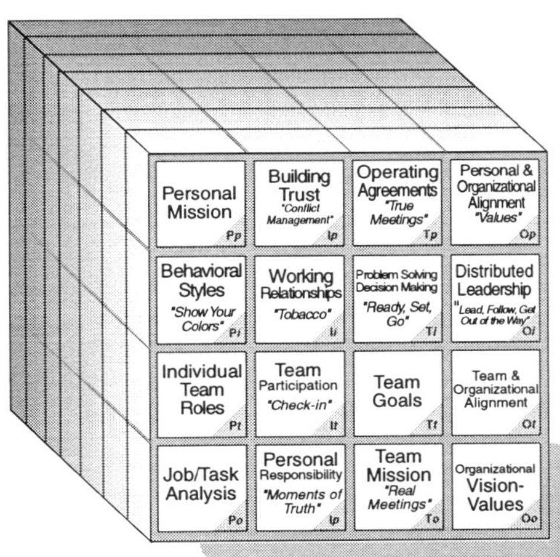

Chapter Eleven

Building Blocks and Tools: An Experiential Approach

Building Blocks and Tools: An Expriential Approach

The purpose of this chapter is to integrate and consolidate the theoretical and practical information contained in the previous chapters into various tools, skills, and models that will facilitate the creation of new, or the transformation of existing organizations into more Truthful Organizations. I call the process *trueing*, because it involves aligning the disparate components of the organization according to a comprehensive visionary plan designed to fulfill the potential of the organization and its stakeholders.

The model is the Organizational Development and Analysis Matrix (ODAM). Modeled after a spreadsheet, a vertical column of seven criteria is compared to a horizontal list of each functional area (divisions, departments, teams, or workgroups) within the organization. At the intersecting coordinate of each criterion and every functional area is both a planning opportunity and data point suitable for assessment.

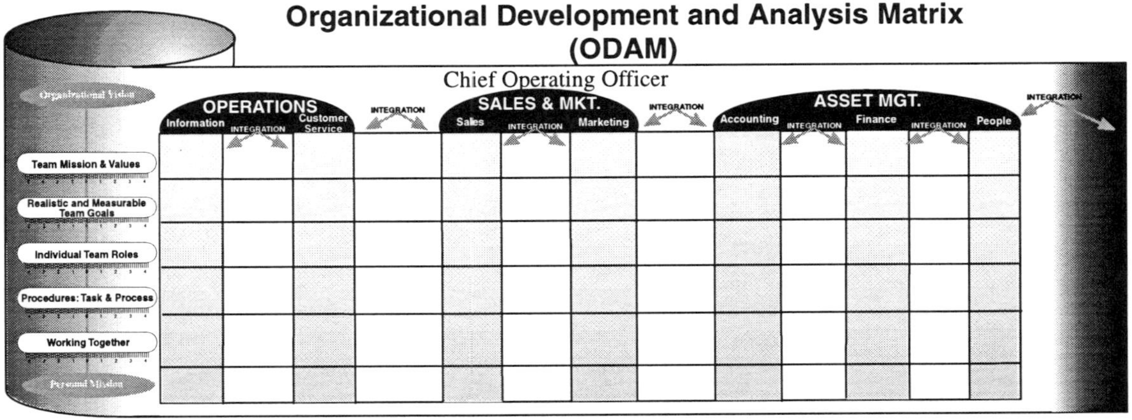

Organizational Development and Analysis Matrix (ODAM)

Chief Operating Officer

OPERATIONS: Information, INTEGRATION, Customer Service
INTEGRATION
SALES & MKT.: Sales, INTEGRATION, Marketing
INTEGRATION
ASSET MGT.: Accounting, INTEGRATION, Finance, INTEGRATION, People
INTEGRATION

Organizational Vision
Team Mission & Values
Realistic and Measurable Team Goals
Individual Team Roles
Procedures: Task & Process
Working Together
Personal Mission

Don't play for safety—it's the most dangerous thing in the world.
— Hugh Walpole

This is not a typical organizational chart. It is not designed to illustrate relationships between individuals. However, it comes closer to the organic model of the trellis and ivy discussed in Chapter One (See pages 30 - 33) because it describes both the planned structure and the organic quality of the organization. Notice that a key function of managers is to facilitate integration between the vertical columns.

In the example illustrated (from an actual organization), Rick, the operations manager, is responsible to make sure information services (and all back-office systems) are well integrated with the substantial customer service requirements of (in this case) an Internet Service Provider (ISP). Rick and all managers are focused on the usually hidden aspects of the relationship between different departments.

Note that Pat, who is the COO, facilitates a meta-integration process among all three silos. Ultimately, the graph needs to be thought of as a cylinder, or birthday cake. With the birthday cake analogy, all silos are integrated with each other, and every layer of the seven-layer cake represents a level of functionality that every department works on and measures.

Organizational Development and Analysis Matrix (ODAM) Criteria

The seven criteria encompass and allow assessment of all Sixteen Building Blocks of a Truthful Organization. To appreciate the essence of the trueing process, think of a rubber band stretched between two anchoring points: Organizational Vision at the top, and Personal Mission at the anchor position. Except possibly for the founding entrepreneur, no one person's mission is likely to be 100% aligned with the vision of any organization. There will always be some tension between what any individual wants to do and what the organization requires of the person.

Now imagine that on this elastic band are affixed the following five labels:

Elements of Organizational Alignment

Team, Departmental, or Workgroup Focus - **Team Mission**
Realistic and Measurable **Team Goals**
Team Roles of Individuals
Precisely Delineated **Tasks and Procedures**
Working Together

Using this exact model, I have created a simple alignment instrument that can quickly reveal the relative degree of alignment among group members.

Imagine that each of the five elements is represented by a slider bar, like the volume control on a radio. On the graphic here, notice that the center position, zero, represents perfect alignment. The element is clearly defined and is perfectly aligned. However, the positions to the left indicate a lack of specificity or confusion. Therefore, position four, to the *left*, indicates the user has no idea how what is going on aligns with the vision of the organization, let alone their own personal mission. In the other direction, position four, to the *right*, indicates the situation is well articulated, but is NOT aligned with the organizational vision or the individual's personal mission.

Experiential Activity:

Assessing Team Alignmeent

On individual sheets, each person can make a mark to indicate where they would put the slider bar to represent how aligned they feel with each element. When the dots are connected, a pattern is made visible. Try using a large blow-up to capture (in different colors) the results from individual sheets collected from an entire group. Remember, in an ideal world, all participants will generate a straight line up and down the middle (position zero) of each sheet.

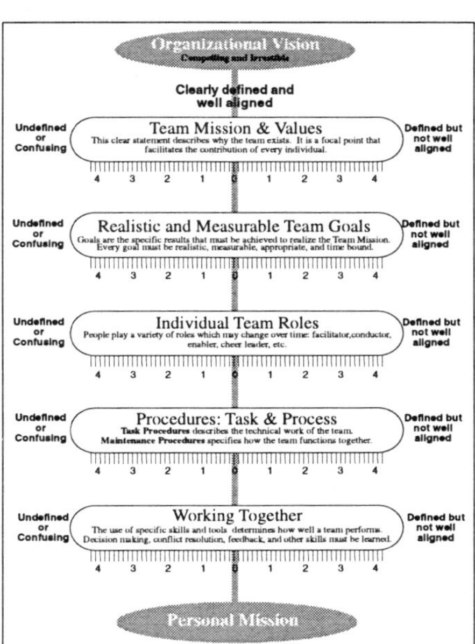

The Sixteen Building Blocks of a Truthful Organization

A closer look at the seven criteria reveals the sixteen blocks. In some cases, a single element, such as the Team Role of Individuals is comprised of five building blocks. Of the sixteen building blocks, ten involve specific tools, while the remaining four describe skills vital to the health of an organization.

A Compelling and Irresistible Vision (pp: 156 - 159)

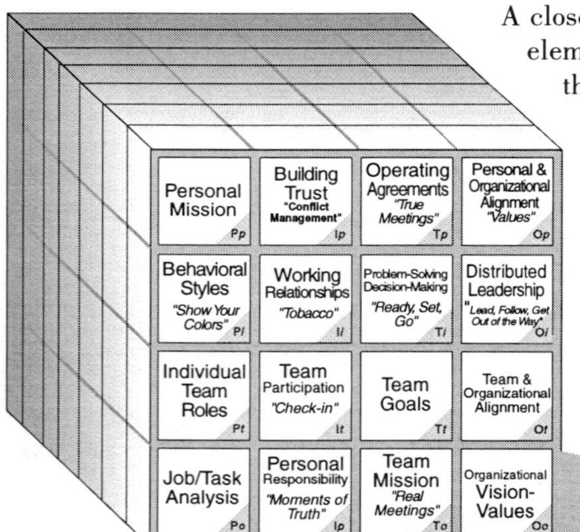

Sixteen Core Building Blocks and Tools

Many organizations have beautifully wordsmithed Vision Statements engraved on plaques, business cards, and annual reports. Most were crafted by executive teams, some evolved out of an arduous process involving representative members of the whole organization. Sadly, some were written by public relations departments or marketing consultants.

Very, very few say anything that means much to the front-line worker. Fewer still motivate a worker to do a better job, almost none give a worker the guidance necessary to make difficult decisions when no one of higher rank is available for consultation. In the final analysis, nearly every organization has a vision statement, but precious few operate in accordance with their vision—those that compensate their people for living up to the vision are few and far between.

A vision statement is an internal document. If profit is more important to management than customer satisfaction, the vision statement should make the position clear—at least it should not talk about happy, satisfied customers. It exists to help every employee understand what they are working for, and how they are expected to achieve the goals of management. It must form the core of an organization's stability. It typically describes a future situation that is far enough off (timeless is even better) that it can remain in force for a long period of time—unaffected by market shifts, economic factors, or emerging technologies. While describing the future fulfillment of the organization, the vision statement should describe or clearly imply something about WHY the organization exists as well as what the organization VALUES in its work and employees.

It is not necessary to say "... we will be profitable," or "... a dominant force in the market." It is assumed that the organization shall exist in perpetuity, serve its customers' needs, be profitable, be law abiding, and continually increase real profits. An organization that feels the need to include profitability, market share, or any other of these "givens" is demonstrating a special interest in the subject and doing so to inform the people of the organization what is held at the highest value.

Without adventure civilization is in full decay.
—Alfred North Whitehead

It is my observation that even though most vision statements are irrelevant or non-existent, most members of organizations share a common unspoken understanding about what is *really* important to management. Remember the Social Field Theory? (See Pages 37 - 57.) The organizational field makes it inevitable that everyone in the field becomes acclimatized to the field. What is valued, is rewarded. As a result, even when working with groups within larger organizations, it is possible to discuss alignment issues, even if the larger organization has an irrelevant or inarticulate vision.

Team, Departmental, or Workgroup Focus (Mission)

Building Block: Team Mission
Every team needs a mission statement. It is similar to a Vision Statement for the organization, but it specifically describes why this team exists and delineates what work the team does to support the Vision of the Organization.

Tool: *Real Teams*
Teams are a common feature of the modern work environment. Unfortunately, there has

Experiential Activity:

Establishing A Team Performance Baseline

A wide variety of team problem-solving initiatives can be used to assess and baseline a team's performance. For example, popular team events like the blind square or spider web are effective reflectors of a team's performance baseline. Add this feature: Appoint (or have team select) an official observer who is furnished with the following score card. After regular debrief questions, discuss the results of the observer's scores.

(0–9) ***Real Team Score Card***

- ❒ Personal and team agendas are clear to everyone.
- ❒ To achieve the shared goal, everyone is willing to shift their own agenda.
- ❒ Everyone supports each other; no one competes with others.
- ❒ People respect each other; everyone listens and seeks the input of teammates.
- ❒ Dissent is encouraged; conflict is seen as an opportunity to grow, learn, and improve one's self and the team.
- ❒ Processes are in place to facilitate disagreements, seeking win/win outcomes.
- ❒ Trust is nurtured by encouraging rational risk taking. When trust is present, fear disappears.
- ❒ In addition to consensus building, a variety of decision-making processes are used, but agreed upon up front.
- ❒ Leadership is distributed according to defined roles and rotated often.
- ❒ The team is on a quest for continual improvement; getting stuck is out of the question.
- ❒ When the work is done, when will the team disband?
- ❒ Members of the team have fun!

been so much emphasis on teambuilding that few teams learn team*work*. So many organizations and leaders are so focused on results that it is difficult to think about, much less implement, new processes to facilitate cooperation and co-ordination between team members.

Discuss Reasons Why Some Teams Never Get Real

- The larger organization is committed to a management style that is incompatible with teams.
- Team is so focused on tasks that processes and relationships are never fully developed.
- Members of the team are unwilling to accept responsibility for their own behavior and results.
- Team members are fearful and unable to bond or build trust.
- The team is so large that processes are difficult to implement.
- Team is not wholeheartedly supported by management.
- Team members are not given enough training.
- Leaders do not place enough emphasis on team development.

Building Block:
Team & Organization Alignment

Nearly every team or work group operates according to plans, goals, or other guidelines. In most organizations, it is the responsibility of an upper-level manager to coordinate the work of individual teams or departments to make sure their efforts are focused, effective, and appropriate, as well as to make certain that everything that should be done to achieve organizational goals is being done.

Where most organizations fail to achieve alignment is by leaving the coordination process to individual managers instead of creating a proactive system to assure alignment throughout the organization. The Organizational Development and Analysis Matrix (ODAM) was created to provide just such a system. The supplied example describes a small, simple organization. All that is required for more complex organizations is more columns and possibly layers to describe how a corporate office with multiple departments (or functional divisions) manages a number of regional organizations with multiple departments of their own.

Business is like riding a bicycle—either you keep moving or you fall down.

— Anonymous

The ODAM Matrix is enlarged and mounted in a convenient meeting area or conference room. When the chart is six or eight feet long, the "cells" are about the size of "sticky notes" that can be easily added, changed, and deleted. Ultimately, the developmental process of the organization is made visible for anyone to see. Currently, we are developing an intra- or internet replacement that can be made accessible to anyone in the organization. By "clicking" on any cell, it will be possible to see the work completed or in progress of any department or team in the organization. When everyone sees the process and gets a bigger picture, it is easier to engender buy-in and more passionate participation.

Realistic and Measurable Goals

Building Block: Team Goals

Beyond a mission, every member of the team must have specific goals to work toward. Each goal is a milepost that each team member, as well as the whole team, can use to measure individual and team progress. Remember, goals must be measurable, achievable, appropriate, and time restricted.

Individual Team Roles

How each person contributes, participates, and works with others must not be left to chance. How problems will be solved and decisions made must be carefully articulated and agreed upon up front!

Building Block: Individual Team Roles

Functional and *Process* roles are necessary for every team. Most effort is focused on functional roles. In most teams, almost no energy is expended on developing process roles. Functional roles are defined by the work the team does to contribute to the larger organization. Who does what is usually defined by training and experience (occasionally by temperament or other factors). Process roles are a different story. Since none of us were actually trained for these roles, anyone who is willing and trained should be able to fill any role.

A wide variety of process roles are played by members of every team. Some team leaders try to fulfill more than their share of these roles. Other team members are not likely to object—but they will not feel fully engaged either. Once the roles are delineated, high-performing teams rotate the duties among all team members.

Consider these roles as a starting point for your team:

Agenda Builder

Every meeting should have an agenda. Splitting the task of agenda builder from facilitator offers a greater chance that everyone's issues will be included and no one will be left out. In the old "top-down" management environments of the past, control of the agenda was a sought after role because it meant power and control.

Facilitator

The role of the facilitator is to begin meetings, promote the agenda, and close sessions. The facilitator's responsibility is to the goals of the team and the robust participation of the team members.

Recorder

The recorder captures vital issues and outcomes for two reasons. One, to bring new or absent team members up to speed. Second, to keep an accurate record that may be consulted in the future to better understand the historical fine points of an issue that may emerge in the future.

Timekeeper

The timekeeper starts meetings on time and ends them punctually. Throughout the meeting, with a copy of the agenda, the timekeeper can keep the team posted on their progress.

Observer

The observer watches how the meeting proceeds. She or he pays special attention to the processes, relationships, and "human side" of the meeting. The observer does not interject, unless called upon by the facilitator or other member. Instead, they offer a brief overview of their observations at the end of the meeting. A good observer takes care to avoid negative comments and instead acknowledges what worked well along with some suggestions for improving the next session.

Mission Keeper

This person's focus is the opposite of the Observer. Where the observer watches the process and flow of the meeting, the mission keeper watches all decisions related to tasks, output, and work. The mission keeper offers observations, asks open-ended questions, and polls the team about whether the work of the meeting is aligned with the goals and mission of the team and the vision of the organization.

A good mission keeper understands their job is not to be a judge or authority figure, but by holding up a "mirror" and asking questions, instigates the team to ask the kinds of questions that will keep everyone focused and on schedule.

Humorist (A.K.A., Corporate Jester)

The idea of having someone designated to keep meetings "up" and hearts light may seem odd in a business environment, but those organizations which have tried it usually appreciate the results. Think about how much the gesture says about the organization's commitment to quality-of-life issues!

Aside from the fact that a great deal of research indicates people are more productive when they are happy, humor is a wonderful way to let off steam and release stress. It is interesting to note that in organizations where humor is repressed or off-limits, stress builds up. When humor does emerge, it is often dark—full of half-truths, and sarcastic. It still relieves stress, but promotes cynicism by disempowering staff by casting them in the role of victims.

All authority belongs to the people.
— Thomas Jefferson

A good humorist takes the job seriously. They plan icebreakers and jokes, prepare puzzles, and often expand their role to include celebrations. Humor is both healthy and valuable. Try it, you'll like it—no kidding!

Building Block: Operating Agreements

At the core of high-performing teams is a set of agreements that guide team processes through the details of day-to-day work as well as the occasional calamity. Agreements are not the same as rules—they do not limit, they liberate the individual. Here is how:

In a Truthful Organization, people take the time, up-front, to talk about how they want to work together—especially how they want to deal with the tough stuff. Stuff like group problem solving, decision making, who's in charge, disagreements, failures, mistakes, misunderstandings, asking for help, telling co-workers when they are in the way, and so on. Agreements also establish boundaries around gossip, criticism, pointing blame, privacy, etc.

A set of operating agreements should be the agenda for one of the first meetings for a new team. And like the U. S. Constitution, it should be a "living" document, always subject to change, amendment, and deletion.

Example Agreements

- Use “I” statements, such as “I feel,” “I think,” “I need” instead of “You, they, them.”
- Let go of personal agendas, work together for the common good.
- Listen to the complete ideas of others, do not interrupt.
- Be as willing to hear the disagreement of others as you expect them to hear you.
- Accept responsibility for your own experience, avoid blame.
- Remember that NO may be the response to any request.
- Confidentiality, what happens of a personal nature in the meeting stays there.

Tool: *True Meetings*

True meetings are meetings with a clearly articulated and shared purpose. True Meetings have processes in place that promote the full participation of all involved, leading to a “true meeting” of the minds and hearts of everyone in attendance. In a true meeting, the common focus is to promote the mission of the team and the vision of the organization.

Suggested Meeting Elemeents

Conduct a meeting about meetings. Using the suggested meeting elements, conduct a meeting with your group. The singular outcome is only that a format for future meetings be established. Of course, following this outline provides important practice for future meetings with more substantial and practical content.

Building the agenda

Agenda building is best when not conducted in a vacuum. If real participation is desired, advance input to the agenda by participants is required.

Experiential Activity

Meeting Meeting

Conduct a meeting about meetings. Using the "Suggested Meeting Elements," conduct a meeting with your group. The singular outcome is only that—a format for future meetings is being established. Following this outline provides important practice for future meetings with more substantial and practical content.

Defining outcomes
Everyone should know why the meeting is called and what the purpose may be. The person who called the meeting, or the facilitator, must articulate this purpose. Otherwise, everyone is left assuming, reading minds, and/or acting as if they know. Clarity is power.

Resolutions and Actions
Every item on the agenda must be addressed and either resolved or postponed until a future meeting. Managing time to leave no item untouched is the responsibility of the facilitator.

Ending the meeting
Meetings should be completed, as they begin, on time. No more than ten minutes over time can be used to wrap up the agenda and hear the observer's report—and then, only with the consensus of those present. If people start leaving, consensus has not been reached and a strong message is being sent: commitments are unimportant.

Incomplete agendas
Ask the group whether the item really needs to be addressed. Sometimes it has been resolved by a previous resolution. If it does need time, find out how much time will be sufficient. Propose to put it under "old business" at the next meeting, for the agreed upon amount of time. Is there consensus with this course of action?

Tardiness
Most tardiness occurs because meetings start late and/or end late. When meetings get on-track, it does not take long for participants to realize how important being on time is.

Absences
Some absences are unavoidable, others are a result of meaningless meetings that are unproductive. Make sure that at least two people take responsibility to contact the missing

person and discuss the meeting with them. Make sure the notes or minutes of the meeting are distributed in a timely manner. Make sure there is a reason for meeting and that each meeting generates results.

Guests

Few meetings need to be private, but make sure permission is granted from other attendees before firming up an invitation to a guest.

Confidentiality

How decisions are made, the discussion that takes place prior to a resolution, should always remain confidential. Only those resolutions which the team agrees to should be made public. Otherwise, people will not trust the security of the meeting and might withhold ideas or hesitate to fully participate.

Pagers, Phones, and Interruptions

Something must be done. Find consensus about how these issues will be dealt with BEFORE the problem arises.

Non-exempt (hourly) staff

If people need to attend, they need to be paid.

Special Meetings

Stand-up Meetings (5 - 10 Minutes)

Quick check-ins are appropriate at shift changes or at the beginning and/or ending of the day. They are a great way to keep a team feeling connected and on the same wavelength after a teambuilding event.

Weekly Meetings (20 - 60 Minutes)

If the team meets daily for a stand-up, it is possible to get a lot done in a brief weekly meeting because there is no need to "connect" through stories, anecdotes, etc. It is possible to get right to the agenda and begin to generate results.

Deep Focus Meetings (3 - 8 Hours)
On a quarterly basis, these can be enormously valuable, especially if facilitated by an outsider, for example, someone from another department. These meetings can generate an enormous leap in productivity, and like retreats, refresh rather than exhaust.

V/Space Meetings
When it is necessary to get a moderately large group together, a fixed agenda tends to alienate participation. This technology, developed by Ward Flynn, combines the traditional fixed agenda with a participant-built agenda inspired by the Open Space meetings developed by Harrison Owen.

Every great advance in natural knowledge has involved the absolute rejection of authority.
— Thomas Huxley

Teleconferences, Video-conferencing, and Cyber-meetings
New and emerging technologies make it possible to meet across great distances. The same etiquette described here works well in all media, but no matter how effective the technology, there is no substitute for face-to-face meetings. Sending e-mail to someone ten feet away is a misuse of a powerful technology.

Building Block: Problem Solving/Decision Making
In the final analysis, the effectiveness of teams has more to do with their ability to solve problems and make decisions than with how they get along. Much of my work is with technical (medical, software, financial, engineering, etc.) organizations. Each of these organizations is comprised of individuals trained and experienced at problem solving. Yet few have developed their group problem-solving potential. Solving problems in groups requires an agreed-upon methodology that all understand and are willing to support. Without an up-front agreement, the group tends to waste energy bickering about how to

proceed. Ironically, the reason most groups do not agree upon a problem-solving methodology is a fear of wasting time. The work ethic of most groups forces the participants to try to achieve results quickly. Beginning in Chapter Six, on pages 138 - 139, there is a discussion of this subject and an example of a problem-solving model:

1. Specify the problem or situation
2. Define resolution as a specific outcome
3. Collect alternative solutions
4. Evaluate and prioritize alternatives
5. Take action on the best alternative
6. Evaluate the results

Decision making requires the same kind of up-front effort, but it is not as simple as agreeing on a single model. Instead, the group must develop a repertoire of decision-making methods: ranging from the boss making the decision, to consensus and unanimity, all the way to no decision being made at all. On pages 140 - 145, also in Chapter Six, a variety of decision-making scenarios are highlighted. Those commonly encountered processes include the following:

Decision Making Processes

Boss makes decision
Boss makes decision after input
Majority rules (voting)
Unanimity
Consensus with leader's constraints
Consensus without constraints
Decision is delegated to "experts"
Non-decision

Tool: *Ready, Set, Go*

READY

Roles and Relationships

According to Edwards W. Demming, the father of TQM, the influence of the first 15% of a project has a greater influence on the outcome of the project than the remaining 85%. The most difficult, yet most important thing a group can do to tackle a problem is to get READY. The first inclination is to jump into solutions or strategies. Nobody wants to talk about who's playing, their roles, and how we will work together.

- Who is going to participate?
- What roles will we play...?
  Facilitator, Recorder, Timekeeper, Observer, Mission Keeper, Humorist, others.
- Is anyone unable or unwilling to participate?
- How will we solve problems?
- How will we make decisions?
- How will we evaluate our *process*?

SET

Strategy & Sequence

Using the problem-solving and decision-making processes:

- What shall we do first?
- How will we know when we are finished?
- How will we evaluate our *progress*?

GO — Go for it!

The greatest obstacle to teamwork is going directly to "GO" and skipping the previous steps. The second greatest problem is continuing to "GO" when the circumstances have changed. Think of Ready, Set, Go as a flowchart loop. When any of the following situations arise, go back to READY and start again:

- Failure (or lack of desired results)
- Loss of group enthusiasm
- The loss or addition of a participant
- Significant learning or perspective shift
- Rules or expectations change
- The unexpected occurs
- Whenever anyone wants to

Building Block: Distributed Leadership

Those organizations that have conducted teambuilding programs should think again. People do not need to be taught how to work together—we have been doing that for years. The real shift is how the teams deal with power.

When power is centralized and used to "drive" the team, it is difficult for the team to become truly high performing; they remain dependent on the strong leader.

This can be a trap, especially for those people with a penchant for control or overwork. These people reinforce their need to control and overwork by pointing at their subordinates. They always seem unruly, undisciplined, and unmotivated when compared to the boss who retains possession of the big picture, strategic information, experience, and special skills.

Not My Father's Job

My dad, Howard, had a difficult time understanding what I do for a living. I tried to explain about the "new economy" empowerment, teams, etc. He has been retired for half a decade, but spent his career as a department manager in a large hospital. He was the manager of the laundry, the "hottest," as he described it, "most uncomfortable place anyone could imagine working for half a century." His crew was comprised largely of unskilled laborers, mostly women.

With some pride, he described that no one had to teach them to work as a team. Each knew exactly what to do, when and how. "I kept them running like a well-oiled machine," he said.

"Aha," I said, "How did they work when you weren't around?"

"They didn't," he said, "at least not for many years."

"That's what I do," I explained, "I teach teams to operate with less supervision; I teach bosses how to share power and distribute leadership." This reduces the cost of management and tends to hasten the development of employees.

Excellent leaders learn to distribute power, responsibility, and accountability across the whole team. I call this distributed leadership as opposed to centralized control, or management. Yet it is more than *situational leadership* which has recently come into vogue. Real distributed leadership does not merely shift from one person to another, but rests collectively with the whole group. It is the team who apportions roles and responsibilities among team members as appropriate to specific tasks. Hence the turn of Lee Iacocca's phrase to Lead, Follow, AND Get Out Of The Way!

"Following," even "getting out of the way," is a vital aspect of team behavior because it allows the natural distribution of leadership to emerge and shift. Unfortunately, situational leadership sometimes becomes a competition among team members for temporary dominance, where individual agendas overshadow the team mission and goals.

> ***Experiential Activity:***
> **A Developmental Approach To Skill Building**
>
> Most experiential training is little more than a collection of events. At most, the trainer will weave a theme throughout the training program. Consider this innovation. Take a specific "tool" such as Ready-Set-Go and through reminders, check-ins and debriefings, make sure it is applied throughout all events for a whole training program. For example, an ice breaker can be used to baseline the group's performance. Then as each subsequent event increases the challenge, the group or team gains more and more experience using the tool. Make sure each debriefing focuses the dialogue on how well the Ready-Set-Go tool was used and how it may have helped.

Tool: *Lead, Follow, AND Get Out Of The Way*

Distributing leadership across the team creates a "leaderful" team. It is a key responsibility of every manager, supervisor, and designated team leader.

LEAD	Leaders are facilitators, visionaries, and champions. They seldom have comprehensive plans or new answers. They do not get people to move in a particular direction through coercion, control, manipulation, or the direct application of power. They help a team see the power of collaboration and cooperation by getting everyone to participate and contribute in their own, best way. The leader's vision, attitude, and skills invigorate the team and offer every follower newfound power.
FOLLOW	Following is about fully participating in a group or team effort without letting your personal agenda get in the way. It is about wholeheartedly supporting the efforts of the leader and other

followers. When others get in your way, it is about constructively and compassionately asking them to set their agenda (ego) aside so work can continue. Likewise, it is being willing to hear others remind you when you get in the way. Ultimately, it is about proactively finding ways to contribute to the success of the project and the development of the team.

GET OUT OF THE WAY

The ability to get out of the way means setting aside your individual agenda to embrace the agenda of the team. Getting out of the way is NOT about checking out. *Always check in before checking out!* It is about shifting from follower to leader or leader to follower. It is about getting your ego out of the way so the team can benefit from your unique contribution.

> ***Experiential Activity:***
> **Who's In Charge**
> During a wide variety of experiential activities, it is possible to challenge the existing pecking order by asking those who take charge to avoid that role so others can try out their leadership skills. You can use the "winds of change" technique (by telling all participants that without notice, the wind could blow in new rules, expectations, or other changes) that alerts the team that anything may change at any moment. So there is no problem if it becomes necessary to take the ability to speak or see away from some participants. By manipulating the "field" (de-scribed earlier in Chapter 3) in this way, it easy to create a wide range of opportunities for participants to Lead, Follow, and Get Out Of The Way.

Building Block: Team Participation

Between the creation of individual roles within a team and the actual tackling of team goals lies the spirit of participation. While it seems natural enough for a team to move directly from roles to action (see Ready, Set, Go, above), the level of individual participation on a team varies day by day, hour by hour, even minute by minute. Although some of this can be attributed to behavioral styles (see below), it is simply natural that people's attention, motivation, and interest will vary.

The most important way to keep participation at a high level is to help individuals align their personal missions with a compelling organizational vision. But that is not enough. It is also important to make sure every individual knows the importance of their singular contributions. People must be acknowledged and rewarded for their efforts. And all this is still not enough.

Not everyone wants to participate. Those who do want to participate will find their level of commitment deviating. Even the most motivated will waver occasionally. What is vital is that every team know this about itself and be able to recognize it when it occurs.

Experiential Activity:

Check In Before You Check Out

Everyone is furnished a card and told that any time they feel as though things are not going well, it is okay, they should not feel guilty, they should just check in. Maybe they feel left out, ignored, bored, or otherwise not engaged. All they have to do is hold up their card. When anyone sees a card (red or green), they are asked to hold theirs up in response. This way, very quickly and silently, an individual holding up a red card has a way of (non-verbally) saying: "I am not happy with what's going on, does anyone else agree?" A lot of green cards send back the message that the problem is the individual's, whereas sympathetic red cards may indicate the need to go back to "Ready" and discuss what is going on. Such a response should not be construed as a lack of compassion for the individual's situation; it is only feedback that lets them know how to proceed to a resolution.

Note that anyone can hold up a card at any time. If someone sees others talking or not focusing, they may hold up a card. If someone sees another person staring off into space, they may hold up a green card to see if that person responds. Some check-ins might consist of an open-ended question: "I feel a need to check-in to see how everyone else is doing . . . are we on target?" "Is everything ok?"

After a while, it is not necessary to use the cards. Participants begin to realize the value of checking-in by saying, "I want to check in," or "I am calling a 'red card' here." The important thing to remember is always check in before checking out.

Everyone needs to be encouraged to check in with the team BEFORE the check out. Likewise, everyone needs to see how important it is to check in with individuals who seem to be wavering, not to bring them into line or embarrass them, but to confirm the assumption rather than to just believe it to be true. Many people look as though they are checking out when they are not. When reminded, even those checking out often return to full attention. Either way, checked-in or checked-out is okay, as long as the team knows what is going on.

Tool: *Check-in*

One of the most powerful ways to illustrate the technique and power of check-in is to issue the members of a team check-in cards. These are shirt-pocket-sized cards, red on one side, green on the other. The team is asked to use these cards to check in before they check out.

Precisely Delineated Tasks and Procedures

Job/Task Analysis can be relatively simple or highly complex. However, a simple job description is NOT it. Where a job description is general in its language, a Job/Task analysis is as specific as possible.

Working Together

A careful analysis of how teams move beyond team building to achieve a level of effective teamwork reveals a number of critical building blocks and vital tools.

Experiential Activity:

Job/Task Analysis

When I work with groups, we undergo a three-phased process. It is only fair to point out that these phases often take several months to drive home, and are never really complete.

Phase One - Identification of All Tasks

Each person is asked to make a list of the tasks they perform on an hourly, daily, weekly, monthly, quarterly, annual, and as-needed basis. This is a wonderful experience for most workers, because they have never seen such a list. It is usually quite extensive and it pleases them that their supervisor will see it!

After these lists are complete, the team meets and each person circulates a list of their tasks and discusses the list. They solicit input from other members of the team, seeking to remove the extraneous and to add items they may have overlooked.

Phase Two - Documenting Critical Tasks

Each team member now works their list in several ways:

- Identify all critical tasks
- Identify tasks that need to be documented
- Prioritize the documenting process

The next time the team meets and shares their lists, input is again sought regarding missing tasks, suggestions about priorities, and input on how to combine tasks into natural groupings or "clumps."

After this meeting, the team agrees to work individually or in affinity groups to complete the documentation process according to the established priorities.

Phase Three - Delineating the Continuum of Tasks

During the documentation period, the team should consider meeting regularly for five to ten minutes for the purpose of checking in with each other and coordinating the documentation process. Up to this point, the team has met regularly for an hour or so on a weekly basis. Some teams elect to continue carving out an hour or so each week, not for the purpose of meeting, but to work on documentation. The last ten minutes of these sessions are reserved for a fast-paced stand-up meeting to share with each other what has been accomplished.

All the while, team leaders, supervisors, and managers concern themselves with coordinating the documentation process into a comprehensive project management scheme that is integrated into the ODAM Matrix.

> ***Experiential Activity:***
> **Tobacco Talks**
>
> Create a big grid on a piece of poster board. Along the top, enter the names of each member of the team as a header for each column. Along the left-hand vertical axis, enter the same list of names for each row. At the intersection of each column and row can be entered an appointment time for each scheduled Tobacco Talk. This grid can also be placed on a web site on your intranet.
>
> When each Tobacco Talk is complete, a big red check mark can be placed in the box (or electronically noted on the web site) to let everyone know the talk has taken place. This way, everyone knows who is talking to whom. Make sure to set a deadline for completion of all talks and schedule a meeting that allows people to share the results (not the details of the conversation), followed by a celebration.

Building Block: Working Relationships

Traditional wisdom holds that workers need to be as self-sufficient as possible. In a Truthful Organization, we work relationships for all they are worth.

Building a strong working relationship requires going far beyond familiarity, courtesy, and cooperation. Each worker on every team needs to be encouraged to explore the boundaries, limitations, and expectations of every relationship.

The tool we use to do this is the TOBACCO model derived from indigenous Native American cultures (see Chapter Five, pages 107 -113). As an organizational tool, it is not enough to merely encourage people to have "tobacco talks"; at the very least, managers and supervisors must agree to engage staff in an ongoing series of "tobacco talks."

Tools: Tobacco

The purpose of TOBACCO is to provide a step-by-step guide to having a conversation with a co-worker, supervisor, or customer in order to move toward deeper understanding, greater cooperation, and a genuine working relationship. The seven steps are:

T *Talk straight*
Create rapport.
Get past all assumptions.
Find out what is real.

O *Old Business*
What could get in the way?

B *Be clear on the details*
This is Ready, Set... not go.
What is really going on?

A *Accurately reflect back what you understand*
The only way to know you understand is to ask.

C *Conditions for your participation*
What resources, authority, time, tools do you need?

C *Communicating the hard truths*
If something goes wrong who do you tell? How?
What can you say to whom, about what?
Are there sacred cows? Black holes?

O *Overview of the agreement and relationship*
Summarize the current and concluding state of affairs.

Building Block: Building Trust

Trust is at once the most difficult quality to engender in an organization and the most vital. Yet trust must be genuine and appropriate. Genuine because when feigned, it can be dangerous. Appropriate because not everyone deserves our trust.

It is important to understand that contrary to public belief, trust is difficult, often impossible to earn. It is much easier to give trust. To be sure, giving absolute trust is imprudent. The most workable model may be the "trust account." Like a bank account, consider creating an account for each person you know. For some, you would fill the account—indicating no limit to trust. At the other end of the spectrum, people you have just met or people who have let you down in the past will merit only a limited "good faith" deposit. This way, the behavior of each person has an effect on the account that varies over time, but each has "wiggle room" rather than being saddled with the obligation to prove themselves from the start.

Tools: Conflict Management

Most approaches to conflict are about resolution—ways to bridge the gap, mend the fences, and make everything nice. The notion of conflict management is different because its starting point is the belief that conflict is not only natural, but vital to the health of relationships and organizations.

Many people avoid conflict but actually fear hostility and violence. Conflict is natural. When proactively managed, it is unlikely to escalate into either hostility or violence. A Truthful Organization is a conflict-positive environment where conflict is creatively used to elicit new ideas, generate fresh points of view, and promote renewed levels of communication and cooperation.

Many conflicts are prevented with the use of Tobacco Talks. Those conflicts that do arise require at least one of the parties in conflict to desire a reconciliation.

Conflict Conference

A conflict conference (private or with facilitator/observer) is a method to proactively deal with a conflict or dispute. A private conference is initiated by at least one party who speaks only with "I" statements:

Preamble:	"I would like to talk with you about something that is troubling me."
What I perceive	"There were a lot of sharp words and pained looks yesterday."
What I believe	"I think I must have done something to upset you."
What I feel	"I feel bad about this."
What I wish	"I wish we could find a way to work this out and get back to work."

Conflict Management

Some conflicts interfere with the business of the team. The behavior of some individuals may require intervention and/or disciplinary action. In any case, the process is the same as a one-on-one conversation, but may involve others in accordance with a due process procedure mandated by the organization and/or the state government.

Steps of Escalation in During Due Process

Private, one-on-one	Initiated by any proactive participant in the dispute. If resolved, it goes no further. If unresolved, do not allow an escalation to hostility to occur. Stop the process and make a good-faith statement, such as, "I regret ending this, but it is going nowhere. I will revisit this in the future if we can find someone to help us work through this." Any party may invite a facilitator or observer to a follow-up meeting.
With observer/ facilitator	The second meeting uses the same model described above, especially "I" statements. These meetings usually proceed more smoothly because all parties to the dispute are usually on their best behavior in the presence of impartial observers. It may be necessary to have an impartial facilitator to help even the most deeply entrenched find common ground.
With facilitator	If a meeting with an impartial observer or facilitator fails to find a solution (not every conflict will be resolved, but a working agreement is usually possible), it may be necessary to try again with the passively observing, preferably not engaged or facilitating so that if it becomes necessary to intervene, the supervisor has heard from both sides and has seen the participants' level of commitment to resolution.

He who is firmly seated in authority soon learns to think security, and not progress, the highest lesson of statecraft.
— *James Russell Lowell*

Experiential Activity:

Switch Hitters

The above questions lead to fascinating convers-ations, but as mentioned earlier, tend to reinforce behaviors. I find it valuable to set up an experiential "team challenge" of some kind (game, simulation, new learning, puzzle, etc.) but I assign participants (or enlist the team's help to select) alternate styles for each individual to "role play" during the challenge. When a person who is usually the *thinker* is now expected to be the *friendly*, it changes not only team dynamics, but dramatically raises aware-ness about how important other roles are to team performance.

Building Block: Behavior Styles (pages 47 - 57)

There are a variety of ways that we can look at individual behaviors in a group setting. Instruments have been developed that reveal complex patterns of interpersonal behaviors. When used by trained professionals, these instruments can uncover important information to help the team function more effectively. Whether it is the simple self-assessment tool I use or the sophisticated Myers-Briggs, DISC, and other instruments, it is clear that anything that offers realistic feedback to members of a team can be a useful tool in enhancing individual and team performance because it makes the invisible, visible. These tools can reveal the personal, interpersonal, team and organizational fields so that our true colors can show through!

Tools: Show Your Colors

An easy self-assessment tool to help people show their true colors is the Thinker, Doer, Friendly, Visionary or TDFV model. Most people readily identify with a dominant characteristic that drives their business behavior. In groups, I ask each person to distribute ballots (with their name on each) to five or six co-workers who can indicate whether they believe the person is a T,D,F, or V. These are anonymously returned to the person whose name is on the ballot to tabulate for themselves. In this way, a group of seven would require approximately 42 ballots.

The opportunities for discussion are great. Is there a preponderance of "votes" for a single characteristic? Does your own self-assessment align with what your team indicated? What kinds of behaviors are generally associated with each "style"? Are all styles represented on your team? Do you need more (or less) of any one style? How do the number and grouping of styles on your team affect team function?

Thinker, Doer, Friendly, Visionary Model

Thinker

General Behavior:

Mr. Spock exhibits a generally cerebral approach to life. He tends to approach technical issues and relationships in the same "logical" way.

Up Side:

These people are capable of enormous contributions to problem solving. They tend to be task oriented, loyal, and highly motivated. They are never at a loss for ideas. They tend to be optimistic.

Down side:

Thinkers are easily distracted and get caught up in details. They may get bogged down in semantic arguments and find it difficult to articulate what is on their mind. They often second-guess decisions. Their logical approach to relationships may be ineffective.

Compatibilities:

Thinkers work well with doers. They may not understand or grasp a visionary's world view, but they can be motivated to follow. The greatest challenge to a thinker is the friendly, who seems frivolous and focused on the "wrong" things.

Doer

General Behavior:

John Wayne knew what had to be done and he wasted no time getting it done. He had little patience for anyone or anything that got in his way—his world was generally black or white.

Up Side:

Stuff gets done. No obstacle seems too great. They have an enormous effect on those around them. Real doers tend to make believers of even the most pessimistic.

Down side:

When people get in the way, or do not agree with a doer, they tend to get run over. They may be directive, overbearing, and insensitive. There are always a few casualties left in the wake of a doer. Doers are so focused on tasks, that processes, people, and procedures are difficult for them to comprehend.

Compatibilities:

By definition, doers are impatient. They have little insight into the motivations of "visionaries" but can form alliances with "friendly" and "thinkers" as long as they are able to focus on the task.

Friendly

General Behavior:

An ideal example of a friendly is Counselor Deanna Troy from Paramount Television's *Star Trek: The Next Generation.* Friendly people may be better described as "feeling" because they can be quite moody and, occasionally, not friendly at all. They are sensitive to the feelings of others and have a keen sense of interpersonal, group, and organizational dynamics.

Up Side:

The friendly helps a team operate by providing feedback to team members about how others feel and how well the group is functioning. They are the peacemakers and the bridge builders. They can often offer innovative, "lateral" ideas and solutions far from the prevailing paradigm.

Down side:

Sometimes they get so caught up in "process" that the task and even the mission is lost. When unskilled at communication, or poorly accepted by the rest of the team, their behavior may seem erratic and counter-productive.

Compatibilities:

By definition, "friendly" people have no trouble getting along with others.

Visionary

General Behavior:

John F. Kennedy was a quintessential charismatic visionary because he envisioned a distinct shift from the post-war world to what he called the "New Frontier." Accordingly, he was able to articulate ideas ("Ask not...") and embody innovative new programs (Peace Corps). Visionaries force the rest of us to ask difficult questions of ourselves, and for their trouble, they are often martyred (literally or figuratively).

Up Side:

They mix things up. They get us out of old "comfortable" troubles by creating a vision of possibility that strikes chords of understanding in many others. They motivate others. They make life interesting.

Down side:

Sometimes their ideas are so far from the norm that they are deeply misunderstood. They often raise more questions than they can answer and leave people frustrated and angry. Interesting is often uncomfortable and never easy.

Compatibilities:

Articulate visionaries are often easy to admire, but difficult to get close to. Visionaries are often solitary and apart. Their closest alliances are with friendlies and sometimes thinkers; what they need most are doers to make their visions real. Visionaries can create a vision that is so powerful and compelling that thinkers, doers, and friendlies will work together.

Building Block: Personal Responsibility

Empowerment cannot come from another; it can only be asserted from one's self. The "power" in empowerment comes from the deepest part of our self. Those who allow themselves to live powerless lives are forced to assert themselves by complaining, blaming, and playing the role of the victim until the rage gets so great that they are "forced" to lash out at others.

Every time an otherwise "normal" person goes berserk and kills people at a fast food restaurant, post office, or other public place, the media pundits apply words like unforeseen, unexpected, and bizarre. But except for the extreme use of violence, millions act out the same scenario every day with angry gestures, pounding fists, high-speed lane changes, and other "minor" acts of violence at home, work, and play.

The challenge for participants of a truthful organization is to accept personal responsibility for themselves—their safety, success, happiness, and life.

One way people often come to accept personal responsibility is through some kind of adversity or failure. Whenever we run into an insurmountable obstacle and feel frustrated, we experience what I call a Moment of Truth. It is during a moment of truth that we often realize the choices (or apparent lack of them) that we have. Most people fail to learn from their moments of truth, but a valuable tool offers valuable support.

Tools: Moments of Truth (pages 116 - 124)

Every unworkable situation, every challenge, every obstacle, and every crisis is an opportunity to have a Moment of Truth. During Moments of Truth, we get in touch with what is really important to us and, most of all, with the power and influence of the choices we make.

What I know is that when things are at their worst, it seems as though there are no options left. When I feel powerless, I try to remember that there are *always* at least four alternative choices.

Each choice can dramatically alter the outcome of any situation.

Change Your Self

Every one can, if they choose, change themselves. This may mean altering a cherished core belief (something about our self-worth, perhaps) or it may be as innocuous as acknowledging the point of view of someone else, or choosing not to take a stand and just going along with the group.

Change The Situation

A variety of actions can change the situation. One of the most commonly employed is to negotiate a change in expectations. For example, if the boss wants a project completed by Thursday, asking for an additional day changes the situation. A day, a helper, a few dollars, extra equipment, etc., not only change the situation, but may make the difference between success and failure.

Get Out

This is not about quitting, but the real option that always exists when you have changed yourself and the situation to no avail. Some jobs, situations, and opportunities are not for

Experiential Activity:

Moments of Truth

Occasionally a team is so set in their ways (the field is stable) that they need to be brought to their knees (strongly perturbed) before they can really consider changing. An ordinary training event such as the Spider Web or Maze can be ratcheted up to make the challenge so difficult that the team's politeness dissolves and the field begins to fluctuate.

On the Spider Web, for example, some of the holes may be a little smaller than usual and the event may be set up before lunch or dinner with an agreement from the team that they will work through and complete the event before going to eat. Then, as they run out of options and blood sugar levels drop, the team begins to get a little more real and moments of truth emerge.

Make sure your facilitation skills are up to this task. You, the facilitator are likely to take the brunt of all frustration, so it is best to check out your plan with a representative from the team. I often ask this person to act as a reality check to give me feedback as to whether the team has been perturbed enough.

us. Sometimes the geatest wisdom is the ability to know when we should decline an opportunity.

Stay And Suffer

The least desirable and all together too often selected option is to stay and suffer, I can handle it. Things will get better. It is just the way things are. I made my bed, I will have to lie in it. This option is unhealthy for the organization and the team, but perhaps the greatest casualty is the mental and even physical well-being of the person selecting this option. How many people have sacrificed themselves to bring home the paycheck, only to be so unhappy as to not enjoy their family, or worst of all, to simply die so young that they never realize the benefits of their efforts? We must never encourage or even tolerate this option.

Personal Mission

Building Block: Personal Mission

When a person is crystal clear about their mission—their reason for living—they are able to articulate that mission with passion and power. The reason for going to the trouble of clarifying and articulating a personal mission is that it is the foundation for every action and all achievement. Without a mission, a person lives a reactive life, constantly fighting the winds of change. People without missions are setting themselves up to be victims.

Building Block: Personal & Organizational Alignment

In a Truthful Organization, every level of the organization is in alignment. Every employee has taken the time to craft a personal mission for themselves and considered the degree of alignment that exists between their personal mission and the vision of the organization. In between, the team mission, team goals, individual team roles, tasks, procedures, and general team behavior are all in the process of being aligned.

The process of trueing or aligning the organization is an ongoing process that every member of the organization must be involved in and take ownership for. While there are a thousand technical reasons and a myriad of situational crises that can get in the way, it is vital that the organization be committed to investing some portion of time to this process on a regular basis.

Tools: Driving Forces

In addition to the core building blocks and tools, every organization is driven by a business argument such as those listed here. Note, feel free to re-write any statement to make it appropriate and to transcend symantics. Few organizations would not claim at least one of these as a driving force. The trick is getting clear about which *one* or *two* are the primary driving forces. It is too easy (and totally unproductive) to say the organization

Experiential Activity:

Show Me Your Passion

In the Business & You Seminars developed by Marshall Thurber, he developed a wonderful experiential event that I have adapted here. After participants have written a personal mission, they are told they will have an opportunity to articulate (not read or trade papers) their mission for others.

Tables are arranged with three chairs on one side. Groups of four are assigned to each table/chair setup. One person stands in front of the table and three partners. Nothing is on the table but three cards (red on one side, green on the other). At the beginning, all three cards are green. As the presenter discusses his/her personal mission, the panelists listen carefully, not for content, but between the lines for passion. When anyone hears real gut-level passion, they turn over the card. When all three cards are red, the presenter is complete. If at the end of a pre-determined amount of time (5, 7, 10 minutes) all the cards are not red, the presenter ends and switches off with one of the panelists. It is important to remember that this is NOT a dialogue, panelists must not coach, ask questions, or offer any verbal or non-verbal feedback to the presenter. Being a truthful, fair panelist is as great a challenge as being the presenter. Remind everyone this is not about speaking skills, drama, or earning brownie points—this is about passion, integrity, and truth! Remind everyone that what is discussed is not the point and should remain private within each group of four.

After everyone is finished (it is best to have one timekeeper so that everyone rotates to the next presenter at the same time), save time for an opportunity for everyone to talk about their experiences.

Experiential Activity:

Personal Inventory

When a person leaves their job, they are faced with the cold hard reality of competing in the open job market. In order to compete, it is vital that the worker perform an self-inventory of experience and skills (in order to create a resume), and determine what the value of these skills are on the open market (in order to make a salary/benefit request or to know which offer to accept).

In a Truthful Organization, every employee is keenly aware of their personal skill-set and their value on the open market. The reason why this is such an important activity is because it is at this level that every employee's personal empowerment interfaces with their organization. Employees who do not know precisely how they add value to the organization and what their value is operate with a significant handicap.

Take the time to carefully and completely list the following in two columns, side by side. Leave a narrow third column blank, on the right:

	Assets		**Liabilities**
	(elements that add value to your ability to do your job)		(elements generally expected in your job position)
1.	Education, training, and certificated skills	1.	Missing education, training, and certificated skills
2.	Attitude, interpersonal, and team skills	2.	Challenges to attitude, interpersonal and team skills
3.	Task-related, technical, job-related skills	3.	Limitations of technical job-related skills
4.	General work-related skills (non-certificated)	4.	Missing general work skills
5.	Experience, past jobs, projects, responsibilities, etc.	5.	Limitations to past experience, jobs, projects, etc.

Analyze the Net-Value of Your Skill-Set

Compare each of the five items in both columns. In the blank right-hand column, enter a plus or minus to indicate whether the net value is positive or negative. If you wish, you can even enter numerical values.

Assess the Economic Value of Your Skill-Set

Ultimately, you must research the job market in your own geographical area. This research will result in a salary/benefit range. Using your list of pluses and minuses, determine your location on the salary/benefit range—lots of pluses lead to the high end, negatives to the low end of the scale.

subscribes to them all. Now is the time to get specific and truthful about what drives your company.

Priority	Driving Forces
❐	Growth
❐	Sales and Marketing
❐	Innovation and Creativity
❐	Equity and Financial Return
❐	Customer Acquisition and Retention
❐	Quality and Continuous Improvement
❐	Citizenship, Community, and Participation

We live in a wonderful world that is full of beauty, charm and adventure. There is no end to the adventures that we can have if only we seek them with our eyes open.
—Jawaharlal Nehru

Once the top driving forces are identified, they need to be integrated into all organizational development initiatives and become part of all ongoing training efforts. The driving forces are best utilized as an integrating theme across all departments, missions, goal sets, skill levels, and tools.

The Ready-Set-Go tool, discussed earlier, is used differently depending upon the identified driving force-theme. For example, if the driving force is *Innovation & Creativity*, the tool is used to explore the boundaries of prevailing assumptions, current technology, and know-how. This is done by posing a problem to the team requiring out-of-the-box thinking. On the other hand, when the driving force is *Quality & Continuous Improvement*, Ready-Set-Go can be easily integrated into the (Shewhart-Deming) Plan-Do-Measure-Adjust cycle by using the tool to participate in business simulations and analyze case studies.

Bibliography & Index

BIBLIOGRAPHY

Ackoff, Russell. *The Democratic Corporation.* New York: Oxford Press, 1994.

Aguayo, Rafael. *Dr. Deming.* New York: Simon & Schuster, 1990.

Angeles, Arrien. *Signs of Life.* Sonoma, CA: Arcus, 1992.

Avery, Michel. *Building United Judgment.* Madison, WI: Center for Conflict Resolution, 1981.

Axelrod, Robert. *The Evolution of Cooperation.* New York: HarperCollins, 1987.

Barker, Joel A. *Paradigms.* New York: HarperBusiness, 1992.

Barrentine, Pat (ed.). *When The Canary Stops Singing.* San Francisco: Berrett-Koehler, 1993.

Beale, Lucy & Rick Fields. *The Win/Win Way.* New York: Harcourt, 1987.

Belasco, James A. *Teaching The Elephant To Dance.* New York: Crown, 1991.

Bellman, Geoffrey M.. *Getting Things Done When You Are Not In Charge.* San Francisco: Berrett-Koehler, 1992.

Below, Patrick J., George L. Morrisey & Betty L. Acomb. *The Executive Guide To Strategic Planning.* San Francisco, CA: Jossey-Bass, 1987.

Block, Peter, *Stewardship*, San Francisco: Berrett-Koehler, 1993.

———. *The Empowered Manager.* San Francisco: Jossey-Bass, 1987.

Bohm, David. *Wholeness and the Implicate Order.* New York: Routledge, 1994.

———. *Thought As A System.* New York: Routledge, 1994.

Bradshaw, John. *Healing The Shame That Binds You.* Deerfield Beach, FL: Health Communications, 1988.

Bristol, Claude. *The Magic of Believing.* New York: Simon & Schuster, 1985.

Campbell, Joseph. *The Hero With A Thousand Faces.* Princeton, NJ: Princeton Press, 1973.

———. *The Inner Reaches of Outer Space.* New York: HarperCollins, 1986.

Capezio, Peter & Debra Morehouse. *Taking The Mystery Out Of TQM.* Hawthorne, NJ: Career Press, 1993.

Carlzon, Jan. *Moments Of Truth.* New York: HarperCollins, 1987.

Carse, James P. *Finite and Infinite Games.* New York: MacMillan, 1986.

Chang, Richard Y., Gloria E. Bader & Audrey E. Bloom. *Measuring Team Performance.* Irvine, CA: Richard Chang Assoc., 1994.

Chopra, Deepak. *Quantum Healing.* New York: Bantam, 1990.

Collins, James C. & Jerry I. Porras. *Built To Last.* New York: Harper Business, 1994.

Covey, Stephen R. *Principle Centered Leadership.* New York: Summit Books, 1991.

———. *The Seven Habits of Highly Effective People.* New York: Simon & Schuster, 1989

Crum, Thomas F. *The Magic of Conflict.* New York: Simon & Schuster, 1987.

Davidow, William H. & Michael S. Malone. *The Virtual Corporation.* New York: HarperBusiness, 1992.

Deal, Terrence E. & William A. Jenkins. *Managing The Hidden Organization.* New York: Warner Books, 1994.

DeBono, Edward. *Conflicts A Better Way To Resolve Them.* New York: Penguin, 1985.

Delavigne, Kenneth T., & J. Daniel Robertson. *Deming's Profound Changes.* New York: Prentice-Hall, 1994.

DePree, Max. *Leadership Is An Art.* New York: Dell, 1990.

Drucker, Peter F. *The New Realities.* New York: Harper Row, 1989.

Frankl, Viktor E. *Man's Search For Meaning.* New York: Washington Square Press, 1984.

Fritz, Robert. *The Path Of Least Resistance.* New York: Fawcett-Columbine, 1989.

Gerber, Michael E. *The E Myth Revisited.* New York: HarperCollins, 1995.

Gerson, Richard F. *Measuring Customer Satisfaction.* Menlo Park, CA: Crisp Publications, 1993.

Goldstein, Jeffrey. *The Unshackled Organization.* Portland, OR: Productivity Press, 1994.

Goleman, Daniel. *Emotional Intelligence.* New York: Bantam Books, 1995.

Grinder, John & Richard Bandler. *Trance-Formations.* Moab, UT: Real People Press, 1981.

Haas, Howard G., *The Leader Within*, New York: HarperCollins, 1992.

Hall, Edward T. *Beyond Culture.* New York: Doubleday, 1976.

Hammer, Michael & James Champy. *Reengineering the Corporation.* New York: HarperCollins, 1993.

Handy, Charles. *The Age Of Unreason.* Boston, MA: Harvard Press, 1990.

———. *Understanding Organizations.* New York: Penguin, 1991.

Harrington-Mackin, Deborah. *The Team Building Tool Kit.* New York: American Management Association, 1994.

Harris, Thomas A. *I'm Ok—You're Ok.* New York: Harper & Row, 1969.

Hart, Lois. *Learning From Conflict.* Reading, MA: Addison-Wesley, 1981.

Head, Glenn E. *Training Cost Analysis.* Denver, CO: Marlin Press, 1985.

Heider, John. *The Tao Of Leadership.* New York: Bantam, 1988.

Hillman, James (ed.). *Facing The Gods.* Dallas, TX: Spring Publications, 1988.

———. *Kinds Of Power.* New York: Doubleday, 1995.

How To Manage Conflict. Hawthorne, NJ: Career Press, 1993.
Jacobs, Robert W. *Real Time Strategic Change*. San Francisco: Berrett-Koehler, 1994.
Kawasaki, Guy. *How To Drive Your Competition Crazy*. New York: Hyperion, 1995.
———. *Selling The Dream*. New York: HarperCollins, 1991.
Kearns, David T. & David A. Nadler. *Prophets In The Dark*. New York: HarperCollins, 1992.
Kiersey, David & Marilyn Bates. *Please Understand Me*. Del Mar, CA: Prometheus Books, 1984.
King, Bob. *Hoshin Planning The Developmental Approach*. Methuen, MA: Goal QPC, 1989.
Kohn, Alfie. *No Contest*. New York: Houghton Mifflin, 1992.
Koopman, A. D., M. E. Nasser & J. Nel. *The Corporate Crusaders*. Johannesburg: Lexicon, 1987.
Korman, Abraham K. *Human Dilemmas In Work Organizations*. New York: Guilford Press, 1994.
Kostner, Jaclyn. *Knights Of The Tele-Round Table*. New York: Warner Books, 1994.
Kuhn, Thomas, S. *The Structure of Scientific Revolutions*. New York: W. W. Norton & Co., 1967.
Latzko, William J. & David M. Saunders. *Four Days With Dr. Deming*. Reading, MA: Addison-Wesley, 1995.
Lewis, Clarence Irving. *Mind And World Order*. New York: Dover, 1990.
Maltz, Maxwell. *Psycho-Cybernetics*. N. Hollywood, CA: Wilshire Books, 1960.
Maslow, A. H. *The Farther Reaches of Human Nature*. New York: Viking Press, 1971.
Maturana, Humberto R. & Francisco J. Varela. *The Tree Of Knowledge*. Boston, MA: Shambhala, 1987.
Mindel, Arnold. *The Leader As Martial Artist*. San Francisco: HarperCollins, 1992.
Morrisey, George L., Patrick L. Below & Betty L. Acomb. *The Executive Guide To Operational Planning*. San Francisco: Jossey-Bass, 1987.
Nelson, Robert B. & Peter Economy. *Better Business Meetings*. New York: Irwin, 1995.
Nirenberg, John. *The Living Organization*. San Diego, CA: Pfeiffer & Co, 1993.
Osborn, Carol. *Inner Excellence*. San Rafael, CA: New World, 1992.
Peck, M. Scott. *A World Waiting To Be Born*. New York: Bantam Books, 1994.
———. *The Road Less Traveled*. New York: Simon & Schuster, 1978.
Pokras, Sandy. *Systematic Problem-Solving And Decision-Making*. Menlo Park, CA: Crisp Publications, 1989.
Prigogine, Ilya & Gregiore Nicolis. *Exploring Complexity*. New York: W. H. Freeman & Co., 1989.
Quinn, Daniel. *Ishmael*. New York: Bantam/Turner, 1993.
Reed, Stanley Foster. *The Toxic Executive*. New York: HarperCollins, 1993.
Robbins, Anthony. *Awaken The Giant Within*. New York: Simon & Schuster, 1992.
Rogers, Carl R. *Client-Centered Therapy*. Boston, MA: Houghton-Mifflin, 1965.
———. *On Becoming A Person*. New York: Houghton Mifflin, 1961.
Rummler, Geary A. & Alan P. Brache. *Improving Performance, How To Manage The White Space On The Organization Chart*. San Francisco: Jossey-Bass, 1990.
Schaef, Anne Wilson. *When Society Becomes An Addict*. New York: Harper & Row, 1987.
Schein, Edgar. *Process Consultation*. Reading, MA: Addison-Wesley, 1988.
Senge, Peter M. *The Fifth Discipline*. New York: Doubleday, 1990.
——— [et.al.]. *The Fifth Discipline Fieldbook*. New York: Doubleday, 1994.
Shefsky, Lloyd E. *Entrepreneurs Are Made Not Born*. New York: McGraw-Hill, 1994.
Shewhart, Walter A. *Statistical Method from The Viewpoint of Quality Control*. New York: Dover, 1986.
Simon, Sidney B., Leland Howe, Howard Hirschenbaum. *Values Clarification*. New York: Warner Books, 1995.
Stack, Jack. *The Great Game Of Business*. New York: Currency Doubleday, 1992.
Steiner, Claude. *Scripts People Live*. New York: Grove Press, 1974.
Talbot, Michael. *The Holographics Universe*. New York: HarperCollins, 1991.
Taylor, Frederick Winslow. *The Principles Of Scientific Management*. New York: W. W. Norton & Co., 1967.
Walton, Mary. *The Deming Management Method*. New York: Perigee, 1986.
Wares, Bruce R. *Partner $ell*. Dubuque, IA: Kendall Hunt, 1994.
Weidlein, Marianne. *Empowering Vision*. Boulder, CO: Amari Press, 1991.
Weiss, Laurie & Jonothan B. Weiss. *Recovery From Co-Dependency*. Deerfield Beach, FL: Health Communications, 1989.
Wheelis, Allen. *How People Change*. New York: Harper & Row, 1973
Wick, Calhoun W. *The Learning Edge*. New York: McGraw-Hill, 1993.
Woititz, Janet Geringer. *Struggle For Intimacy*. Pompano Beach, FL: Health Communications, 1985.
Zukav, Gary. *The Seat Of The Soul*. New York: Simon & Schuster, 1989.

Index

Symbols

A

B

C

D

E

F

W

Z